3

CV

CLARENDON LAW SERIES

Edited by
H. L. A. HART

CLARENDON LAW SERIES

Introduction to the Law of Property
By F. H. LAWSON

Introduction to the Law of Contract
Second Edition
By P. S. ATIYAH

The Concept of Law
By H. L. A. HART

Precedent in English Law
By A. R. N. CROSS

Criminal Law and Punishment
By P. J. FITZGERALD

An Introduction to Roman Law
By BARRY NICHOLAS

Law in Society
By GEOFFREY SAWYER

An Introduction to the Law of Torts
By JOHN G. FLEMING

Constitutional Theory
By G. MARSHALL

LEGAL REASONING
AND
LEGAL THEORY

BY

NEIL MacCORMICK

ERRATUM

p. 232. The penultimate paragraph on this page
should begin

'If we are to achieve a clear conceptual
distinction between'

CLARENDON PRESS · OXFORD

1978

Oxford University Press, Walton Street, Oxford OX2 6DP

OXFORD LONDON GLASGOW
NEW YORK TORONTO MELBOURNE WELLINGTON
IBADAN NAIROBI DAR ES SALAAM LUSAKA CAPE TOWN
KUALA LUMPUR SINGAPORE JAKARTA HONG KONG TOKYO
DELHI BOMBAY CALCUTTA MADRAS KARACHI

© Oxford University Press 1978

British Library Cataloguing in Publication Data
MacCormick, Neil
  Legal reasoning and legal theory. — (Clarendon law series).
  1. Legal reasoning
  I. Title
  340.1   [Law]   78-40235
ISBN 0-19-876080-9

Typeset by Hope Services Ltd., Wantage
Printed in Great Britain
by Richard Clay & Co. Ltd., Bungay

PREFACE

In this book, I try to describe and explain the elements of legal arguments advanced in justification of decisions, or claims and defences put to the courts for decision; to relate that to the general theory of law; and to do all that in the framework of a general theory of practical reason which owes a great deal to David Hume. I hope that my efforts will be of some interest to lawyers, jurisprudents, and philosophers. I have therefore tried to write it in such a way that it will be comprehensible to non-philosophical lawyers and to nonlawyer philosophers. Each group will find a great deal which is from its own point of view rather elementary and obvious, for which I apologize in advance. Conversely, I hope that neither group will find undue obscurities in the less familiar points of the text.

The book originated in a series of lectures given in Queen's College, Dundee (now the University of Dundee), under the guidance of Professor I.D. Willock in 1966 and 1967; various parts of it have been tried out in various forms in lectures in Oxford University from 1967 till 1972, and in Edinburgh University from 1972 till the present. I intended to finish it long ago, but a combination of laziness and administrative responsibilities delayed me, perhaps to good effect.

Naturally, I owe a lot to innumerable students who put up very courteously with my efforts to master my thoughts on the topics discussed, and gave all manner of useful criticisms. Even more I am indebted to many colleagues for helpful discussions and criticisms, in particular to: J. Bjarup, Z.K. Bankowski, A.A.M. Irvine, H.L.A. Hart, D.R. Harris, N.R. Hutton, Ch. Perelman, G. Maher, R.M.J. Kinsey, M.J. Machan, D. Small, I.D. Willock, W.A.J. Watson, and A. Zuckerman. Karen Mac-Cormick suffered my earliest attempts to cast the first version of the lectures in acceptable form, and prodded me into finally completing the present version, and Isabel Roberts gave all manner of help. To them all, I am profoundly grateful. Naturally, I accept full responsibility for any defects remaining in the book as it now appears.

Edinburgh, 2 May 1977   NEIL MacCORMICK

CONTENTS

	Table of Cases	ix
I.	Introduction	1
II.	Deductive Justification	19
III.	Deductive Justification—Presuppositions and Limits	53
IV.	The Constraint of Formal Justice	73
V.	Second-Order Justification	100
VI.	Consequentialist Arguments	129
VII.	The Requirement of 'Coherence': Principles and Analogies	152
VIII.	The Requirement of Consistency and the Problem of Interpretation: Clear Cases and Hard Cases	195
IX.	Legal Reasoning and Legal Theory	229
	Excursus	259
X.	Law, Morality, and the Limits of Practical Reason	265
	Appendix: On the 'Internal Aspect' of Norms	275
	Index of Statutes Cited	293
	General Index	294

TABLE OF CASES

Alfred Crompton Amusement Machines Ltd. v. *Commissioners of Customs and Excise* (1972) 2 Q.B. 106A-116G: 134
Allen v. *Flood* [1898] A.C.1: 40
Anisminic v. *Foreign Compensation Commission* [1969] 2 A.C. 197: 143-4, 193, 195-6, 193, 199, 210, 219, 223, 232.
Att. Gen. v. *Wilts United Dairies* (1921) 37 T.L.R. 884: 178
Avery v. *Bowden* (1885) 5 El.Bl. 714: 173
Barker v. Bell [1971] 2 All E.R. 867: 206
Barwick v. *British Joint Stock Bank* (1886) L.R. 2 Ex. 259:225-6
Bates & anor. v. *Batey & Co. Ltd.* [1913] 3 K.B. 351: 127
Beith's Trustees v. *Beith* 1950 S.C. 66: 137, 193
Blackburn v. *Att. Gen.* [1971] 2 All E.R. 1380: 132-3
Blacker v. Lake & Elliott (1912) 106 L.T. 533: 127
Bland v. *Moseley* (1587) 9 Co.Rep. 58a: 190
Borland v. Borland 1947 S.C. 432: 98
Bourhill v. *Young* 1942 S.C. (H.L.) 78: 163
Brandon v. *Osborne Garret and Co.* [1942] 1 K.B. 548:162
British Railways Board v. Pickin [1974] A.C. 765 132
B.T.C. v. *Gourley* [1956] A.C. 185: 174-8, 217-8, 254
Cameron v. *Young* [1908] A.C. 176; 1908 S.C. (H.L.) 7: 121
Cassell & Co. Ltd. v. *Broome* [1972] A.C. 1027: 179
Cavalier v. Pope [1906] A.C. 428: 121
Chaplin v. *Boys* [1971] A.C. 356: 83
Chapman v. *Sadler & Co.* [1929] A.C. 584: 127
Charter v. Race Relations Board [1973] A.C. 868: 154-5, 235
Conway v. *Rimmer* [1968] A.C. 910: 134, 137, 183, 255
Cutler v. *United Dairies (London) Ltd.* [1933] 2 K.V. 297: 162
Dalton v. *Angus* (1881) 6 App.Cas. 740: 189, 219
Daniels & Daniels v. *R. White & Sons & Tarbard* [1938] 4 All E.R. 258: 19-33, 36, 37, 41-5, 64-5, 74, 197-8, 200, 216-7, 267
Derry v. Peek (1889) 14 App.Cas. 337: 223-4
Dixon v. Bell (1816) 5. M. & S. 198: 127
Donoghue v. *Stevenson* [1932] A.C. 562; 1932 S.C. (H.L.) 31: 42, 69-70, 80-2, 85, 108-28, 140, 148-9, 157, 159-60, 186, 198, 200, 216, 224-5, 235, 251-4, 256
Drummond's J.F. v. *H.M. Advocate* 1944 S.C. 298: 165
Duncan v. *Cammell, Laird & Co. Ltd.* [1942] A.C. 624: 134
Dynamco Ltd. v. *Holland & Hannen & Cubitts (Scotland) Ltd.* 1971 S.C. 257: 140-2
Ealing London Borough Council v. *Race Relations Board* [1972] A.C. 342: 66-8, 77-9, 147-9, 210-3

Earl v. *Lubbock* [1905] 1 K.B. 253:   127
Elder Dempster & Co. Ltd. v. *Paterson, Zochonis & Co. Ltd.* [1924]
    A.C. 552   150-1
Elliott v. *Hall or Nailstone Colliery Co.* (1885) 15 Q.B.D. 315:   127
Esso Petroleum Co. Ltd. v. *Mardon* [1975] Q.B. 819; [1976] Q.B.
    801 (C.A.):   224
Gallie v. *Lee* [1969] 1 All E.R. 1062:   215
George v. *Skivington* (1869) L.R. 5 Exch. 1:   127
Glasgow Corporation v. *Central Land Board* 1956 S.C. (H.L.) 1:   135
Glendarrock, The [1894] P. 264:   145
Gordon v. *M'Hardy* (1903) 6 F. 210:   109-110
Grant v. *Australian Knitting Mills* [1936] A.C. 85:   22, 25, 30, 225
Grote v. *Chester & Holyhead Rail Co.* (1848) 2 Exch. 251:   127
Hambleton v. *Callinan* [1968] 2 All E.R. 943:   50-1
Haseldine v. *C.A. Daw & Co. Ltd.* [1941] 2 K.B. 343:   85, 225
Haskins v. *Lewis* [1931] 2 K.B.1:   204-5, 236
Hawkins v. *Smith* (1896) 12 T.L.R. 532:   127
Haynes v. *Harwood* [1935] 1 K.B. 146:   162
Heaven v. *Pender* (1883) 11 Q.B.D. 503:   125, 127
Hedley Byrne & Co. Ltd. v. *Heller & Partners* [1964] A.C. 465:   224
Henderson v. *John Stuart (Farms) Ltd.* 1963 S.C. 245:   142-3
Home Office v. *Royal Dorset Yacht Co. Ltd.* [1970] A.C. 1004:
                                                          158-60, 167, 178
Hotel & Catering Industry Training Board v. *Automobile Proprietary
    Ltd.* [1969] 2 All E.R. 582   178
Hughes v. *The Metropolitan Railway* (1887) 2 App.Cas. 439:   193
Joseph Constantine Steamship Line Ltd. v. *Imperial Smelting Cor-
    poration Ltd.* [1942] A.C. 154:   144-6
Kerr v. *The Earl of Orkney* (1857) 20 D. 298:   193
Langford v. *Dutch* 1952 S.C. 15:   222-3
Langridge v. *Levy* (1838) 4 M. & W. 337:   127
Le Lievre v. *Gould* [1893] 1 Q.B. 491:   125
Lee v. *Bude & Torrington Rly. Co. Ltd.* (1871) L.R.C.P. 576:   132
Lloyd v. *Grace Smith & Co.* [1912] A.C. 716:   226
London Street Tramways v. *L.C.C.* [1898] A.C. 375:   115, 134, 137
Longmeid v. *Holliday* (1851) 6 Exch. 761:   127
Lyndale Fashion Mfrs. Ltd. v. *Rich* [1973] 1 All E.R. 33:   217-8
MacCormick v. *Lord Advocate* 1953 S.C. 396:   130-2
Macdonald v. *David MacBrayne Ltd.* 1915 S.C. 716:   220-2
Macdonald v. *Glasgow Western Hospitals* 1954 S.C. 453:   137
M'Glone v. *British Railways Board* 1966 S.C. (H.L.) 1:   216-7
Maclennan v. *Maclennan* 1958 S.C. 105:   93-4, 147-8, 198
Malloch v. *Aberdeen Corporation* 1971 S.C. (H.L.) 85; [1971] 2 All
    E.R. 1278:   179, 193-4, 223
Marbury v. *Madison* (1803) 1 Cranch 137:   129-30
Menzies v. *Murray* (1875) 2 R. 507:   137
Miliangos v. *George Frank (Textiles) Ltd.* [1976] A.C. 443:   138
Moore v. *D.E.R. Ltd.* [1971] 3 All E.R. 517:   173-4

Morelli v. *Fitch & Gibbons* [1928] 2 K.B. 636: 20, 30, 74
Mostyn, The [1928] A.C.57: 151
Mullen v. *Barr & Co., McGowan* v. *Barr & Co.* 1929 S.C. 461: 113
Mutual Life etc. Co. v. *Evatt* [1971] A.C. 793: 224
Myers v. *D.P.P.* [1965] A.C. 1001: 164
Nagle v. *Fielden* [1966] 2 Q.B. 633: 237–8
Norwich Pharmacal Ltd. v. *Commissioners of Customs & Excise*
    [1972] Ch. 182; [1974] A.C. 182: 182–7, 193
Orr v. *Diaper* (1876) 4 Ch.D. 92: 184–6
Phipps v. *Pears* [1964] 2 All E.R. 35: 189–91, 219
Qualcast (Wolverhampton) Ltd. v. *Haynes* [1959] A.C. 743: 96–7
Quinn v. *Leathem* [1901] A.C. 495: 39–40
Read v. *J. Lyons & Co. Ltd.* [1947] A.C. 156: 167–9, 179, 226
Reavis v. *Clan Line Steamers* 1925 S.C. 725: 141
Reidford v. *Magistrates of Aberdeen* 1935 S.C. 276: 137
R. v. *Arthur* [1968] 1 Q.B. 810: 180–2, 186
R. v. *Pardoe* (1897) 17 Cox C.C. 715: 180
R. v. *Voisin* [1918] 1 K.B. 531: 89
Ridge v. *Baldwin* [1964] A.C. 40: 223
River Wear Commissioners v. *Adamson* (1887) 2 App. Cas. 743: 151
Rondel v. *Worsley* [1969] 1 A.C. 191: 157–8, 160, 189
Rylands v. *Fletcher* (1868) L.R. 3 H.L. 330:168–9, 193, 226, 232
St. John Shipping Corpn. v. *Joseph Rank Ltd.* [1957] 1 Q.B. 267: 146–7
Scala Ballroom (Wolverhampton) Ltd. v. *Ratcliffe* [1958]
    3 All E.R. 220: 237
Scruttons Ltd. v. *Midland Silicones Ltd.* [1962] A.C. 446: 150–1
Smith v. *East Elloe R.D.C.* [1956] A.C. 736: 199, 200, 210
Steel v. *Glasgow Iron & Steel Co. Ltd.* 1944 S.C. 237: 161–3, 186, 220–2
Temple v. *Mitchell* 1956 S.C. 267: 200–6, 210, 213–4, 223, 232
Thompson v. *Glasgow Corporation* 1962 S.C. (H.L.) 36: 49–50, 119
Upmann v. *Elkan* (1871) L.R. 2 Eq. 140: 184
Webb v. *Bird* (1861) 13 C.B.(N.S.) 841: 190
White & Carter (Councils) Ltd. v. *McGregor* [1962] A.C. 413; 1962
    S.C. (H.L.) 1: 169–73, 254
Wilkinson v. *Kinneil Cannel & Coking Co. Ltd.* (1897) 24 R. 1001: 162
Winterbottom v. *Wright* (1842) 10 M. & W. 109: 113, 127
Woods v. *Caledonian Rly.* (1886) 13 R. 1118: 162
Yetton v. *Eastwoods Froy Ltd.* [1966] 3 All E.R. 353: 173–4

I

INTRODUCTION

(a) *The Perspective of the Inquiry*

The idea that reason has a part to play in the ordering of human affairs has a long history. It is associated with the view that some things are 'by nature' right for human beings; others so, merely by convention or by enactment. Whether or not there were enforced laws prohibiting murder, it would be wrong for human beings wantonly to take each others' lives. On the other hand, it seems strange to suppose that parking a car in a particular street could be considered a wrongful act in the absence of some consciously adopted scheme of regulations.

If there are some actions which are always wrong simply in virtue of the nature of human beings—or, more generally, the 'nature of things'—it may be thought to follow that the exercise of reason should suffice to disclose which actions are by nature right or wrong. And even in case of more apparently arbitrary matters such as parking regulations, or regulations concerning weights and measures, it can be argued that reason discloses to us the need to have some rule as a common standard.

If there are numerous private cars, lorries, etc., there will be grievous congestion if parking is quite unrestricted, and no amount of attempts at intelligent self-denial by individuals will resolve the problem: let there then be some public enactment of parking regulations aimed at securing over-all public convenience by balancing the inconvenience of restraints on parking against the inconvenience of excessive congestion of the streets. If there is a market in commodities, let there be some established common system of weights and measurements reasonably suited to the measurement of the range of quantities most commonly marketed.

The idea, expressed in one form by Lord Stair in the terms that 'Law is the dictate of reason determining every rational being to that which is congruous and convenient for the nature thereof',[1] is at least as old as the writings of Plato and Aristotle, and has of course exercised a profound influence upon the development of western legal thought, in which it has been stated and restated many times and in many forms. Whether or not it is well founded, it is a belief which has profoundly influenced the form and the substance of the legal systems (in their various 'families') which have developed in Europe, and been carried therefrom to the ends of the earth.

It is not, however, a belief which has gone unchallenged, nor has the challenge in its turn failed to be influential. To David Hume, above all others perhaps, belongs the credit—if such it be—for the most fundamental scepticism about the limits of reason in practical affairs.[2] Reduced to its essentials, his argument is that our faculty of reasoning can operate only upon given premises; assuming certain premises, we can by reason ascertain the conclusions which follow from them. And indeed reason can guide us in seeking to verify or falsify assertions concerning matters of fact or existential propositions generally. In the latter case, however, reasoning has a secondary role, since it can work only with evidence already given in our various sense impressions.

So too in relation to practical affairs: if I have an appointment which I ought to keep on Wednesday, then if today is Wednesday, today is the day on which I ought to keep my appointment. The necessity of that conclusion is indeed a matter determined by reasoning. But the conclusion has *practical* force for me (*Am* I going to keep my appointment?) only so far as the premises have: that I ought to keep appointments is in effect one of these premises, no doubt in its turn derived or derivable from 'Everyone ought to keep appointments'. but wherein consists the rational demonstration of that proposition?

---

[1] James, 1st Viscount Stair, *Institutions of the Law of Scotland* (2nd edn., Edinburgh, 1893, or subsequent edns., also Edinburgh) I.i.1.

[2] See especially David Hume, *A Treatise of Human Nature* (many edns.) Book II, Part III, § III; and Book III, Part I, § § I and II, and Part III, § § I and II; for a clarification and partial retraction see Hume, *Enquiry Concerning the Principles of Morals* (many edns.), Appendix I. Hume himself regarded the *Enquiry* as his own best and final statement on the topic in question.

Perhaps it can be shown that the use of various forms of speech whereby people can 'make appointments' with each other makes possible great convenience for people in ordering their affairs, provided only that people do treat as binding their appointments made (or other types of promise). But is it a matter of 'reason' to prefer that general convenience to the alternative, the inconvenience of leaving it to chance to determine when we shall meet even those with whom we have business to do? Is it not rather a matter of a disposition of the will founded upon some simple sentiment of preference or approbation which we feel toward the former state of affairs, a sentiment which indeed we express in calling it 'convenient'?

And so too in the simpler cases: why say that reason tells us we ought not to kill each other? Is it not rather the case that we have in ordinary circumstances a simple and direct sentiment of revulsion from acts of violence perpetrated by human beings upon human beings? And indeed, if that were not so, is it conceivable that we would ever *do* anything about it? Conceivable that we would actually make a point of keeping appointments, or of reining in our more violent reactions towards our fellows? Or that we would take steps to censure others for breaking appointments or to restrain them from violence toward others?

Such, in summary, are the arguments whereby Hume sought to justify his well-known remarks about 'reason' being 'the slave of the passions',[3] and about the underivability of an 'ought-statement' from an 'is-statement'[4]

To Hume's arguments there has been only one effective reply, first advanced by his younger contemporary Thomas Reid[5] (successor to Adam Smith in the Chair of Moral Philosophy at Glasgow University). What Reid said was that Hume was correct in asserting that reasons cannot be given for ultimate moral premises; there are no statements of 'pure fact' which we can give to back up whatever we set forth as

---

[3] Hume, *Treatise* Book II, Part III, § III, 5th paragraph.
[4] Hume, *Treatise* Book III, Part I, § I, final paragraph.
[5] See Thomas Reid, *Essays on the Powers of the Human Mind* (Edinburgh, 1819), vol. iii, Essay V, esp. ch. VII (i.e. Essay V of the *Essays on the Active Powers*); on 'is/ought', see p. 578 of vol. iii of the 1819 edition of the Essays.

our ultimate premisses in moral arguments. Moreover, it is
the case that these ultimate moral premisses are necessarily
associated with dispositions of the affections and of the will.
But it is not true that they are not also apprehended by
reason and in that sense rational. Our adherence to general
principles—e.g. that no acts of violence ought to be perpetrated on human beings save in certain justifying or excusing
circumstances—is a manifestation of our rationality, by
contrast with our merely impulsive and animal reactions to
circumstances. Reason for Reid is not and certainly ought
not to be the slave of the passions. (In part this is, not
uncharacteristically of Reid, an unfair rejoinder to Hume,
who certainly recognized (e.g.) a difference between our
more settled 'calm passions' and the more violent and impulsive of our reactions to circumstances. There remains an
important difference between them on the question whether
all our more cool and consistent attitudes to conduct are an
aspect of our 'reason'.)

It deserves to be added that the work of thinkers such as
Adam Smith,[6] Adam Ferguson,[7] John Millar,[8] and Karl
Marx[9] has pretty convincingly demonstrated a strong correlation between the moral opinions and legal norms actually
subscribed to by human beings, and the changing forms of
social and economic life. That people ought to be left as
far as possible free to conduct their own affairs by means of
voluntary contracts which ought, once made, to be rigorously
and impartially enforced by public authorities is, for example,
an opinion both characteristic of and indeed peculiar to
that mode of social organization which Smith called 'commercial' and Marx 'bourgeois':

Whether this should be interpreted along Humean lines as

---

[6] Adam Smith, *Lectures on Justice, Police, Revenue and Arms*, ed. E. Cannan
(Oxford, 1896); a new text edited by P.G. Stein and R. Meek is due to be published at Oxford in 1977 or 1978. For an illuminating account of Smith's views
on this matter, see Andrew Skinner, 'Adam Smith: Society and Government', in
Perspectives in Jurisprudence, ed. Elspeth Attwooll (Glasgow, 1977).

[7] Adam Ferguson, *Essay on the History of Civil Society* (1st edn., Edinburgh,
1767; a new edition by Duncan Forbes, Edinburgh, 1966).

[8] John Millar, *The Origin of the Distinction of Ranks* (Edinburgh, 1806);
reprinted, together with selections from other works in W.C. Lehmann, *John
Millar of Glasgow* (Cambridge, 1960).

[9] See E. Kamenka, *Marxism and Ethics* (London, 1969).

implying that the dispositions of our sentiments and wills are simply and inevitably shaped by the social environment in which we find ourselves, or along lines more favourable to Reid (or Smith, or Marx) as implying that only in certain circumstances can reason achieve its full development, is a question which need not for the moment detain us. Suffice it that we have sketched the essentials of our problem: the problem how far the determination of order in human affairs is a matter of reason. There are, as we see, substantial arguments on either side; and both sets of arguments have been in important ways influential.

In the ensuing chapters of this book, I shall follow the point which is common to both Hume and Reid in assuming that any mode of evaluative argument must involve, depend on, or presuppose, some ultimate premisses which are not themselves provable, demonstrable, or confirmable in terms of further or ulterior reasons. In that sense, our ultimate normative premisses are not reasoned, not the product of a chain of logical reasoning.

As we shall see, that does not mean the same as saying that no reasons at all can be given for adhering to such ultimate normative premisses—'principles'—as grounds for action and judgement. But the reasons which can be given are not in their nature conclusive, nor equally convincing to everyone. Honest and reasonable people can and do differ even upon ultimate matters of principle, each having reasons which seem to him or her good for the view to which he or she adheres.

To that extent I go along with Hume in supposing that a determinant factor in our assent to some or another normative principle lies in our affective nature, in our sentiments, passions, predispositions of will—whatever be the proper term. That people have different affective natures, differences of sentiment, passion, predisposition, can then be advanced in explanation of fundamental moral disagreements. Moreover, that our affective natures are in important ways socially moulded, if not entirely socially determined, so that our individual attitudes contain much that is rather a reflection of than a reflection upon the material conditions set by the economic forms of the society to which we belong seems also to be true.

Nevertheless, the point which Reid and after him Kant[10] alike urged as to the significance of 'practical reason' cannot be overlooked. That our adherence to ultimate principles in the evaluative and normative spheres is not derived by reasoning from ulterior factual or scientific knowledge of the world nor justifiable by reasoning of that sort, does not show that our adherence to such principles is other than a manifestation of our rational nature.

Human beings are not organisms set in motion by mere reaction to stimuli in the environment. Not merely can we give explanatory reasons to account for the actions of humans as for the ebb and flow of the tide; but it is also the case that human beings act *for reasons* when they act at all, and no 'explanation' or human behaviour which omits reference to the subjective reasons for which it is performed can be a full or adequate one. To any variety of behaviourism which expressly or impliedly denies that, there is a conclusive reply as devastating as it is simple; that it cannot be wrong to be anthropomorphic about people.

Whatever the basis of our adherence to such principles of conduct as we take to be ultimate, it is the case that for human beings they belong among the category of reasons for acting and of reasons for judgments about and critical or approbative reaction to others' actings. What is more, because they are not *ad hoc* or *ad hominem* but universal in their tenor and their reference to human beings as such, or categories of human beings, there is indeed (as Reid and Kant urged) good ground for distinguishing them from simple emotional or animal reactions to immediate circumstances, and even from what Hume called 'calm passions'. They represent an attempt to impose a rational pattern on our actings—rather as scientific endeavour imposes general schemata on observed events in an effort to provide a rational and structured explanation of them. At least at the formal level, there are worthwhile analogies to be drawn between 'practical' and 'pure' reason.

The attempt to articulate principles for action belongs

[10] See H.J. Paton, *The Moral Law* (London, 1948), being a commentary on and translation of Kant's *Groundwork of the Metaphysic of Morals*; also Jeffrie G. Murphy, *Kant: the Philosophy of Right* (London, 1970).

in the realm of reasoning concerning the practical affairs of life; it is concerned with the guidance of decisions, judgments, appraisals, and all the rest of it. That is not to say that all our reasons for acting are principled, nor to say that people do not often act in a merely impulsive way. But to the extent that we do, sometimes at least, act and judge upon principle rather than for some *ad hoc* reason, it is our rational as well as indeed our affective nature which is manifested in such acting. That is so even though it must be admitted that affectivity at least as much as rationality is engaged in our adherence to some particular principles rather than others.[11]

All that has been said so far is unavoidably abstract and rarefied. Even if intelligible, it is in no sense proved or justified as yet. It is in effect a programmatic declaration of the opinion to be advanced in this book, with reference to one particular sphere of practical activity: the making and justifying of decisions in law.

The book has therefore two purposes. One is to explain, concretize, and justify the thesis already sketched in abstract form about practical reasoning. The other is to advance an explanation of the nature of legal argumentation as manifested in the public process of litigation and adjudication upon disputed matters of law. In so far as I am a jurist, I hope in particular to contribute to a better understanding of what is often called 'the judicial process', and if I am even partially successful in that endeavour this book will have served some purpose. But I do not believe that one can say much that is illuminating about the rationality of the judicial process without some wider philosophical perspective of the kind sketched already. Accordingly I hope also to make some contribution to practical philosophy in elaborating that perspective. At least I may perform some small service in making more accessible to philosophers who are not lawyers some elements of what is perhaps a uniquely public and published form of reasoning, and therefore a resource of great potential interest to philosophers:

---

[11] Subject to the assertion of a more active role of 'reason' than Hume admits, this view is not at all dissimilar from that stated in *Enquiry*, Appendix I; but see also Chapter X of the present book.

namely, the recorded judgments and justifying opinions of courts of law.

(b) The Subject Matter of the Inquiry

The subject matter of my inquiry is the process of reasoning which is revealed to us in published decisions of Courts of Law. There are two legal systems, English law and Scots law, with which I am reasonably familiar, and most of my examples will be drawn therefrom, though I shall also advert to aspects of other legal systems, including that of the U.S.A., and other 'common law' countries within the Commonwealth; and, so far as my little knowledge will carry me, to Roman law and modern civilian systems, in particular the French.

The conclusions which I reach, so far as based on particular evidence, are therefore going to be restricted in range, and I do not pretend to be demonstrating necessary truths about legal reasoning everywhere. Nevertheless, in so far as I am able to explain my particular instances in terms of more general philosophical premises, I shall be aiming to give suggestive hypotheses worthy of testing for their explanatory value in relation to other legal systems, a task which would call for comparative study beyond my present compass. If any legal systems are illuminated by this approach it must be those of the contemporary United Kingdom; and if they are not explained and illuminated satisfactorily, the book is of no value whatever; if they are, it may be of more general value and interest.

Over the past three centuries at least, there has developed a practice of reporting on the decisions of the superior courts in England and Wales and in Scotland; and the same is true of other western countries. No doubt a particular reason for the practice of reporting decisions has been the importance of precedent as a formal source of law in the British systems (historically, more so in England than in Scotland); but there has also been a development of similar reporting in other jurisdictions such as the French, in which there is no similar doctrine of binding precedent—not in the strict and formal sense, at any rate.

Such reports always contain some recital of the facts relevant to the matter at issue in the case reported, often some outline of the arguments of advocates in either side, and invariably (in more recent times) a report of the opinion stated by the judge in justification of his decision as well as (invariably) a statement of the specific decision given as between the parties to the litigation.

A feature of the British systems, shared by most 'common law' systems of law, is that most trials, both civil and criminal, are conducted at first instance before a single judge who may or may not be assisted by a jury responsible for deciding on matters of fact where there is a dispute about facts. It is only when one of the parties to a case chooses to challenge the decision at first instance by way of an appeal that a dispute normally comes before a court which comprises more than one judge.

By contrast, in most civilian systems, the normal rule is that all save the most insignificant cases are taken by collegiate courts having more than one professional judge, and there is a further rule normally observed that the Court itself pronounces a single judgment which in no way discloses any disagreement among the members of the Court as to the appropriate decision for the case. That rule—or convention—holds good at all levels of the court system in such jurisdictions, so that even (e.g.) the Cour de Cassation in France publishes only a single statement—and that a very schematic one—for its most important decisions as the final court of appeal on civil and criminal matters in France.

In Scots or English law, on the other hand, appellate courts follow quite the opposite pattern. In them there almost invariably sit several—three or more—judges, each of whom normally states in a discursive way his own opinion on the points raised in the case, so that the decision of the court is based on simple majority decision among the judges, who may elaborate quite different, even opposed points of view in arguing for the decision which they favour.

This style of judging makes it much more candidly and publicly visible than does the continental style that in many disputed legal questions more than one point of view is possible; more than one answer may be given and supported by reference to 'the law'. Few if any continental lawyers would deny that, but many would strongly support the practice of keeping judicial argument over right and wrong answers behind closed doors, so that the Court's judgment as eventually presented shall contribute rather to faith in the relative certainty of the law than to revelation of its relative uncertainty.[12]

Without entering into any debate upon the merits of alternative approaches in this matter considered as a technical legal-cum-political question of the organization of a legal system, I might mention an advantage for my purposes in the British tradition. It follows from the practice of permitting each judge to state publicly his own opinion, that the judges in effect enter into public argument among themselves: in a difficult case each judge is stating what seem to him the best reasons for one way of deciding the case, and also countering any reasons which tell in the opposite direction. One strong reason for clearly articulating these counter-arguments is that a dissenting judge may have articulated in a strong form the very reasons which need to be countered for the justi- fication of the majority view to stand up.

Unless it were supposed that, in a collegiate system of judging, the types and grounds of disagreement which go on behind closed doors are fundamentally different from those which take place openly in the British systems, one may therefore take the latter systems as making more public some aspects of legal argumentation than do the former.

Certainly, it is a consequence of the dialectical setting of the British appellate judgment that, characteristically, a much more thorough exploration of arguments one way and the other is set forth than in those systems which in effect express only a set of sufficient justifying reasons for what may be only a majority decision, and which need neither rehearse nor counter any possible opposed arguments.

Another peculiarity which marks off the systems with which I am primarily dealing from continental systems is

---

[12] For an interesting discussion of the relative inexplicitness of judicial argumentation *as reported* in France, and for suggestions as to reform, including the admission of dissenting opinions, see A. Touffait and A. Tunc 'Pour une motivation plus explicite des décisions de justice', *Revue trimestrielle de droit civil* (Paris, 1974), p. 487.

the absence of a career judiciary. Whereas in the 'civilian' tradition—setting apart such 'mixed' systems as the Scots—it is normal for young and highly qualified men and women to enter directly into the judicial service of the state upon completion of their basic legal training (normally extended over a longer time than is common with us), the tradition of the U.K. and the 'common law' world is that the judiciary is recruited from among those who have established themselves as successful legal practitioners, and among them predominantly if not entirely from those who have specialized in the profession of advocacy before the courts. It is characteristically the senior and successful barrister or advocate in England and Wales or in Scotland who is in middle life elevated on to the bench.

It should therefore hardly be surprising if in some considerable degree the style of judicial argumentation in that tradition mirrors the style of advocative argument. Indeed, each would be expected to exercise some degree of reciprocal influence on the other; the able advocate constructs for his side of the case an argument which he hopes will weigh with the Court, as being the kind of argument which the Court will see good ground to adopt, doubtless with modifications, as a strong or compelling reason for a decision in favour of that side. The judge or judges faced with a choice to make between two sides in whose interest such arguments have been made have to decide for one side or the other and by convention (if not by law as is commonly the case in continental Europe) have to give their reasons for so deciding. Not surprisingly, the reasons which they offer owe much to the reasoning which has been offered by counsel appearing before them; even when rejecting an argument, they commonly do counsel the courtesy of indicating why they do not accept it.

Even if there were no sociological evidence (as in fact there is[13]), that in some degree common normative expectations

<hr/>

[13] On this, I am entirely indebted to Dr. A.A. Paterson's as yet unpublished D.Phil. thesis 'A Sociological Investigation of the Creative Role-Performance of English Appellate Judges in Hard Cases' (Oxford, 1976), which I had the good fortune to see as supervisor in the concluding stages of Dr. Paterson's research.

are held by bench and bar as to what constitutes a relevant and acceptable argument at law upon a given point, the facts already mentioned would lead one to infer that there are shared norms among judges and as between judges and counsel which determine what types of argument do and ought to carry weight in contested matters of litigation. There is indeed within every legal system, and within the same one at different points of time, an observable common style of argumentation. There are from place to place and from time to time more or less noticeable differences of style, or differing ranges of style.

I shall not here be mainly concerned with local or temporal variations of style, interesting though that is as indicating e.g. shifts in the definition of judges' or advocates' roles: my attempt will be to bring out what seem to me to be more invariant elements in legal argumentation (in relation to which I shall indicate grounds for thinking that they are and ought to be invariant).

My point in mentioning the matter of style is rather that it makes obvious what is on reflection obviously true: that reasoning in the sense at least of public argumentation is itself an activity conducted within more or less vague or clear, implicit or explicit, normative canons. We distinguish between good and bad, more sound and less sound, relevant and irrelevant, acceptable or unacceptable arguments in relation to philosophical, economic, sociological, or, above all, legal disputation over given foci of dispute. That is possible only given some criteria (as often as not both vague and inexplicit criteria) of goodness or badness, more or less soundness, relevancy, acceptability, and so forth. At the most superficial level, criteria of acceptable modes of presentation are also in play, and observance of these is in some measure determinative of style. (At the most basic level, one might also observe, the rules of formal logic function as criteria distinguishing the unsound-because-self-contradictory from that which is valid as being undeniable without self-contradiction: that we ought to reject illogical arguments follows only if or because we recognize that there are good reasons for avoiding self-contradiction.)

Any study of legal reasoning is therefore an attempt to expiscate and explain the criteria as to what constitutes a good or a bad, an acceptable or an unacceptable type of argument in the law.

That said, a question immediately poses itself as to the type of inquiry upon which we are embarked: is it *about* norms, or itself normative? Am I simply to seek by the most comprehensive possible study of the courts in action an exhaustive description of the norms actually operative among the judiciary and the bar? Or am I to offer my own account of how people who argue in law ought to argue in law?

There is a middle road between these two possibilities, and it is the one which I shall pursue: I neither aim at, nor purport to give, an exhaustive description of every possible element in legal reasoning as concretely pursued in the courts and evidenced in the Law Reports. Equally, I do not cut myself adrift from the actualities of legal systems and issue from on high my own ukases as to how judges and lawyers ought to argue. Rather, I set forth an account of certain features of legal argumentation which are actually instantiated within the law reports, and explain the reasons why I think they ought to be fundamental features of legal argumentation given its function; these reasons I further offer as explaining why such features are in fact highly common in the practice of legal argumentation, as can be shown by a plethora of examples. My conclusions therefore present a double face: they are both in their own right normative and yet I believe them to describe norms actually operative within the systems under study. In the latter aspect I am offering eminently falsifiable hypotheses. If they do falsely represent the process of argumentation in any system, there must be a mass of available evidence to that effect. Of course, one single, or one or two, counter-examples would not necessarily falsify the hypothesis, for if the only counter-examples were few in number, it is plainly open to me to argue that they are genuinely examples of cases deviant from actually operative norms rather than that I have erred in stating what I take to be operative norms. In my own right, I can simply treat them as instances of bad arguments.

(c) *The justificatory function of legal argumentation*

A moment ago I spoke of features of legal argumentation which I think 'ought to be fundamental features of legal

argumentation given its function'. What then is its function? Is
this whole inquiry predicated upon some naive functionalism?
Arguments in practical contexts are usually advanced in
order to persuade; they are aimed at a particular audience
with a view to persuading that audience to do something;
they are therefore in some measure relative both to audience
and to topic, a point first made in recorded form in Aristotle's
Topica and *Rhetorica*, and ably resuscitated by Professor
Ch. Perelman in his many contributions to 'La Nouvelle
Rhétorique'.[14] Everyone knows that different styles and even
tricks of arguing are suited to jury trials and to appeals before
the House of Lords. But in each situation the advocate is out
to persuade the tribunal to decide in favour of his side of
the case.

Underlying the practical aim of persuasion there is, it
appears to me, a function of *justification*, at least ostensible
justification. If a citizen brings an action against another for
example claiming damages for some alleged injury inflicted
by the other, it is a logical condition of the success of his
claim that he be able to show it a justified claim; if the other
party denies liability he must in his turn demonstrate that the
claim is not justified and accordingly his demand to be
absolved from liability is a justified demand. The judge or
court before whom the action is brought must—so far as
there is a dispute as to what actually happened—reach some
findings on the evidence as to what did happen, and must in
the light of that decide whether the claim is justified or the
defence (in the sense given) justified; the reasoning stated in
the judicial opinion actually supports the decision to the
extent that it shows why the order given—whether an order
awarding damages as claimed, wholly or in part, or absolving
the defender—is justified given the facts established and the
relevant legal norms and other considerations.

At all points in such a process, insincerity is an evident
possibility: a skilled lawyer may be able to persuade a judge
that a claim which he himself does not regard as a good

---

[14] See e.g. Ch. Perelman and L. Olbrechts-Tyteca, *La Nouvelle Rhétorique:
traité de l'argumentation* (1st edn., Paris, 1958; English translation, Notre Dame,
Indiana, and London, 1969); Ch. Perelman, *Logique juridique: nouvelle rhétorique*
(Paris, Dalloz, 1976).

one is justified in law; a judge may (as we have often enough been told) give a decision in favour of a pursuer with a pretty face or a given class background, really because he likes the face or the class (yet more insidiously, because of an unconscious prejudice in favour of the face or the class), but ostensibly because the reasons for his decision and such and such...(here follows a carefully articulated and ostensibly flawless chain of legal reasons for his decision). So it may be; so, sometimes, it must almost certainly be.

But insincerity is even more revealing than sincerity. Why is it that a lawyer who wants to win a case in order to be sure of his fee rather than because he really believes in it does not say so? Why does the judge not make his reason explicit by granting Mrs. McTavish her divorce just because she has a ravishingly pert retroussé nose? Because such are not accepted as good reasons within the system for sustaining claims or granting divorces. Whether sincerely advanced or not, only those arguments which show why x ought to be done are reasons for demanding that it be done, or doing it. Those who work within such a system persuade precisely by convincing the relevant audience that there are reasons of overriding weight why x *ought* to be done; or at least, by showing that there are good ostensibly justifying reasons in addition to such other elements in the case as may appeal to unstated prejudices and predispositions.

Hence the essential notion is that of giving (what are understood and presented as) good justifying reasons for claims defences or decisions. The process which is worth studying is the process of argumentation as a process of justification.

There is no need to labour unduly a point often made before about the difference between processes of justification and processes of discovery.[15] Archimedes may indeed have discovered his celebrated principle in a blinding flash of insight resulting from the overflowing of his bath due to his own immersion therein. (He may even have so forgotten himself as to set off into the street of Syracuse with many a

[15] See R.A. Wasserstrom, *The Judicial Decision* (Stanford and London, 1961), esp. cc. 1 and 2; D.H. Hodgson, *Consequences of Utilitarianism* (Oxford, 1967), esp. pp. 83–5.

happy cry of 'Eureka') But many a flash of insight has been rudely brought to earth when relevantly tested. What justified Archimedes, or anyone else, in believing that bodies immersed in fluids receive an upthrust equivalent to the weight of fluid displaced, is that it can be proved experimentally (which for those who follow Sir K. Popper means that many instances of experimental evidence have corroborated it, and none falsified it[16] —but theories as to the nature of scientific 'proof' are not our present concern).

Likewise, what prompts a judge to think of one side rather than the other as a winner is quite a different matter from the question whether there are on consideration good justifying reasons in favour of that rather than the other side.

Of course, it could in principle be the case that in their nature, legally justifying reasons are so vague and indecisive as to be always compatible with an actual decision either way, in which case for practical purposes the 'process of discovery' would always have primacy over the 'process of justification'—a view which Jerome Frank on occasion came dangerously close to asserting.[17] But we could establish that as true only if we had first given serious study to the type of ostensibly justifying reasons which are given for legal decisions —that would be a necessary condition of demonstrating them to be not merely open textured but positively tattered and torn. So even if all justifying reasons in law never function as more than ostensibly justifying reasons operating to cloak decisions always motivated upon other grounds, the only possible way of establishing that would be by reasonably exhaustive study and analysis of what are, on any view, at least *ostensibly* justifying reasons. So we may as well get on with it, to see what turns up.

So far as the foregoing is predicated on beliefs about what is required within 'the system', it dangerously courts denunciation as an instance of naive functionalism.

---

[16] K.R. Popper *The Logic of Scientific Discovery* (revised edn., London, 1968); cf. also P.D. Medawar, *Induction and Intuition in Scientific Thought* (London, 1969), M.J. Lessnoff, *The Structure of Social Science* (London, 1974), ch. 1.

[17] See Jerome Frank, *Law and the Modern Mind* (New York, 1936), pp. 100, 128.

Functionalist in a sense it may be, but not naive, far less wrong. Judges present themselves as the impartial determiners of disputes between citizen and citizen, or of prosecutions by public authorities of citizens. They so present themselves at least because within the dominant political tradition that is what they are expected to be. They are appointed to do 'justice according to law', and the watchdogs of the public interest are continually alert to yap at their heels if they appear to do any other thing.

To put it at its very lowest, there are therefore strong pressures—apparently very effective pressures—on judges to appear to be what they are supposed to be. The reasons they publicly state for their decisions must therefore be reasons which (so far as taken seriously) make them appear to be what they are supposed to be: in short, reasons which show that their decisions secure 'justice according to law', and which are at least in that sense justifying reasons.

Equally, therefore, lawyers who want to win their cases are on notice that they had better give reasons on behalf of their clients which could consistently with the required appearances commend themselves to the judiciary. In short, justifying reasons.

There is a certain sort of not altogether uncommon silliness which, observing the veracity of such observations as these, leaps to the conclusion that appearances are all that is to it. That could be true, but would require proof of a kind which has yet to be offered. In the absence of much good evidence, it seems reasonable to suppose that judges and lawyers are, like all humans, capable of occasional fits of humbug and hypocrisy, or of interpreting rooted prejudices as revealed truths. But equally, they are more commonly honest and honourable, capable of real efforts at, if never total achievement of, impartiality and objectivity; through practice, moreover, they have normally done more to develop habits of impartiality than many of those who are most strident in their denunciation.

Whether the system which they administer is systematically non-impartial, that is, unjust, is not a question of fact at all. When Hume observed that careful attention to transitions from 'is' to 'ought' would 'subvert all the vulgar systems of morality.[18] he did not know half of the truth of what he spoke—nor with his eighteenth-century faith in progress could he have had any anticipation of the vulgarities to come.

[18] Loc.cit. *supra*, p. 3 n. 4.

II

DEDUCTIVE JUSTIFICATION

In Chapter I, it was stated that, in relation to legal reasoning, 'the process which is worth studying is the process of argumentation as a process of justification.' As a value judgment that is doubtless disputable, but it demarcates the main area of inquiry of this book. In relation to all manner of acts and activities, claims and rebuttals, citizens of a society may be called on to show legal justification for what they do. In particular since judges are required to give only such decisions as are justified according to law, they must apply thought to the question which of the decisions sought from them by the parties to a case in Court is so justified. Since they are required to state the reasons for their decisions, they must not merely reason out, they must publicly state and expound, the justifying reasons for their decisions—hence their eminent accessibility to study.

As will be mentioned shortly, some people have denied that legal reasoning is ever strictly deductive. If this denial is intended in the strictest sense, implying that legal reasoning is never, or cannot ever be, solely deductive in form, then the denial is manifestly and demonstrably false. It is sometimes possible to show conclusively that a given decision is legally justified by means of a purely deductive argument. To demonstrate the *possibility* of purely deductive justification, it is sufficient to produce a single example of such justification. Without more ado I shall therefore produce an example of it, analysis of which will serve to elucidate the concept of 'deductive reasoning'.

My example is the case of *Daniels and Daniels v. R. White & Sons and Tarbard* ([1938] 4 All E.R. 258). The facts of the matter were as follows. Mr. Daniels went to a pub, and there bought a bottle of lemonade (R. White's lemonade) and a jug of beer. These he took home, and there drank some of the lemonade himself and gave a glass of it to his wife, which she drank. They both experienced burning sensations and became ill. The cause of their sickness was subsequently established as being the fact that the lemonade which they had consumed was heavily contaminated with carbolic acid. Examination of the remaining contents of the lemonade bottle showed the lemonade to contain a large admixture of carbolic acid.

The plaintiffs, Mr. and Mrs. Daniels, subsequently sued the manufacturer of the lemonade and the publican who sold it to them for damages in compensation for their illness, treatment expenses, and loss of earnings when ill. The defendant manufacturer was absolved from liability (as will appear in due course); the defendant publican was held liable and ordered to pay them damages. With what justification?

Let me first of all quote the whole relevant passage of Lewis J.'s opinion, with a view subsequently to analysing its logical structure:

> She [i.e. the publican, the second defendant] was, of course, entirely innocent and blameless in the matter. She had received the bottle three days before from the first defendants, and she sold it over the counter to the husband, and the husband, of course, is the only one who has any rights in contract and breach of warranty against her. There is no issue of fact between the husband and Mrs. Tarbard. They entirely agree as to what happened—namely, that Mr. Daniels came into the public house, the licensed premises, and said, 'I want a bottle of R. White's lemonade,' and R. White's lemonade was what she gave him. The question which arises is, on those facts, the bottle in fact containing carbolic acid, and the lemonade, therefore, not being of merchantable quality, whether or not the second defendant is liable.
>
> To my mind, it is quite clear that she is not liable under sect. 14 (1) of the Act, because Mr. Daniels did not rely upon her skill and judgment at all. He asked for and obtained exactly what he wanted. If a man goes in and asks for a bottle of R. White's lemonade, or somebody's particular brand of beer, he is not relying upon the skill and judgment of the person who serves it to him. In spite of the argument which has been put forward by counsel for the second defendant, I have some difficulty in seeing—particularly in view of the cases which have been cited to me, and more particularly *Morelli* v. *Fitch & Gibbons* ([1928] 2 K.B. 636)—why this was not a case of sale by description within the Sale of Goods Act, 1893, s. 14(2). If it is a case of goods sold by description by a seller who deals in goods of that description, there is an implied condition that the goods shall be of merchantable quality. Unfortunately for Mrs. Tarbard, through no fault of hers, the goods were not of merchantable quality. It was suggested by Mr. Block [Counsel for Mrs. Tarbard] that there was an oppportunity of

examination so as to bring the matter within the proviso to sect. 14(2) of the Act, and he cited an authority to me, but I do not think that that authority takes him the length which he would wish it to do. I therefore find that this was a sale by description, and therefore hold— with some regret, because it is rather hard on Mrs. Tarbard, who is a perfectly innocent person in the matter—that she is liable for the injury sustained by Mrs. Daniels through drinking this bottle of lemonade. However, that as I understand it, is the law, and therefore I think that there must be judgment for Mr. Daniels, who is the only person who can recover against Mrs. Tarbard.

Judgment for the male plaintiff against the second defendant for £21. 15s., and judgment for the first defendants against both plaintiffs. Costs on the High Court scale.

The above-quoted passage from Lewis J.'s opinion is the whole of what appears in the Report in relation to the husband's claim against the publican, the second defendant (other than the more discursive account of the 'facts' given earlier in the opinion, and summarized above.) The passage is sufficiently concise to facilitate the task of analysing its elements in reasonably small bulk. There is no reason to suppose that its shortness disqualifies it as a relevant example.

It appears on the face of it that the argument quoted has conclusive force; the learned judge certainly thought so, as appears from his expression of regret that 'there must be judgment' against Mrs. Tarbard, despite the fact that she was 'entirely innocent and blameless in the matter'. The question which must now be discussed is whether the superficial appearance of conclusiveness is accurate or is deceptive. Is it possible to show that the argument presented is logically conclusive? Since the task which I have set myself is to demonstrate that it is possible for some legal decisions to be justified by deductive arguments, I shall now attempt to answer my most recently posed question by showing that the passage quoted from Lewis J.'s judgment is an example of a valid deductive argument.

A deductive argument is an argument which purports to show that one proposition, the conclusion of the argument, is implied by some other proposition or propositions, the 'premisses' of the argument. A deductive argument is valid if, whatever may be the content of the premisses and the conclusion, its form is such that its premisses do in fact imply (or entail) the conclusion. By that is meant that it would be self-contradictory for anyone to assert the premisses and at the same time to deny the conclusion.

To illustrate and explain, let me take one phrase from Lewis J.'s above-quoted opinion: 'the bottle in fact containing carbolic acid and the lemonade, therefore, not being of merchantable quality'. Lewis J. in effect asserts two propositions:

> The bottle of lemonade bought by Mr. Daniels contained carbolic acid
>
> Therefore the bottle of lemonade bought by Mr. Daniels was not of merchantable quality.

For what reason can it be said so confidently that the first of these propositions implies the second? The answer is, of course, that Lewis J. takes for granted the meaning which the phrase 'of merchantable quality' bears for legal purposes in the context of s.14(2) of the Sale of Goods Act 1893. A convenient dictum of Lord Wright's in the 1936 case of *Grant* v. *Australian Knitting Mills* ([1936] A.C. 85 at p. 100) gives an account of the legal meaning of the phrase which would have been relevant at the time of the *Daniels* decision: A thing 'is not merchantable. . .if it has defects unfitting it for its only proper use but not apparent on ordinary examination.' To restate that in an equivalent proposition:

> (A) In any case, if goods sold by one person to another have defects unfitting them for their only proper use but not apparent on ordinary examination, then the goods sold are not of merchantable quality.

Let us now suppose that Lewis J.'s assertion that the bottle of lemonade in the *Daniels* case contained carbolic acid can be restated as follows:

> (B) In the instant case, goods sold by one person to another had defects unfitting them for their only proper use but not apparent on ordinary examination.

It will be obvious that it would be impossible to assert as true both proposition (A) and proposition (B) above without at the same time conceding the truth of the following proposition (C); it would be plain self-contradiction to assert both (A) and (B) and, at the same time, to deny (C);

> (C) Therefore, in the instant case, the goods sold are not of merchantable quality.

Let it at once be observed that the self-contradictory character of denying (C) while asserting (A) and (B) is not dependent on either (A) or (B) being *actually* true. Even if either or both of (A) and (B) were actually false, somebody who asserted them (mistakenly, in that case) as true, would be unable without self-contradiction to deny (C). That (A) and (B) taken together imply (C), is necessarily true, and is true whether or not either or both of (A) and (B) is actually true.

To recognize that is to recognize that the argument is *formally valid*. Any argument of the same form as our argument would be equally valid, whatever the substance of the premises. To reveal the form of the argument it is helpful to use some very simply symbols. For the proposition (A) above, let us substitute the following partly symbolic expression:

In any case, if *p* then *q*.

It will be seen that *p* is substituted for the proposition contained in the first clause of (A) ('goods sold by one person to another have defects unfitting them for their only proper use but not apparent on ordinary examination'); likewise *q* for the proposition contained in the second clause ('the goods sold are not of merchantable quality'). It will also be seen that the assertion of the compound proposition which we have now represented by the symbolic propositional form 'In any case, if *p* then *q*' in no way involves the assertion that the state of affairs denoted by *p* (or by *q*) has ever been, is now, or will ever be the case. (To revert to our concrete example, we can at least imagine the world's being such that no goods with hidden defects which make them unfit for use are ever sold by one person to another.) All that 'In any case, if *p* then *q*' says is that whenever *p* is true, *q* is also true; *p* cannot be true without *q* being in consequence, true as well. The legal systems of the U.K. can (e.g. by legislation) make it true that goods sold cannot have hidden defects unfitting them for their proper use without being in consequence 'unmerchantable' in the specific sense ascribed to that term within the legal system. It is unlikely that legislators would bother to do so if they did not think it likely that, on occasion, such goods would be sold, but to make it true that the one proposition implies the other is not to make it true that such goods are ever sold. It may even make it less likely that they will be. That is why proposition (B) gives us information not contained in proposition (A). To state that in a given case proposition (B) held good is to state that once somebody did sell goods with such hidden defects. So *for that case* (C) was also true. But (B) and (C) are assertions, of the simple propositions which, yoked together with 'if...then...' form the clauses of (A). So the whole argument could be expressed symbolically as:

(A)   In any case, if p then q
(B)   In the instant case p
(C) $\therefore$, in the instant case, q

These symbols 'p' and 'q' were introduced as symbols substituted for the specific propositions of the argument reviewed. But it is now clear that we could in turn substitute for p and q any propositions whatsoever, whether propositions of law, of science, of sociology or whatever; without regard to the content of the propositions, an argument of the above form is a valid argument. For any proposition p and any other proposition q it must be self contradictory to assert 'In any case, if p then q; and in *this* case, p but not q'.

The specific task of logic as a branch of knowledge is to study the forms of valid argument. At least since the time of Aristotle, it has been recognized that an argument of the form 'If p then q, p, therefore q' is a valid deductive argument; the logicians of the Stoic school who came after him gave that form of valid inference the name 'modus ponens'. But full understanding of 'propositional logic' did not come until the present century, when Russell and Whitehead and others worked out a systematic account of the 'calculus of propositions'.[1] Within the calculus, it is possible to show that arguments of the form discussed are necessarily valid given certain more fundamental definition and axioms.

[1] See Russell and Whitehead, *Principia Mathematica* (London, 1910), and L. Wittgenstein, *Tractatus Logico Philosophicus* (tr. C.K. Ogden and I.A. Richards, London, 1922), and cf. Anthony Kenny, *Wittgenstein* (London, 1973), cc. 2 and 3. On propositional logic in general, see any modern introduction to logic, e.g. David Mitchell, *An Introduction to Logic* (London, 1962).

In the present context, however, we are concerned not with the demonstration of logical truths but with their application, that is with the application of logically valid forms of argument in legal contexts. It is important therefore to emphasize that the logical validity of an argument does not guarantee the truth of its conclusion; that the argument is valid entails that if the premisses are true, the conclusion must be true; but logic itself cannot establish or guarantee the truth of the premisses. Whether or not they are true is (or at least may be) an empirical question. Let us therefore reconsider the argument to see on what ground its premisses might be held to be true:

(A) In any case, if goods sold by one person to another have defects unfitting them for their only proper use but not apparent on ordinary examination, then the goods sold are not of merchantable quality.

(B) In the instant case, goods sold by one person to another had defects unfitting them for their proper use but not apparent on ordinary examination.

Therefore (C) In the instant case, the goods sold are not of merchantable quality.

The 'major premiss' (A) of that argument is, as we saw above, a restatement in different words of the same proposition as that stated by Lord Wright in *Grant's* case ([1936] A.C. 85), by way of an authoritative explanation of the meaning of the term 'merchantable quality' for legal purposes. By giving an authoritative explanation of the term, Lord Wright *ascribed* a particular meaning to it. Now it is certainly the case that Lord Wright's act of ascribing meaning to the term is not in itself either true or false;[2] but given the authoritative character of a ruling on such a point by a Lord of Appeal, even in a Privy Council case, *his* ascription of a particular

---

[2] Compare the case of a lady launching a ship, and saying 'I name this ship *Helen of Troy*...' The act of naming the ship is not true or false. It is simply performed. But *if* the act is performed 'validly', i.e. by the correct person, giving it the agreed name, then it is thereby *made* true that (thenceforward) the ship's name is *Helen of Troy*. Cf. J.L. Austin, *How to do Things with Words* (Oxford, 1962), and also his essay 'Performative Utterances' in *Philosophical Papers* (Oxford, 1961, ed. J.O. Urmson and G.J. Warnock) pp. 220–9, esp. at 222–7.

meaning to the term *makes* it true at least for lower courts and legal writers, that for legal purposes that *is* the meaning of the phrase. Therefore premiss (A) may be said to have been a true proposition of law, at least in the year 1938.[3]

What of the 'minor premiss', (B)? That is not a proposition of a kind which can be 'made' true by an authoriative utterance such as the dictum of a superior judge or an enactment by a Parliament. It is a proposition relating to a particular historical moment which must therefore be proved, if at all, by recourse to particular relevant evidence. But at that rate, it can hardly be said that proposition (B) was *directly* proved by the evidence in the case. What was proved, or deemed proved because the parties did not disagree about it, was that a bottle of lemonade was sold by Mrs. T. to Mr. D., and that the lemonade in the bottle sold was contaminated with carbolic acid. Since carbolic acid is a clear liquid, its presence would not be detectable by visual inspection. It was assumed as being incontestably true that the 'proper use' of lemonade is to be drunk as a refreshment.[4] It was proved that as a result of drinking the lemonade, Mr. and Mrs. D. became ill; if on no other ground, it seems true that the lemonade was, by virtue of the presence of the carbolic acid, unfit for its 'proper use'. It appears, therefore, that in the instant case, our proposition (B) was true only if it is true: (i) that a bottle of lemonade belongs to the category 'goods'; (ii) that the bottle of lemonade was sold by one party to the other; (iii) that a bottle of lemonade in which there is an admixture of carbolic acid has a defect in that it is unfit for its only proper use; and (iv) that that is a defect of a kind which does not appear on ordinary examination.

One of the advantages of having selected a very simple example as a starting point of the inquiry, is that each of these four assumptions is on the face of it indubitably true. But it is worth observing, a point which will be resumed

---

[3] The temporal reference is important, since legal rules, and legal rulings can be changed. Thus, e.g., in 1973 Parliament gave a new definition of merchantable quality in the Supply of Goods (Implied Terms) Act 1973. See s. 7(2).

[4] That is a fact of the kind of which judges are entitled to 'take judicial notice', i.e. to assume without proof on the ground that they are a matter of common knowledge.

later, that the events which transpired in the *Daniels* case might have been marginally different. What if the poison present in the lemonade had been such as slightly to discolour the lemonade? Then a problem could have arisen whether or not the 'evidentiary facts' of the instant case were truly instances of the 'operative facts' of the proposition of law stated as premiss (A). Then the truth of proposition (B) as an assertion about the instant case could be doubted.

Be that as it may, we can be satisfied that the facts proved did fit unequivocally within the categories used in proposition (B) and therefore proposition (B), as asserted about the instant case was true. We ought perhaps to say that it was accepted for legal purposes as being true, the point of putting it that way being as follows: the legal process of 'Proof' results in some authorized individual (judge or jury) making 'findings of fact' on the basis of evidence presented or admissions of parties in a case. The 'facts' which he 'finds' are then taken to be established as true for the purposes of the litigation, and have to be accepted as such unless and until 'set aside' by some body of superior authority in the context of an appeal. The process of 'proof' is a process of establishing that certain propositions are for legal purposes to be considered true, specifically for the purpose of the litigation in question.

We may therefore conclude that the argument considered is both a logically valid argument of the form 'If p then q; p; $\therefore$ q.' and an argument of which both premisses are, given criteria adopted for legal purposes, true. It accordingly follows that the conclusion must also be, given these criteria, true.

But the argument so far considered is only a tiny element in the reasoning of Lewis J. in the case. What is more, taken in isolation that argument presupposes certain conclusions of law as already established—e.g. that the bottle of lemonade was 'sold' by one person to another. In order to show that the whole argument is a valid deductive argument, it will be necessary to set out every step in the argument; for simplicity's sake, the argument will throughout be presented in the same form as has been discussed so far, but subject to one further refinement which must be noted. The refinement concerns the possibility of a particular legal provision being made conditional on the fulfilment of two (or perhaps more) jointly sufficient conditions. Take s. 14(2) of the Sale of Goods Act 1893:

Where goods are bought by description from a seller who deals in goods of that description. . .there is an implied condition that the goods shall be of merchantable quality.

To bring that section into operation, it is not sufficient to prove only that goods were bought by description, nor sufficient to prove only that the seller of the goods in question is a person who (habitually) deals in goods of the kind sold. As is obvious, both of these propositions must be proved. A more logically tidy way of stating s.14(2) would therefore be the following:

'If goods are bought by description by one person from another, and if the seller is a person who deals in goods of the relevant description; then there is an implied condition (which must be fulfilled by the seller) that the goods shall be of merchantable quality.'

If that were to be expressed symbolically according to the convention already used, it would take such a form as

In any case, if (*p* and *q*), then *r*.

In logical terms, (*p* and *q*) is a compound proposition, which is true if and only if each of *p* and *q* are true. So, for legal purposes, if each *p* and *q* were held to be proven in a given case, the argument could be completed thus:

In the instant case *p* and *q*

∴ in the instant case *r*.

One final preliminary which may be helpful, if only as an introduction to an estblished logical usage, will be to explain a further piece of symbolic shorthand. Instead of writing 'if in any case. . . .then. . .' we can adopt the sign '⊃' which is standardly used to express the relationship of 'material implication' between two propositions *p* and *q*.[5] Instead of

---

[5] It has been rightly pointed out that the material implication sign '⊃' as defined in the calculus of propositions has a more extensive meaning than 'If. . . then. . .' in English usage, including legal usage; but for present purposes, nothing turns on that. See David Mitchell, *An Introduction to Logic*, (2nd edn., Oxford, 1964), pp. 61−8. It is also the case that legal norms of the form 'If *p* then *q*' belong, strictly speaking, to the category of 'open hypotheticals' and therefore do not strictly belong within the calculus of propositions. But no importance need be attached to that in the present context.

writing 'If in any case p then q' we can then use the formula '$p \supset q$'. Again, the symbol '.' can be used to express conjunction, so that instead of writing 'p and q' we write '$p \cdot q$'. To avoid confusion, brackets are introduced into more complex formulae. 'If p and q then r' is symbolically expressed thus: '$(p \cdot q) \supset r$'. This is distinguishable from, and must be distinguished from: '$p \cdot (q \supset r)$', which means 'p, and if q then r'. The symbol $\therefore$ will be used, as hitherto, to stand for 'therefore'.

These preliminary points being settled, we are in a position to show that the entire argument of Lewis J. in the *Daniels* case so far as it related to the action between Mr. D., the plaintiff, and Mrs. T. the publican, can be restated in the most ruthlessly deductive form; and that each step of the argument, and the argument as a whole, are logically valid. All of the major premisses involved in the argument, not all of which were expressly stated, are rules of law for which contemporary authority can be cited. The minor premisses are either statements of proven 'primary fact' or conclusions of 'secondary fact' derived from the former by deduction via some major premiss which is a rule of law. Re-examination of the passage quoted from Lewis J.'s opinion reveals that there are three assertions of 'primary fact' on which the whole edifice is ostensibly built:

(i)   Mr. D. came into the public house. . .and said 'I want a bottle of R. White's lemonade' and R. White's lemonade was what [Mrs. T] gave him.

(ii)   The bottle in fact contain[ed] carbolic acid.

(iii)   [Mrs. T. is] a seller who deals in goods of that description [viz. bottles of lemonade].

To these we have to add one further tacit finding of fact which is so trivially obvious that its omission from the express statements of Lewis J. is scarcely surprising—namely that the transaction described in (i) above was intended by each of the parties to be a purchase by Mr. D. from Mrs. T. and a sale by her to him. To express that in strict terms:

(iv)   Mrs. T. transferred the property in the bottle of lemonade to Mr. D. for a money consideration.

It will be seen that each of these propositions appears in the following statement of the argument, expressed in logical form. Beside each stage of the argument, a symbolic expression of the syllogism is stated, indicating that it exhibits a valid form. In the case of major premisses which are rules of law, the source will be indicated.

(1)   If one person transfers the property in goods to another person for a money consideration, then a contract of sale of those goods exists as between those parties, called 'the seller' and 'the buyer' respectively. (See Sale of Goods Act, s. 1(1).)

(2)   In the instant case, one person [Mrs. T] transferred the property in goods [a bottle of lemonade] to another person [Mr. D.] for a money consideration. (See 'fact (iv)' above.)

$p \supset q$
p
$\therefore q$

(3) $\therefore$ In the instant case a contract of sale of those goods [a bottle of lemonade] existed as between those parties, [Mrs. T] 'the seller' and [Mr. D] 'the buyer'.

(4)   If a contract of sale of certain goods exists as between a seller and a buyer, if the goods in question are a form of bottled drink, and if the buyer in purchasing the bottled drink asks for a bottle of a certain named beverage, then the goods in question are bought and sold by description (see[6] *Morelli* v. *Fitch & Gibbons* [1928] 2 K.B. 636).

$[(q.r).s] \supset t$
$(q.r).s$
$\therefore t$

(3)   In the instant case a contract of sale of certain goods [a bottle of lemonade] existed between a seller and a buyer [Mrs. T. and Mr.D.].

and

(5)   The goods in question were a form of bottled drink [viz. a bottle of lemonade]. (See 'fact (i)' above.)

and

(6)   The buyer in purchasing the bottled drink asked for a bottle of a certain named beverage ['Mr. D. . . .said "I want a bottle of R. White's lemonade" ']. (See 'fact (i)' above.)

(7) $\therefore$ In the instant case, the goods in question [a bottle of lemonade] were bought and sold by description.

(8)   If goods are bought and sold by description, and if the seller of the goods is a person who deals in goods of that description, then there is an implied condition (which must be fulfilled by the seller) that the goods shall be of merchantable quality. (See S.G.A. s. 14(2).)

(7)   In the instant case, goods [a bottle of lemonade] were bought and sold by description.

[6] The general proposition stated above is implied by, but not expressly stated in the case. For a more general proposition, see *Grant* v. *Australian Knitting Mills* [1936] A.C. 85 at 100, *per* Lord Wright: 'a thing is sold by description, though it is [a] specific [article], so long as it is sold not merely as the specific thing but as a thing corresponding to a description.'

and
(9) The seller of the goods [Mrs. T.] was a person who dealt in goods of that description [viz. bottles of lemonade]. (See 'fact (iii)' above.)

$(t.u) \supset v$ (10)   ∴ In the instant case, there was an implied condition
$t.u$ (which must be fulfilled by the seller) that the goods
$∴v$ should be of merchantable quality.

(11) If goods sold by one person to another have defects unfitting them for their only proper use but not apparent on ordinary examination, then the goods sold are not of merchantable quality.

(12) In the instant case, goods sold by one person to another [a bottle of lemonade] had defects [contamination with carbolic acid] unfitting them for their only proper use [human consumption] but not apparent on ordinary examination. (See 'fact (ii)' above, and the discussion at pp. 7−8 above.)

$w \supset x$ (13)   ∴ In the instant case the goods sold were not of
w merchantable quality.
$∴x$

(14) If a contract of sale of goods exists between two parties, and if there is an implied condition (which must be fulfilled by the seller) that the goods shall be of merchantable quality, and if the goods sold are not of merchantable quality, then the seller has broken a condition of the contract which he was required to fulfil. (Tautological, dependent on legal concept of 'condition'.)

(3) In the instant case, a contract of sale of goods existed between two parties [Mrs. T and Mr. D.].

and
(10) There was an implied condition (which must be fulfilled by the seller) that the goods should be of
$[(q.v).x] \supset y$ merchantable quality.
$(q.v).x$ and
$∴y$ (13)   The goods sold were not of merchantable quality.
        (15)   ∴ In the instant case, the seller has broken a condition of the contract which she was required to fulfil.

(16) If a seller has broken a condition of a contract which he was required to fulfil, the buyer is entitled to recover damages from him equivalent to the loss directly and naturally resulting to him from the seller's breach of the condition. (See S.G.A.;ss. 11(1) (a), and 53(1) and (2); the buyer has other rights which are of no present concern.)

(15)   In the instant case, the seller has broken a condition
        of the contract which she was required to fulfil.

$y \supset z$ (17)   ∴ In the instant case the buyer is entitled to recover
y damages from her equivalent to the loss directly and
∴z naturally resulting to him from the seller's breach of
                 the condition.

The converse of proposition 17, which is therefore immediately
entailed by it is: 'The seller is liable to pay damages to the
buyer equivalent to the loss directly and naturally resulting
to him from the seller's breach of condition.' And that in
turn is precisely the conclusion expressed by Lewis J. when
he said 'I...therefore hold...that [Mrs. Tarbard] is liable
for the injury sustained by Mr. D. through drinking this
lemonade.'

It will be observed that in the above analysis of the argument each stage in the argument is a valid hypothetical
argument the premisses of which are either statements of
propositions of law which at the material time were true for
legal purposes, or findings of fact which are also for legal
purposes taken to be true, or intermediate conclusions derived
from such premisses. Since each step in the argument is valid,
the whole argument is valid; since each premiss is (given the
relevant legal criteria) true (either because it is a true proposition of law, or a finding of fact, or a conclusion derived
from such premisses), the final conclusion drawn, in addition
to being validly established by deductive reasoning, must also
be true by those same criteria.

Of course, it may be said that the ultimate conclusion is
not merely that Mrs. T. is liable to Mr. D., but as the judge
said, that 'there must be judgment for Mr. Daniels'. What
about that? The answer is that it is not difficult to assert a
major premiss which will lead in turn to that conclusion. Let
us start with the banal proposition that judges must do
justice according to law, and let us suppose that one proposition entailed by that is: 'If in any case one party to
litigation establishes that the other party is legally liable in
damages to him, then the judge must give judgment in favour
of the successful litigant.' To that we can in virtue of the
foregoing argument add the minor premiss that 'in the
instant case one party to litigation has established that the

other party is legally liable in damages to him.' By the same form of reasoning as before it then follows that 'in the instant case the judge must give judgment in favour of the successful litigant [Mr. D.].'

But let us beware. That 'must' is not the 'must' of causal necessity or of logical necessity. It is the 'must' of obligation. The judge has a *duty* to give that judgment. It is merely banal to observe that his having a duty so to give judgment does not mean or entail that he does or that he will give, or that he has given, such a judgment. It is neither physically nor psychologically nor logically impossible that an individual will not act as he ought, will not act in accordance with his duty. All that strictly follows is that the judge would be acting in an unjustifiable way if he failed so to give judgment.

The importance of making that observation is obvious. It would be wrong to suggest that the actual decision given by the judge in the case, if by that is meant the order issued by him to the defendant to pay damages to the plaintiff, is logically entailed by the premisses. That the defendant is liable to pay damages is established by the argument reviewed; that the judge's duty is to order her to pay such damages is established by the subsidiary argument (if its major premiss is accepted); but the judge's giving that order is not entailed by any argument at all. The judge's issuing an order is an act which he performs or does not perform, and in so acting he either fulfils or does not fulfil his duty. Acts are not determined by logic, they are determined by the choices of agents, and by whatever, if anything, determines those choices. The normative quality (good or bad, right or wrong, justified or unjustified) of an act performed or under contemplation by an agent can be established logically given appropriate normative premisses, such as propositions of law of the kind set out above. Logic does not 'establish' the act.

It would be strange if a judge's opinion as to the normative quality of the alternative decisions confronting him in litigation were not for him a motivating factor in making up his mind what decision to give, that is, what order to make. He does after all have to state publicly in open court the reasons for which he is deciding the case as he is. Given the institutional pressures within the legal system—the opinion of the profession, the possibility of an appeal, etc.—and given the external pressures of adverse press publicity and Parliamentary comment and the like, it would be so strange as to be barely imaginable that a judge having established the justifiability of one decision by logical argument from sound legal premisses and findings of fact should then issue some diametrically different order. So institutionally and psychologically it is highly unlikely that a judge will so conduct himself, but it is not impossible; and even if it were, the impossibility would not be logical impossibility. The court's order is not a logical product of the argument which justifies it.

That and much which precedes it may seem to be an instance of labouring the obvious. Indeed it is. But the surprising fact is that although obvious, it has been misunderstood and misrepresented. For example, in his *Logic of Choice*[7], Dr. Gottlieb takes the following set of statements:

'X did A' (fact)
'All who do A are guilty of B' (rule)
'Verdict: X is guilty of B' (decision)

and he asserts that 'the conclusion of [that] set of statements does not follow from the two premisses.' That is either total nonsense, or at best a very dim and obscure approach to the truth. No person having the elementary gift of consistency in thought could possibly assert the first two *expressis verbis* and deny the conclusion 'X is guilty of B.' That conclusion, conceived as a proposition, is necessarily true if the premisses are.

Of course, Dr. Gottlieb may be understood here as making the point, in a rather obscure way, that a jury which returns a verdict of 'Guilty' or 'Not Guilty' is performing an act which constitutes the authoritative determination of the legal result of a trial. By so doing the jury makes it the case that X is, for the purposes of the law, guilty or not guilty; and accordingly the judge will have either to pass sentence on X, or to discharge him. The law ascribes to the jury the function of deciding on the basis of the evidence and the law whether

---

[7] London, 1968: The passage quoted is from p. 70, but has been amended in that in the published text the second line reads 'All who do X are guilty of B', an evident misprint. I find the whole argument from p. 66 to p. 77 entirely opaque.

the accused person is to be convicted or acquitted, and so the utterance by the jury of its verdict has the effect of making it true that the accused is for the further purposes of the law guilty or not. (In that sense, the pronouncement of a verdict is what J.L. Austin called a 'performative utterance': it is an instance of the performing of an institutionally defined act through the use of words, not an instance of the use of words to make a (true or false) statement of fact.)

As was said already, 'acts are not determined by logic, they are determined by the choices of agents', and that is as much true of the act of a jury pronouncing a verdict as of the act of a judge in deciding upon a claim or passing a sentence. But what verdict is a jury *justified* in pronouncing? If it is satisfied that X did A and that *according to the law* all who do A are guilty of B, it can hardly be justified *in law* if it gives any other verdict than 'Guilty'.

But since juries do not have to, and indeed may not, give reasons in public for their verdicts, it is certainly the case that a jury can return the verdict 'Not Guilty' without any ostensible contradiction, even when it privately believes that X actually did A, and that doing A constitutes an offence. What they do in such circumstances is not justified in law, though it may well be more than amply justified on moral grounds (the law in question may be unduly harsh or oppressive, the prosecution may have been merely vindictive, etc.). It is sometimes said to be a peculiar virtue of juries that they can, and do sometimes, act in just such a way to nullify the effect in practice of an unjust law or an unfair prosecution.[8]

For my own part, I am glad that that is so. But let that not obscure our realization that the logic of deductive inference is certainly relevant to the justification in law of a jury's verdict as much as of a judge's decision. Nor should we be diverted from that realization by the trivially true observation that the act of pronouncing a verdict, like any other act, cannot be logically necessitated—only performed or not.

It remains true that in case of tribunals of fact or of law or of both which are obliged to state reasons for their decisions, it

---

[8] See, e.g., Patrick Devlin, *Trial by Jury* (revised edn., London, 1966), esp. ch. 6.

would be very odd to find the tribunal setting out findings of fact and propositions of law from which a given conclusion necessarily follows, and then giving a verdict or issuing an order which is unjustified in the face of that conclusion.

Some will say that that merely drives the problem a step further back. A judge knows the proposition of law with which he has to work in a given case. Assume it to be of the form 'If p then q'. He therefore knows that if he 'finds' as facts propositions which entail 'p', he will be committed to the proposition q by way of conclusion. Suppose that q is for some reason a conclusion disagreeable to him in the context of a particular case. His knowledge gives him an obvious escape hatch. He can simply say that he does not find certain facts proven, and therefore p is not the case. Equally, if he is desirous of reaching the conclusion q, he need only say that he finds p true in the instant case. So, logical though his argument will be on the face of it, it is no more than rationalization, since he determined its course by the way in which he chose to 'find' the facts. (All of which is in small bulk the gist of the view of law which Jerome Frank called 'fact skepticism'.[9])

That judges *could* so behave is obvious. That they do sometimes so behave is possible, indeed, likely. That they always so behave is on the face of it extremely unlikely. After all Lewis J. in the *Daniels* case indicated a considerable feeling of regret that the facts of the case and the relevant law led him to a conclusion he thought unfair. Yet he *could* have held, despite the evidence, that there was no carbolic acid in the lemonade, or that its being there did not make the lemonade unmerchantable. It seems a less extravagant hypothesis to suppose that he did, and that other judges do, regularly make sincere efforts to establish a true version of the facts, and do then apply the law accordingly. It is even reasonable to suppose that their findings of fact are quite often correct as well as honestly made.

Strictly, however, that does not matter for the present thesis, which asserts only that the process of legal justification

---

[9] See Jerome Frank, *Law and the Modern Mind* (cit.sup., Ch. I n. 17).

is sometimes purely deductive and logical in character. Even if judges always made wrong or crooked findings of fact (which almost certainly they don't), it would remain an interesting question whether the reasoning by which they then move from those findings via rules of law to conclusions is ever genuinely deductive, or is never so. To demonstrate that in at least one case a conclusive justification of a decision can be given by a purely deductive argument is to show conclusively that deductive justification is possible, and that it sometimes happens. It leaves open the question whether it always happens (which it does not) and also the question what forms of reasoning may be used when a purely deductive justification is not possible, or for some other reason is not adopted by the judge or court.

To summarize what has been established so far: given that courts do make 'findings of fact' and that these, whether actually correct or not, do count for legal purposes as being true; given that legal rules can (at at least can sometimes) be expressed in the form 'if p then q'; and given that it is, at least sometimes, the case that the 'facts' found are unequivocal instances of 'p'; it is therefore sometimes the case that a legal conclusion can be validly derived by deductive logic from the proposition of law and the proposition of fact which serve as premises; and accordingly a legal decision which gives effect to that legal conclusion is justified by reference to that argument.

'But it's not logical'

But is it really *logical* that a decision should be given against Mrs. Tarbard? Somebody might object: 'It's not logical at all to hold the publican liable, when she is in no way responsible for the contents of a sealed bottle of lemonade, and especially not when the manufacturer is, as in the present case, absolved from liability—since he after all is the only person who has any control over what gets into the lemonade bottle before it is sealed.' It will be observed that such an objection echoes the regret expressed by Lewis J. in granting judgment against Mrs. Tarbard, who was, as he said 'entirely innocent and blameless in the matter'.

The imaginary objection which I have stated has a good

deal of force, at any rate if one considers it unreasonable that people should be made liable for states of affairs which are entirely outwith their control. What is more it uses the word 'logical' in what is perhaps its commonest everyday non-technical sense. But how can an argument be logically valid and yet the decision which it justifies be not logical? The answer is obvious, but the moral is worth drawing. The word 'logical' has at least two senses, which are only partially overlapping. In the technical sense of deductive logic (which alone has been dealt with in this chapter), an argument is logical if it complies with the requirements of logic, that is to say, if its conclusion follows necessarily from the premisses. An argument is illogical or logically fallacious if it purports to derive from given premisses a conclusion which is not entailed by them, or which is contradictory of the conclusion which actually follows from them. But, with the sole exception of premisses which are internally self-contradictory, the premisses of an argument cannot themselves be either logical or illogical. In the technical sense, 'being logical' is a characteristic only of arguments; it is applicable to propositions only in the sense that self-contradictory propositions (e.g. 'p and not p') are logically false.

But in everyday usage 'being logical' has a sense which is wider and in some respects different. Some action, or state of affairs can be said to be 'illogical' in that it 'doesn't make sense'. It may be the law that sellers can be held liable for defects in goods sold of which they neither had knowledge nor means of knowledge; but if it is the law, someone might say, 'It's a law which doesn't make sense, and so is "illogical".' One of the things which is true of a technically illogical argument is that it does not make sense, in that to utter it is to utter a self-contradiction. To that extent the two usages overlap. But when it is said that a given rule of law 'doesn't make sense', what is usually intended is that the law sets a standard of conduct which it is silly or unfair or unreasonable to expect of people. And that introduces a new set of values which are outside of the cognizance of 'logic' in the technical sense of the term as the name of a specific philosophical discipline. It is in this everyday usage of the term that the major premiss of a legal argument can be stigmatized as 'illogical' and therefore also any conclusion which follows from its application.

One of the ways in which such a criticism of a law can be justified is by pointing out its inconsistency with the general policies and principles of the law. If it were a generally accepted principle of a legal system that there should be 'No liability without fault', that is, that people should not be made liable for harm suffered by others unless they have caused or contributed to it by some fault of their own,[10] then a specific rule relating to sale of goods in virtue of which the seller may be held liable, albeit without fault, for defects in goods sold is inconsistent with that principle. Different people, different opinions. Some might regard this as a sensible exception to the principle, some again might regard the principle as a bad one and welcome inroads being made into it, and yet others might regard the principle as of being overriding importance in the law and therefore object to rules inconsistent with it as 'not making sense', or being, in the substantively evaluative way, 'illogical'. We shall consider in due course the importance of this conception of over-all consistency or coherence in the law. For the moment, we need only observe that the use of the terms 'logical' and 'illogical' as signifying the presence or absence of over-all consistency in the values and principles pursued by the law is different from, and wider than, the technical sense with which we have so far been concerned. So it is not contradictory to say that a legal argument can be logical and valid, but its conclusion 'illogical'; not if the terms are being used in the two different senses. Hereinafter I shall, to avoid confusion, use the adjectives 'logical' and 'illogical' only in the technical sense, unless I indicate to the contrary.

It has been worth while to tease out the distinction between these two senses of the term, because much of what has been said about the 'non-logical', 'illogical', or 'logical' quality of the law by various writers has been more concerned with the commonsense notion explored above than with the technical sense. When in *Quinn* v. *Leatham*[11] Lord Halsbury

---

[10] This principle is discussed in Chapter VII *infra* at pp. 167–9.

[11] [1901] A.C. 495 at p. 506 '...[E]very lawyer must acknowledge that the law is not always logical at all.'

argued that the law was not logical at all, he was merely justifying his pursuit in that case of a principle inconsistent with that in *Allen* v. *Flood*[12] (in which case he was a member of the minority); when Holmes J. remarked[13] that 'the life of the law has not been logic, it has been experience', he was making the true observation that Anglo-American law as developed by judges has been concerned at least as much with securing decisions which seem to make practical good sense as with showing their derivation from general principles of law whose observation secures a broad consistency and coherence within the law. When Cardozo J. praised the 'Method of Philosophy'[14] as appropriate within its compass, he was thinking of the process of analogical extrapolation of principles from decided cases into new fields, a process which indeed secures a certain broad consistency within this or that branch of the law. By and large English lawyers and writers have tended to think of it as almost a virtue to be illogical, and have ascribed that virtue freely to their law; 'being logical' is an eccentric continental practice, in which common-sensical Englishmen indulge at their peril.

Scotsmen and Scots lawyers by contrast have taken some pride in being logical and in having a legal system which exhibits the virtues of logic.[15] That in turn has been explained by disguised reference to the *Volksgeist*, Scots people being supposed to be of a particularly philosophical cast of mind. Alternatively, it has been ascribed to our exposure over centuries to Continental lawyering in the Civilian schools of France and the Netherlands.

As I have already suggested, there is nothing wrong with the non-technical sense of the words 'logic', 'logical', and the rest; it is in any event so deeply embedded in ordinary speech and writing that no philosophical condemnation could

---

[12] [1898] A.C. 1.

[13] O.W. Holmes, *The Common Law* (Boston, 1881), p. 1.

[14] B.N. Cardozo, *The Nature of the Judicial Process* (New Haven and London, 1921), Lecture I.

[15] See, e.g., Lord Cooper, *The Common and the Civil Law—A Scot's View* (1950) Harvard L.R. 468 at 471: 'The civilian naturally reasons from principles to instances, the common lawyer from instances to principles. The civilian puts his faith in syllogisms, the common lawyer in precedents.' Cf. D.M. Walker, *The Scottish Legal System* (3rd edn., Edinburgh, 1969), p. 122.

expunge it if it would. There is however a danger that observations which are (or may be) true when the terms are used in the non-technical sense are quite false if understood as comprehending also the technical sense. Therefore such attitudes and observations of Anglo-American judges and writers as those noted above must be understood with due caution. That the Anglo-American common law is, or may in part be, 'illogical' in the sense noted is no warrant for supposing that legal reasoning in common-law systems is, or could be, 'illogical' or 'non-logical' in the technical sense.

The Scottish system, and indeed the Civilian systems generally, are less likely to be subject to that mistake; but perhaps such systems are at risk of suffering from the converse equivocation. Since legal reasoning is a form of thought it must be logical, i.e. must conform to the laws of logic, on pain of being irrational and self-contradictory. That is, law must be 'logical' in the technical sense. That established, we may jump illicitly to the conclusion that it is *necessarily* a good thing that law should be 'logical' in the other, nontechnical sense. But the question whether it is good that law should be in that *other* sense 'logical' requires a separate answer and that answer a separate justification; commonly neither is forthcoming.

The logic of acquittal and the burden of proof

Whether or not it makes sound sense, good policy, common justice, or coherent law, to hold a publican such as Mrs. Tarbard liable to her customers for latent defects in goods quite innocently sold by her, we have at least established that there is nothing illogical about it, in the technical sense hereinafter reserved for that term. Is it, however, logical that the first defendant, the lemonade-maker R. White, should be absolved from liability? Let us review the form of the argument which justified dismissal of the action by Mr. and Mrs. Daniels against the first defendant, R. White & Sons Ltd. In that action they claimed damages from the defendant on the ground of negligence, in that 'in breach of the duty which they owed to the plaintiffs, [the defendants] supplied a bottle of lemonade which in fact contained carbolic acid'.[16]

[16] [1938] 4 All E.R. 258 at 259.

'The only evidence in the [plaintiffs'] case,' as Lewis J.
said, accepting a point put by counsel for the defendants,
'[was that] here was a bottle which, when purchased, quite
properly had its stopper in, and also had the label pasted over
the top, but which, on the evidence called by the plaintiffs
[at the close of their case], contained carbolic acid, and that,
as a result of drinking the contents of the bottle, the two
plaintiffs had suffered damage.'[17] The judge having rejected
the defendants' submission that plaintiffs' case was without
more insufficient in law on the ground that it did not cover
or prove any particular act of negligence on the defendants'
part, the defendants then led evidence as to their bottle-
washing process. That evidence was aimed at proving that
they had, in fact, taken reasonable care to secure that their
lemonade was free from contamination with deleterious
substances.

As for the relevant law, the judge observed that

I have to remember that the duty owed to the consumer, or the ultimate
purchaser, by the manufacturer, is not to ensure that his goods are
perfect. All he has to do is to take reasonable care to see that no
injury is done to the consumer or ultimate purchaser. In other words,
his duty is to take reasonable care to see that there exists no defect that
is likely to cause such injury.[18]

The defendants' evidence, which was accepted by the
judge, showed that empty bottles were brought to their
factory, and there washed in a bottle-washing machine which
subjected them to a hot rinse, a hot rinse in caustic soda, and
then a cold rinse. From the washing machine they were
transferred manually to the filling machine, after which
stoppers were put on the filled bottles. 'That method', said
the judge, 'has been described as fool-proof, and it seems to
me a little difficult to say that, if people supply a fool-proof
method of cleaning, washing, and filling bottles, they have
not taken all reasonable care to prevent defects in their commodity'.[19] The only way in which doubt could be cast on that
would be if it could be shown that the machine was not
worked by competent people under adequate supervision.

[17] Ibid. at 260.
[18] Ibid. at 261. The authority for that proposition of law is, of course,
Donoghue v. *Stevenson* 1932 S.C. (H.L.) 31; [1932] A.C. 562.
[19] Ibid. at 262.

But on the evidence presented, the judge was 'quite satisfied that there is adequate supervision.'[20]
Therefore Lewis J. reached the following conclusion:

The plaintiffs. . .have entirely failed to prove to my satisfaction that the defendant company were guilty of a breach of their duty towards the plaintiffs—namely a duty to take reasonable care to see that there should be no defect which might injure the plaintiffs. For that reason I think that the plaintiffs' claim against the first defendants fails.

The form in which the judge's conclusion is expressed is worth dwelling upon for a moment. He does *not* say that it has been demonstrated that the defendants are *not* liable to the plaintiffs. He merely rules that 'the plaintiffs' claim against the first defendants fails', on the ground that they have failed to prove any breach of duty on the defendants' part. In law that is a sufficient justification for absolving the defendant from liability by dismissing the plaintiffs' action. That is so because there is a rule of law that the party who initiates legal proceedings, whether as plaintiff (pursuer) or prosecutor must state and prove his own case; in part that is the point made by saying that he bears 'the burden of proof'.

In the relatively straightforward type of case represented by *Daniels*, there are rules of law having the form $p \supset q$ which the plaintiff invokes. He 'invokes' them by alleging in his pleadings that certain facts have occurred, and that these constitute an instance of the 'operative facts' stipulated in the relevant rule of law, as represented by the symbol p in our formula. (Because he, or his lawyers, know the rule, they know what facts they must aver and prove in order successfully to invoke it.) If he can 'prove' by reference to the required legal standard of proof that facts constituting an instance of p have occurred he thereby justifies asserting that the 'legal consequence' represented by the symbol q applies in his case—and that he has a right to the legal remedy sought. The logic of that process is as we have already demonstrated it.

But what if, as in the action against the first defendants, the lemonade manufacturers, the plaintiffs fail to prove that p (fail to prove that the manufacturers were in breach of the duty of care which, admittedly, they owed to the plaintiffs,

[20] Ibid. at 263.

as consumers)? Suppose the relevant rule of law to be something like 'If a manufacturer of goods breaks the duty of care which he owes to a consumer thereby injuring him, then the manufacturer is liable in damages to the consumer'. That certainly exhibits the form $p \supset q$: but in the given case p is not proven—the manufacturer is not, so far as the law is concerned, in breach of his duty. If we try to set out an argument in the logical form previously discussed, the premisses are

$p \supset q$

$\sim p$ [i.e. 'it is not the case that p]

But from these premisses no conclusion follows. Such premisses neither establish that q is the case, nor that q is not the case. They leave it undetermined.

(That no conclusion follows from premisses having that form is obvious, and can be confirmed by the following example: it is a general truth that if a person swallows 5 grams of arsenic, he will die; of a given individual, Smith, it is at this moment true that he has not swallowed 5 grams of arsenic. But can we say that he will not die? Although taking arsenic is a certain cause of death, abstaining from it is hardly a recipe for immortality.)

Such being the logical position, it is an evident necessity that the law should make some provision about what is to be done when as between two parties and with reference to a particular rule of law the applicability or not of the relevant 'legal consequence' q is not established. It is precisely by means of rules concerning the burden of proof and related matters that the law makes such provision. Since it is a requirement of law that à plaintiff/pursuer must state and justify any claim he makes against a defendant, and likewise a requirement that any prosecutor must frame a specific charge or charges against a particular accused person and prove it or them 'beyond reasonable doubt', it is legally—and logically—justified to absolve or acquit the defendant when that requirement is not met. That is exactly what happened in the *Daniels* case.

There is a considerable and pretty complex body of 'adjectival' law regulating who bears the burden of raising issues of various kinds in a trial, and of proving or disproving points raised. The account of the logic of rule-application here given shows clearly why that body of law should be considered important by lawyers; for it makes provision for matters for which on this account it is an imperative necessity to make provision. No student of the law in books or the law in practice can fail to observe the importance which lawyers actually ascribe to legal provisions of that kind.

Those who deny that deductive logic is relevant to the justification of legal decisions must therefore face up to this challenge: they must show why, on their account of things, there are such legal provisions to which such considerable practical significance is attached. It is a fact which reinforces the credibility of the present thesis, that their existence and importance is compatible with it. If rival theses cannot show why this is so, they are to that extent the less credible.

It has often been argued, and there is no reason to doubt, that all legal rules however formulated in statutes or in precedents can without alteration be recast in the form that if certain facts and circumstances obtain, a certain legal consequence is to follow.[21] The requisite facts and circumstances we may call the 'operative facts' of the rule. Then, with regard to our canonical form *if p then q* ($p \supset q$), the symbol *p* stands for a proposition stipulating a set of operative facts, *q* for the legal consequence which is to follow. The analysis of the action between Mr. and Mrs. Daniels and Mrs. Tarbard given earlier illustrates the feasibility of stating many kinds of rule in the relevant canonical form; and it illustrates how rules may be interrelated by reason of the very fact that a proposition stating the 'legal consequence' of one rule may in turn state the 'operative fact' of another. For example, given certain operative facts, a contract for the sale of goods by description exists; but then, for the purposes of s. 14(2) of the Sale of Goods Act the existence of such a contract together with certain other operative facts entails as legal consequence an implied condition that the goods sold shall be of merchantable quality. And so on.

Some sets of such rules taken together have as their

---

[21] See, e.g., G. Gottlieb, op.cit., pp. 33–49; Twining and Miers, *How to do Things with Rules* (London, 1976) p. 51–5.

ultimate consequence the existence of rights held by persons against each other, and of remedial rights which can be invoked in case of breaches of primary right. Courts are clothed with power to issue mandatory orders to secure the fulfilment of such remedial rights. Other sets of such rules establish that the commission of certain acts in certain circumstances constitutes crimes or offences; and the Courts are clothed with power to impose penalties on those who are convicted of committing crimes or offences.

In a modern industrial society such is the number and complexity of legal rules that no one can suppose that every infringement of right or commission of an offence is noticed as such, far less acted upon. Quite obviously rules are not self applying. To secure their observance, or *a fortiori* their compulsory enforcement, it is indeed necessary that the initiative be taken by somebody.

It would be on the face of it a total practical impossibility to work upon the presumption that everyone who might have committed one of the countless offences for which the law provides, or who might have infringed in some way one of the myriad of rights actually or potentially vested in his fellow citizens, should be required to set about demonstrating that he is free from any such guilt or liability. In some degree at least the boot must be on the other foot.

The legal system must therefore make provision as to who may in what circumstances and by what procedures initiate an action for the vindication of private rights or public duties, or a prosecution for some offence which is believed to have been committed. (Different systems, it need hardly be observed, make different provisions; even as between Scotland and England marked differences exist particularly in respect of criminal prosecutions.) Since the whole point of bringing an action or a prosecution is that it involves the possibility of the coercive force of the state being brought into operation against the other party, the power to do so is one whose exercise may at the very least expose the other party to no little inconvenience. This is so, even though the ground on which the action or prosecution be of the flimsiest character; all the more so, in face of private law actions, if there is provision whereby judgment may be given against a party who neglects to make any answer or defence to an action against him.

In a sense, the counterpoise to that power is the very fact that its exercise necessarily involves the exercise of choice. The pursuer/plaintiff or prosecutor can initiate an action or prosecution as he sees fit. But it is up to him to decide what action or prosecution to initiate. In whatever way he may be offended or aggrieved or outraged by what someone else has done, it is necessary that he settle on some fact or facts which he thinks can be legally proved as against the other party. Then he must be ready and able to show that these proved or provable facts are in some way legally relevant. It is at least the case that *one* way to do that is to show that there is some legal rule $p \supset q$ of whose operative facts p the facts he can prove are an instance.

Again, it is reflection on the deductive logic of rule application which enables us to see in the simplest of possible ways how it is possible for a person to select out of the totality of acts and events in the world those which it is worth averring and offering to prove in relation to a contemplated action or prosecution. In large measure (but not entirely, as will appear in due course) it is knowledge of legal rules which enables the relevant—and unquestionably highly partial and selective—choice to be made from the bewildering and infinitely complex continuum of facts and events with which we are presented. That inevitably puts a large premium on the possession of legal knowledge, or on the capacity to pay, and indeed to capture the effective attention of, those legal professionals who have it.

To those who deplore that fact,[22] the question has to be put how it could be effectively changed. At least the first step is to understand why it is so; one point of the present inquiry is that it shows why it is so. The only remedies for such a state of affairs would be to have less, and less complex, laws; or better knowledge of them.

Be that as it may, we have shown why it is a practical necessity why those who would bring actions or prosecutions must bear the burden of stating what acts and events have

---

[22] See, e.g., Z. Bankowski and G. Mungham, *Images of Law* (London, 1976).

occurred, which they represent as infringements of right or commissions of offence. For reasons already stated, the whole process would lack logical credibility unless enforcement of the remedy or conviction of the offence were made conditional upon proof by the party initiating the action or prosecution of the facts alleged and their legal relevance.

But of course logic cannot tell us what constitutes legal proof of allegations. Logic is necessarily silent as to what constitutes proof of contingent factual propositions (though later in this book there is a brief discussion of the point). It would not even be, in the strict sense, illogical if a legal system provided formally (or operated on the informal assumption) that a prosecutor's averment of p constitutes proof of p unless and until the accused person disproves it. It is a characteristic of totalitarian states that such is in fact, even if not in proclaimed theory, deemed to be sufficient proof. Nevertheless, apart from denouncing such a provision as unjust and tyrannical, one may observe that such a practice is irrational to the extent that it requires purported belief in propositions not supported by evidence. To say that p is deemed to be, or taken to be, true is to invoke a fiction; in such a context as we are considering, the fiction is invoked solely to secure in seemingly impeccable form the necessary logic of rule-application.

Certainly, logic as such uses rather than defines the notions of truth and falsehood. But the use of logical arguments becomes a sham if we truckle with the pretence of deeming contingent averments true without any adduction of evidence for them. The respect for rationality within which respect for logical argumentation is subsumed provides strong, if tangential, support for that conception of the 'burden of proof' in criminal trials to which, however imperfectly in practice, liberal states in public theory adhere.

If we ignored the logic of rule application we should be hard pressed to account for the importance of the idea of the burden of proof, as already stated and now more fully explained. We should be equally hard pressed to account for the problem which legal systems face, and deal with differently, concerning the required degree of specificity of averments in civil pleadings and criminal charges.

In setting out to prove the existence of some set or sets of operative facts to the satisfaction of the tribunal responsible for trying the issue, the party initiating the proceedings must (as we have seen) at some stage prior to judgment commit himself to giving some account or accounts of some part occurrence involving the defending party. If the system contains any tincture of fairness (which is, again, not a point of logic) that account or those accounts will at some stage be disclosed to the party defending. (Here again, respect for rationality may supply a want of fairness if it leads us to suppose that the defending party may be able to contribute some factual information helpful towards constructing a relatively trustworthy account of the relevant slice of history; the 'right to a hearing' has some, albeit again tangential, logical support.)

A crucial point of variation between legal systems can in the light of all that be identified in the rules of procedure which determine the point in the progress of an action at which the initiating party must commit himself to a particular account of the facts which he avers and on which, as averred, he relies; the degree of specificity with which he must give his account; and the extent, if any, to which he must commit himself expressly to invoking specific legal rules as justifying the judgment which he seeks as against the party defending. Such rules serve in part to supplement and in part to concretise the requirements imposed on him by the fact of his bearing the burden of proof.

The Scottish case of *Thompson* v. *Glasgow Corporation* (1962 S.C. (H.L.) 36) indicates well the importance of such procedural rules, and their significance to the present subject matter. The pursuer in the case had been washing clothes in a public wash-house of the defenders'. When she was drying them in a 'hydro-extractor', which whirled the clothes round at great speed in a drum, her arm became in some way involved in the whirling drum just before the process of spinning was due to stop, and her arm was as a result amputated. She sued the Corporation for damages for her injuries, averring that her apron had got caught on the spindle of the drum; the spindle itself revolved with the drum but was surmounted with a guard which, when properly maintained, sat loosely on the spindle and when touched did not revolve with the spindle. The pursuer averred that the guard had not been maintained in proper working order, and that her apron had been wound round it and had involved her arm.

As the action proceeded, it became clear that whatever had caused her injury, it did not happen in the manner which she averred, but must have occurred in some other way; on that ground her action was dismissed, and the Corporation absolved from liability. She appealed, and sought leave on appeal to amend her averments so as to give a different account of the accident and to show that it occurred because of the negligence of a servant of the Corporation who lifted the lids off the extractor drums before they had stopped revolving at a dangerous speed. Her application for leave to amend at that stage was rejected and her appeal dismissed.

Thus it appears that the pursuer might have been able to establish the liability of the Corporation had she initially committed herself to a different or perhaps to a less specific account of the way in which the accident happened. But once she had chosen to give a particular version of the history of her tragic accident as constituting an instance of the operative facts of a particular rule she was committed, and if she could not prove that to which she was committed, the Corporation had a right to be absolved, a right which could not be defeated by the supposition that some alternative version of the cause of the accident might have been true, and on that supposition the Corporation liable.

That was beyond doubt a hard case, and the procedural rules bore hard upon the unfortunate pursuer. But any system in which the logic of rule-application is taken seriously must have some rules covering the problem of specificity of averments.

In criminal causes such rules are likewise important, and operate by and large to the advantage of the accused. Consider the case of *Hambleton* v. *Callinan*, ([1968] 2 All E.R. 943) which so far as here material raised a small question concerning the application of s.1(1) of the Drugs (Prevention of Misuse) Act 1964, in virtue of which if any person has in his possession a substance for the time being specified in the Schedule to the Act, and if certain excusing conditions [here irrelevant] are not fulfilled, he is guilty of an offence. At the material time, amphetamine was a scheduled substance. The accused persons were charged, *inter alia*, with being in possession of amphetamine contrary to s.1(1) of the Act, in that urine samples provided by them at the time of their arrest revealed that at that time traces of amphetamine were present in their bodies. In respect of that part of the charges the Bournemouth Magistrates' Court held that there was no case for the accused to answer, and on appeal their judgment was upheld by the Divisional Court. The Court ruled that a person's being proven to have had traces of amphetamine powder present in his urine at a given point in time does not constitute his having been 'in possession' of it at that time. Accordingly, although the prosecution had proved the former fact, they had not thereby proved the operative fact necessary for conviction of an offence under s.1(1) of the 1964 Act. Therefore those of the accused against which that was the only charge had been rightly acquitted—indeed, *quoad* that charge, all had been rightly acquitted.

Yet, as Lord Parker, C.J., pointed out in his opinion,

I myself can see no reason why in another case the time when the possession is said to have taken place should not be a time prior to the consumption, because as it seems to me the traces of. . .amphetamine powder in the urine is [*sic*] at any rate *prima facie* evidence. . .that the man concerned must have had it in his possession, if only in his hand prior to raising his hand to his mouth and consuming it. (Ibid. at p. 945)

It appears that in this case, the historical account to which the prosecution committed itself was one which could have been so framed as to constitute valid proof of the operative facts required by s.1(1) of the Act, but which in the instant case was so framed as to be irrelevant because not, as recited, an instance of the relevant operative fact. Again, the rules as to specificity of averments may increase the practical weight of the burden of proof. Some might think such procedural requirements unduly stringent and in the bad sense legalistic, but whether they be so or not, it is evident that there must, in criminal as well as in civil cases, be some procedural rules defining the time at which, and the degree to which, the prosecutor must commit himself to some specific historical account as constituting the charge laid. That he must so commit himself enhances the opportunity of the accused to show himself not guilty—that is, not guilty *of the offence charged.*

To conclude: without having purported to demonstrate that all aspects of legal justification in all types of case necessarily involve exclusively the type of deductive argument described in this chapter, it has been demonstrated that arguments of that type are sometimes available to justify decisions. It has further been shown that such an account enables us to understand the significance of the legal notion of 'burden of proof' and related elements of law. Whoever would deny that strictly deductive reasoning is a genuine and important element in legal justification must show some defect in the account here given, and must show that there is some alternative theory which can equally well account for rules about the burden of proof and related matters of so-called 'adjectival law'.

It is not contended that such reasoning is all that is involved in legal justification; it will be for the next chapter to show what presuppositions it involves, and to what limits its utilization is necessarily subject.

III

DEDUCTIVE JUSTIFICATION –
PRESUPPOSITIONS AND LIMITS

(a) The Validity Thesis

Whatever does happen can happen; in giving concrete examples
of deductive justification in the preceding chapter we have
shown that it is a possible mode of legal justification of
decisions. Now therefore we must turn to the question 'What
makes it possible?' To put it in other, perhaps more Kelsenian words, what are the presuppositions we make in
treating deductive arguments as sufficient justification of
legal decisions in certain cases? By examining these presuppositions we shall also put ourselves in a position to
determine the limits of deductive justification and thus to
raise a main question of this book, namely, 'How can decisions
be justified when no deductive argument is sufficient to
justify them?'

Let me return to a point which was made in Chapter II
(pp. 32–3 thereof): having shown the logic by which was
reached the conclusion that Mrs. Tarbard was liable in
damages to Mr. Daniels, I added that to complete the justification of the argument we needed one further premiss. 'If in
any case one party to litigation establishes that the other
party is legally liable to him in damages, then the judge
must give judgment in favour of the successful litigant.' It
seemed reasonable in context to adopt that seemingly obvious
principle as requiring no argument. What makes it so 'seemingly obvious' is that it recites what is on the face of it an
almost tautological proposition about the judicial function.
Behind it there lies what some people would consider basic
presuppositions of legal thinking; that there are rules of law,
and that a judge's job is to apply those rules when they are
relevant and applicable. The notion of 'relevance and applicability' is indeed explicable precisely by reference to the
(deductive) logic of subsumption elaborated at such length
in the first section of Chapter II. A rule of law is general in

terms, stipulating that whenever a given set of operative facts occurs (p), a given legal consequence is to follow (q).[1] When a judge in a given case 'finds facts' amounting to an instance of p, the relevance of the legal rule to the case is established, and the legal consequence q is to be applied.

So what we are in effect presupposing or postulating is that—on this view of the judicial function or the judge's job—every judge has in virtue of his office a duty to apply each and every one of those rules which are 'rules of law' whenever it is relevant and applicable to any case brought before him. And that formulation reveals a second presupposition, without which the 'duty' would lack identifiable reference: that it is possible for the judge to identify all those rules which are 'rules of law'. There must be some criteria settling what counts as a 'rule of law' for this purpose. In two easy jumps we have landed in the heart of legal theory. We have landed on a central tenet of positivistic legal theory (though one which many natural lawyers also adhere to): that every legal system comprises, or at least includes, a set of rules identifiable by reference to common criteria of recognition; and that what constitutes these criteria as criteria of recognition for a legal system is shared acceptance by the judges of that system that their duty is to apply rules identified by reference to them. That thesis is put forward in very similar terms by H.L.A. Hart[2] and Joseph Raz,[3] and bears a recognizable relation to opinions advanced by many other theorists.

There is at least an apparent circularity in what has been said here, however: if we ask 'who is a judge?' in for example contemporary Scotland, or England and Wales, we will be referred to a complicated set of what Hart would call 'rules of adjudication': for example the Court of Session (Scotland) Acts, or the Supreme Court of Judicature Acts. The judges are judges because there are rules that make them so; the rules that make them so—and many other rules—are rules of law because the judges recognize them as such (to put it briefly and crudely).

---

[1] See p. 45 *supra* for the use of this terminology.
[2] H.L.A. Hart, *The Concept of Law* (Oxford, 1961), esp. cc. 5 and 6.
[3] J. Raz, *The Concept of a Legal System* (Oxford, 1970), ch. 8.

The argument would indeed be viciously circular if we left it there. Courts are not self-sustaining institutions endowed with legitimacy by their own say so, clothed with might by their own bodily vigour. They are institutions established (however informally or formally) by a wider community from which they drive their legitimacy and authority as determiners of controversies; the forcefulness of the orders they issue depends in the first instance on acceptance of their authority by those to whom the orders are addressed, and in the second instance (relatively later in historical development) on acceptance of their authority by enforcement officials who do wield some degree (often a considerable degree) of collective might.

That wider community which accords to the Courts their legitimacy and authority is not necessarily the whole 'community of the realm'[4] to use an attractive old phrase. It may perhaps be no wider than that of the power group or ruling class which can by one means or another muster force and fear enough to sustain order within what *they* define as the whole community of the realm. That is the truth which underlies the Austinian or Benthamite notion of the 'habit of obedience' which suffices to constitute political society, or the Kelsenian notion of the 'by and large efficacious' system of norms which is a legal order.

To have 'judges' at all, at the very simplest and most informal analytical level, we must therefore postulate the existence of some group of people who ascribe to some individual or individuals of their number the function of determining controversies; when a dispute or controversy cannot be settled between the disputants and their friends, there must be some socially recognized obligation[5] to refer the question to a particular person, or one from a particular

---

[4] The phrase is one which belongs to traditional Scottish constitutional usage. See G.W.S. Barrow, *Robert Bruce* (2nd edn., Edinburgh, 1976), pp. 23–4 etc.

[5] By a 'socially recognized obligation' I do not mean one that everyone in a society 'recognizes' or 'accepts', but one which *some* persons in a society 'recognize' or 'accept' as applying to *all* members of what they define as 'the society'; such attitudes are significant for other people when held by people who exercise some degree of social power or influence. See the Appendix of this book, and compare MacCormick, 'Legal Obligation and the Imperative Fallacy' in *Oxford Essays in Jurisprudence, Second Series*, ed. A.W.B. Simpson (Oxford, 1973).

group, or a particular group of persons; there must be a socially recognized obligation on that 'judge' or those 'judges' to ordain that the dispute shall be settled in some given way; and there must be a socially recognized obligation on the parties to accept and obtemper that ruling.

Such judges might well (and so far as I know, in primitive societies they do) rely rather on immemorial traditions and notions of equity and fair play than on any sort of formal 'rules' in deciding disputes. But at least it is possible that, just as their obligation to decide disputes is a socially recognized one, so might they also be or come to be regarded by their fellows and by themselves, as being obligated to apply some more or less set code of rules in determining disputes and controversies. If that were so, there would be some socially accepted criteria of recognition—which would of course be effectively operative only if the 'judges' shared in the social recognition that the 'set code of rules' was of mandatory application by them. Moreover, at least in marginal cases it must needs be they themselves who decide the exact effect of the criteria of recognition.

Whether such an analysis would or would not be illuminating in relation to primitive legal orders, it certainly is revealing in relation to the more elaborate and institutionalized judicial structure which characerizes modern states, at least in the 'Western' mode. That the judges who sit in our courts are duty bound to apply, e.g., Acts of Parliament whenever they are relevant and applicable is a norm accepted and daily acted upon by the judges; it is a norm which regulates judges' conduct only; it is a norm whose precise application in cases of doubt can be determined only by the judges themselves. But it is not a norm whose existence depends solely and sufficiently on the will of the judges; it is accepted, and its continued observance is willed, by the substantial majority of at least the most powerful and influential groupings in our society—by the self-same people whose acceptance of the judges as the appropriate authorities for determining all controversies not expressly excepted from their jurisdiction constitutes and sustains their legitimacy and authority as judges whose orders within their competence must be obeyed and shall at need be coercively enforced.

Indeed we have 'formal' and 'institutionalized' Courts precisely in the sense (if I may extend a theme developed elsewhere)[6] that there are recognizable 'institutive', 'consequential', and 'terminative' rules which determine *inter alia*:

1. The establishment of the 'court': on whose appointment persons having what general qualifications may in what circumstances and by what formal procedures become 'judges' of 'the court'.

2. The consequential powers and duties—and also immunities and privileges—which vest in those appointed as judges when they are acting as members of 'the court'. There are three key points here: determination of the competency of the Court—that is, conferment on judges of power to hear and determine disputes and controversies of certain specified classes; the corollary to that is the imposition of an obligation upon citizens to obtemper judicial orders addressed to them in the exercise of that power, which may be backed up by obligations upon subordinate officials under the direction of judges to enforce compliance in cases of recalcitrance; imposition of a duty on judges to 'hear and determine according to law'; to act in accordance with established procedures in hearing cases, and to apply when relevant every 'valid' rule of law.

3. Terminative provisions regulating in what circumstances a judge once appointed, may or must demit his office—here lies a long standing tension between the two values of the accountability of public officials and the independence of the judiciary.

No doubt that is an over-simplified and schematic formulation of a highly complex reality, but it is at least an approximation to the truth, and its utility lies in the way in which it indicates the necessary interrelationship between the judicial and the legislative institutions of modern states. That it is an essential consequence of appointment to judicial office that a judge must apply valid rules of law in exercising his jurisdiction indicates the interrelationship between adjudication and legislation—because legislation is *par excellence* the process whereby valid rules of law are made. Just as there are instituted courts whose central function is the adjudication of disputes in accordance with valid rules of law, so there are instituted legislatures: bodies having existence and membership as determined by institutive rules, upon which bodies 'consequential' rules confer powers of legislating: by carrying out formally defined procedures, legislatures can enact rules which (subject to all conditions concerning manner and form

[6] MacCormick, *Law as Institutional Fact* (1973), Edinburgh University Inaugural Lecture No. 52; also (1974) 90 L.Q.R. 102.

of enactment, and substantive range of competence) constitute 'valid rules of law'. Hence the crucial interrelationship between judicial and legislative institutions: the latter determine the *content* of the duties of the former, while the former in exercising that duty cannot but find themselves defining the range of competence of the latter.

I have said that 'legislation is *par excellence* the process whereby valid rules of law are made'; that for two reasons. Legislation is unique as a source of law in that it yields what have been felicitously called 'rules in fixed verbal form',[7] rules which have a single and uniquely authoritative formulation, their formulation in the *ipsissima verba* of the legislature; and just because legislative power and legislative procedure are formally defined, we have in this case more or less exact criteria of validity which make it possible to distinguish reasonably clearly what is from what is not duly enacted law.

It is worth recalling that to regard legislation as *par excellence* the source of valid law is a distinctively modern view. Even if we go back no further than the seventeenth century we find James, 1st Viscount Stair, arguing in the following terms in his *Institutions of the laws of Scotland*:

Yea, and the nations are more happy whose laws have been entered by long custom, wrung out from their debates on particular cases, until it came to the consistence of a fixed and known custom. For thereby the conveniencies and inconveniencies thereof through a long tract of time are experimentally seen. So that which is found in some cases convenient, if in other cases afterward it be found inconvenient, it proves abortive in the womb of time, before it attain the maturity of a law. But in statutes the lawgiver must at once balance the conveniencies and inconveniences; wherein he may and often doth fall short. . . (*Inst.* I. 1.15)

That is a thesis which depends on a view of the world and of man's place in it, and of the nature of law, which is now wholly out of fashion. It is based on a conception of the scope of deductive legal reasoning substantially different from that sketched in Chapter II. That conception postulates the existence of eternal rational principles governing all rational beings, God included. The rules which men (ought to)

---

[7] W. Twining and D. Miers, *How to Do Things with Rules* (London, 1976) pp. 58–9, 72, 100, 105, etc.

apply in their lives are discoverable by deduction from these first principles of reason. Long custom, especially 'learned custom' evolved by those experienced in handling practical problems (judges in particular), will more securely indicate what are sound deductions from basic principles than will instant legislation. (The more one looks at the statute book of the twentieth century, the more, perhaps, one is inclined to see Stair's point).

That such a view is unfashionable does not make it wrong —and indeed later in this book we shall return to considering the place of 'basic principles' in legal reasoning. For the moment, however, I wish only to observe that in Stair's perspective my conception of the courts being primarily obligated to apply rules which are technically valid as rules of law, e.g. because properly enacted, would seem quite wrong. For Stair, doing justice according to law means simply adjudicating in accordance or with principles of right reason, especially as evidenced by the long custom of the realm (which may for good reason make local and particular variations on that law which is ubiquitous and universal).

It is interesting to see how in the century after Stair's *magnum opus* (derivative in part as that was from the civilian and natural-law traditions of renaissance and early modern Europe, the tradition whose highest point is reached in the writing of Grotius) legal theorists in effect turned the Stair thesis upside down. By the mid-eighteenth century, writers like Erskine[8] in Scotland and Blackstone[9] in England, while still adhering to a vestigial jusnaturalism, expressly recognize within broad limits the supremacy of the national legislature. The principles of natural law are vague, and they leave many things indifferent: the legislature must make law clear in all cases, and must make law for the public benefit in the area of the indifferency of natural law. The legislature's is a supreme, the judges' a subordinate or derivative, power; in so far as custom and precedent function as sources of law, they do so by virtue of a tacit command of the legislature.

[8] J. Erskine *An Institute of the Law of Scotland* (Edinburgh, 1773), I.i *passim*, esp. at I.1.2 and I.i.19–26.

[9] W. Blackstone, *Commentaries on the Laws of England* (16th edn., 1825), vol. i, pp. 90–1, 160–1.

Natural-law thinking having reached such a point as this, it is but a short step to the outright positivism of a Bentham or the more qualified positivism of a John Austin (qualified by his adherence to the conception of Divine Law[10] as 'law properly so-called'—which is a positivistic and voluntarist restatement of the old rationalistic view of natural law; there are already signs of this transition in John Erskine's *Principles* and *Institute*, and there is a strong suggestion in the internal evidence of the texts that Austin had read, and was influenced by, Erskine).

These shifts in attitude belong to politics as well as to philosophy. The insistence that all law is legislated law makes possible the view that all law is changeable, and that is an essential postulate for those who wish to reform the law. In turn it may well be entirely true, and must be at least in part true, that political movements to change law reflect changes in the economic base of societies. But be that as it may, a consequence of the shift in attitude at the level of legal theory is a redefinition of precedent as a source of law. If all law is legislated law, then case-law is legislated law—and it is the judges who legislate it. Bentham[11] and Austin[12] are clear on that point, as against Erskine who denies the binding force of particular precedents[13] and Blackstone who simply equivocates.[14]

That change has a specific effect on the use of precedents. They come in effect to be treated more and more as though they were indeed—as the positivists asserted—a form of delegated legislation, and the scene is set for a century and a half of more or less fruitless pursuit of the elusive notion of *ratio decidendi*—the notion of the clear, valid, rule of law, discoverable in every binding precedent. Custom slides off the stage altogether save as an aid to the construction of private contracts. 'Equity' ceases to be seriously recognizable

[10] J. Austin, *The Province of Jurisprudence Determined* (ed. H.L.A. Hart, London, 1964), ch. 2; or J. Austin, *Lectures on Jurisprudence* (5th edn., R. Campbell, London, 1885), Lecture II.

[11] See, e.g., J. Bentham, *Introduction to the Principles of Morals and Legislation* (ed. J.H. Burns and H.L.A. Hart, London, 1970), pp. 8, 20–3, 308.

[12] Austin, *Lectures* XXXVII—XXXVIII.

[13] Erskine, *Institute* I.i. 44–7.

[14] Blackstone, *Commentaries*, Introduction, § II, division I.

as a source of law, and becomes either the name of a particular set of judicially legislated rules, or the name of a particular power of law-making vested in judges.

The final irony is that the institutional writers' own works, works which could only have been written on the basis of a natural law theory which authorizes asserting as already law all principles conformable with 'reason', themselves come to be reclassified as 'sources of law' in the positivistic sense.[15] The fact that a proposition is advanced in Stair or in Blackstone becomes a justification for regarding it as a proposition of law (if not overridden by some statute or precedent); not 'law' because it truly states what is substantively reasonable—which was its author's ground for stating it; 'law' because of its being stated by that person in that book—which is thus to be deemed a (subordinate) 'formal source of law'. It is almost as though a posthumous power of delegated legislation had been conferred on the institutional writers.

There is a risk that I have pressed too far the antithetical quality of positivistic and jusnaturalist thought by using extreme examples. Looking at it in the perspective of contemporary controversy, one might say this: It is useful to take it as a defining characteristic of legal positivism that every genuine 'positivist' holds that all rules which are rules of law are so because they belong to a particular legal system, and that they belong to the system because they satisfy formal criteria of recognition operative within that system as an effective working social order.[16] 'Natural lawyers' do not necessarily deny that legal systems establish legislative processes the product of which counts as 'valid law' because it satisfies accepted criteria of recognition;[17] but they add that although that is a necessary, it is not a sufficient, condition

[15] For judicial dicta on the authority of Stair and Blackstone see, e.g., *Drew* v. *Drew* (1870) 9 M. 163 at p. 167, and *R.* v. *Sandbach* [1935] 2 K.B. 192 at p. 197.

[16] Cf. e.g. Hart and Raz, locc. citt. *supra*, nn. 2 and 3.

[17] Among contemporary natural lawyers, L.L. Fuller for example would certainly not deny the point—see *The Morality of Law* (rev. edn. 1969, New Haven and London). St. Thomas Aquinas was of the same view, as are his contemporary followers. See *Summa Theologica*, Qu. 95, Art. 1 and 2, and following sections, or *Aquinas: Selected Political Writings* (ed. A.P. D'Entreves, Oxford, 1959), pp. 127–45.

of the validity of enacted rules. To be truly valid, such rules must satisfy or at least not conflict with more basic principles of law, whose status as 'law' is not dependent upon any kind of enactment or 'acceptance' or 'recognition'. There are no doubt many and various ways of explaining the status or justification of such fundamental principles, but that need not detain us here.

It is then a shared thesis as between positivistic and natural law thinking that legal systems have criteria, sustained by 'acceptance' in the society whose system it is, satisfaction of which is at least presumptively sufficient for the existence of a rule as a 'valid rule' of the system. (For shortness I shall hereinafter call that 'the validity thesis'.) It is that shared 'validity thesis' which is presupposed when we treat deductive justification of legal decisions as sufficient and conclusive: given a valid rule *if p then q*, and given that an instance of *p* has occurred, a legal decision which gives effect to *q* (which expresses a legal consequence) is a justified decision.

(b) A *Problem for Positivism*

That said, we have to face a problem for legal positivism: if a positivist theory merely gives a descriptive account of what legal systems actually are, how can the positivist's version of the 'validity thesis' have any reference to 'justification'? If it just *is* the case that whatever is a legal system contains criteria of validity, can that in any sense support the assertion that legal decisions which apply valid rules relevant and applicable to the facts in issue are justified decisions, i.e. decisions which *ought* to be given.

The answer is, of course, that that 'ought' is what Kelsen would call a 'descriptive' ought.[18] Without commitment to (or against) the values of the system in question, the theorist as an observer of it is saying something like: 'From the point of view of those who work within the system, that decision ought to be given'—indeed 'that is a decision which they are committed to treating as justified.' The theorist is not commending it or justifying it for his own part.

---

[18] H. Kelsen, *The Pure Theory of Law* (tr. Max Knight, Berkeley and Los Angeles, 1967), pp. 71–5.

That point is simple and obvious enough, and deals with the problem raised. But it also indicates that a positivistic description of the system as it operates *cannot* answer a particular kind of question which may be raised *internally* to a legal system: the question as it might be raised for a judge in a hard case: 'Why ought *we* to treat every decision in accordance with a rule valid by our criteria of validity as being sufficiently justified?' and that is a question which can be, and from time to time is, raised. Nor can it answer the question yet more frequently raised for judges: 'How ought we to justify decisions concerning the interpretation and application of our criteria of validity?'

For my part I should be reluctant to treat such questions as being non legal simply because of a definitional fiat. As examples in a later chapter will show, they are questions which are concretely raised in actual courts of law; and questions answered by judges resorting to arguments intrinsically similar to those raised in cases not concerned with criteria of validity. To treat such arguments as ideological-but-not-legal (which is what Kelsen[19] and, in effect, Hart do[20]) on *a priori* grounds seems to me unsatisfactory.

For the moment, and still in general terms, it is sufficient to remark that 'from the internal point of view' acceptance of 'the rule of recognition' of a system by the officials of, and (some at least of) the citizens subject to, the system, is not a blind datum, a pure brute fact. They can and do have reasons for accepting it: e.g. 'it is good that judicial decisions be predictable and contribute to certainty of law, which they are and do when they apply known rules identified in accordance with commonly shared and understood criteria of recognition'; 'it is good that judges stay within their assigned place in the constitutional order, applying established law rather than inventing new law'; 'it is good that law-making be entrusted to the elected representatives of the people, not usurped by non-elected and non-removable judges'; 'the existing and accepted constitutional order is a fair and just system, and accordingly the criteria of recognition of

---

[19]   Ibid., pp. 349 f.
[20]   Hart, *Concept of Law*, pp. 114–20.

laws which it institutes are good and just criteria which ought to be observed'; and so on.

The second last of these is peculiarly appropriate to a more or less democratic political system, and to that extent mingles legal with overtly political values; the last involves an overtly political judgment about the justice of the system, yet it is precisely the kind of judgment which for many honest men and women must underpin their acceptance of a legal system all and whole. 'From the internal point of view' acceptance of rules is not unreasoned, though indeed different people may reason differently for acceptance of the same rule. But in so far as arguments of principle figure among such reasons they are certainly (as will be argued in Chapter VI) highly relevant to the law.

I hope I am right in suggesting that for thoughtful people who accept and work within a system of law such reasons as those sketched above are of a kind which would commonly be held and offered as reasons for accepting and adhering to at least the fundamental rules of the system. In *that* sense, and from *that* point of view, it would be fatuous for anyone to pretend that law can be de-moralized—or, for that matter, de-politicized. (Indeed I don't know of any theorist of substance who has even suggested that it can be: certainly not Hart or Kelsen.)

But when we are considering legal argument from such a perspective as that taken in this book—asking with respect to two systems in particular, but with an eye to more general points, 'What are good justification for legal decisions?'—these underpinning reasons, reasons for accepting the system's criteria of validity, have an importance which cannot be overlooked. Only in some few cases—examples of which will be discussed in due course—do the underpinning reasons come overtly to the surface in litigious argument and judicial opinions. Only in these rare cases are the underpinning reasons necessarily offered as essential to the explicit justification of a decision.

Nevertheless, are they not always relevant? Take the plainest and simplest deductively justifiable decision—the decision in the *Daniels* case, or any of the umpteen million like examples (few enough of them reported) which might have been given. The decision is to all appearances conclusively justified by subsuming the particular facts under the relevant and applicable 'valid rule of law', and deducing the conclusion, we simple recite some version of the 'validity thesis', and explain the conclusiveness of the justification by showing how it presupposes the soundness of the validity thesis. But from the point of view of those who have reasons (which they *sometimes* have to argue out in litigious contexts) for accepting and operating the system's criteria of validity, it could be argued that those reasons are *always* tacitly relevant to justifying the decision or accepting it as validly justified.

To go back to where we started: the *Daniels* argument involves the tacit premisses that the judge must decide the case in accordance with the legal rights and liabilities of the parties; that is, the judge must give effect to the consequences deduced from valid rules; that is, more generally, judges must give effect to all valid rules. But if there are reasons why judges ought to respect that duty to give effect to those rules which within the system it is their duty-as-judges to give effect to, the original deductive justification is only as conclusive as these further underpinning reasons. In short, there are presupposed justifying reasons for accepting deductive justification, and these are not themselves explained by our prior explanation of the content of deductive justification. I shall in due course examine and discuss the characteristics of the justificatory arguments relevant to accepting the criteria of validity of a legal system. For the moment it is sufficient that our discussion of the 'problem for positivism' with which this section started should have indicated that deductive justification takes place within a framework of underpinning reasons which it does not explain. That is one limit to deductive justification; but there are others to which I now turn.

(c) *The Limits of Deductive Justification*

It is a very obvious truth that not all legal rules, not even all legislated rules 'in fixed verbal form', can always give a clear answer to every practical question which arises. Almost any rule can prove to be ambiguous or unclear in relation to some disputed or disputable context of litigation. Rules being formulated in language, they are (as H.L.A. Hart has pointed out[21]) both open textured, and vague in relation to some contexts at least.

For example: the United Kingdom's Race Relations Act 1968 prohibits discrimination 'on the ground of colour, race, or ethnic or national origin' in relation *inter alia* to the disposal of housing accommodation. It is clear enough how that provision applies if somebody refuses to sell or let a house to another person because he has a black skin, or Irish ancestors. But what if a local authority in selecting among applicants for council houses applies a rule that only British subjects within the meaning of the British Nationality Act 1948 may be admitted to its housing list? Is that local authority committing a form of discrimination prohibited by the Act? (That very question arose in concrete form in the case of *Ealing London Borough Council* v. *Race Relations Board* ([1972] A.C. 342.)

There are two possible answers:[22] that it is discriminating unlawfully, and that it is not discriminating unlawfully. One or other must be correct and they cannot both be. The trouble is that there are two possible views about the interpretation of the Act: (a) that discriminating 'on the ground of national origins' includes discriminating on the ground of an individual's legal nationality; and (b) that it does not include discrimination on the ground of an individual's legal nationality. (That there are plausible grounds for either interpretation can be confirmed by scrutiny of the report of the case, especially since different judges differed on the proper interpretation and gave reasons for their opposed interpretations).

For simplicity's sake let us translate the enacted rule so far as relevant into the form symbolically expressed as *If p then q*.

If a person discriminates against another on the ground of national origins, then he discriminates unlawfully.

In the problem case which we have identified, that can

---

[21]   Ibid., pp. 120, 124–32, 233, 249.
[22]   Parliament has since resolved the matter by enactment of the Race Relations Act 1976, s.3(1), which determines that discrimination on grounds of 'nationality' is an instance of unlawful discrimination.

in effect be read as equivalent to one or other, but not both, of the following:

  a) if a person discriminates against another on the ground of national origins (including that person's legal nationality) then he discriminates unlawfully.

or

  b) If a person discriminates against another on the ground of national origins (as distinct from that person's legal nationality), then he discriminates unlawfully.

The practical dispute between the parties could be resolved and the decision justified deductively only *after* a decision had been made whether to interpret the enacted rule along the lines of (a) or (b) above.

The problem is that the antecedent proposition p in the enacted rule is ambiguous as between two more detailed but mutually exclusive propositions which we might label p' and p'' (i.e. the antecedent propositions in formulations (a) and (b) above). For some cases it may make no difference which is the 'proper' interpretation of p, but when the very focus of dispute is a case of discrimination between people of differing legal nationalities a resolution must be made.

I have given only one example here but its generalizability is obvious. All legal rules can be formulated as sentences having the structure *If p then q*, stipulating that whenever certain operative facts occur a given legal consequence is to follow. Whatever proposition is substituted for p must be clear in relation to some contexts, but may well be ambiguous in other cases: the rule could be read as meaning *if p' then q* or *if p'' then q*. On the facts which have occurred, p' is satisfied but p'' is not. Therefore assertion of the consequence q can be justified deductively by reference to *that* rule only given *that* interpretation—but not if the rival reading *if p'' then q* is preferred.

In short: rules can be ambiguous in given contexts, and can be applied one way or the other only after the ambiguity is resolved. But resolving the ambiguity in effect involves choosing between rival versions of the rule (*if p'' then q*, or *if p'' then q*); once that choice is made, a simple deductive justification of a particular decision follows. But a complete justification of that decision must hinge then on how the choice between the competing versions of the rule is justified: evidently a deductive justification as analysed in Chapter II is impossible. Our problem then is how such a choice is justified—and that problem, for obvious enough reasons I shall call the 'problem of interpretation'.

Are there any other kinds of problem whose solutions must transcend the limits of deductive argumentation? In relation to some legal systems, one would be inclined to answer in the negative—but that negative would not apply to the systems of the U.K.

Especially within a codified system of law, it may be deemed necessary to refer every dispute and decision thereon to some article or articles of a Code. If the Code is considered as comprehensively covering the whole field of law, then no decision can be held justified unless it is subsumed under an article of written law—on *some* interpretation of that article. The very fact of the comprehensiveness of the Code entails relatively high generality in the terms of its articles, and hence relatively wide latitudes of interpretation and leeways of choice. So it should not be thought that reasoning and argumentation in a codified system is always or necessarily 'formalistic' or mechanical. As consideration of the articles of the Code Civil (1382–6) dealing with 'Délits et Quasi-Délits,' and the judicial development under them of the modern French law of reparation of injuries (torts) would indicate, there may arise under the guise of 'problems of interpretation' of a Code questions of legal policy of the most fundamental and far-reaching kinds.[23]

By contrast, an inevitable feature of a non-codified system of law is that many issues of dispute and decisions thereon arise and are settled without reference to statutory (or 'written') law in any form. In so far as judicial precedent functions as a source of 'valid law' for such systems, deductive arguments applying rules derived from that source are of course frequently resorted to and 'problems of interpretation' as defined above can and do also arise.

[23] For a helpful discussion of this, see F.H. Lawson, *Negligence in the Civil Law* (Oxford, 1950), pp. 231 f. For a particular example relating to Article 1384 see Touffait and Tunc, 'Pour une Motivation Plus Explicite des Decisions de Justice', *Rev. trim.dr.civ.* 1974, pp. 489–90.

But sometimes problems arise and decisions on them are given and justified in a manner which cannot plausibly be represented as involving the simple application of, or even the making of interpretive choices as between different versions of, already established valid and binding rules of law. The kind of problem I have in mind cannot at all plausibly be represented as concerning the question: 'There is here an incontestable rule of law *if p then q*, but what does *p* mean?' The problem is, rather, 'Does the law in any way justify a decision in favour of this party against that party in this context?' The solution of such problems manifestly transcends the possibility of deductive argumentation from established rules of law.

We all know how in *Donoghue* v. *Stevenson* ([1932] A.C. 562: 1932 S.C. (H.L.) 31) the pursuer Mrs. Donoghue raised an action of reparation against the defender, a manufacturer of aerated waters, on the ground that (as she averred) she had drunk some of the contents poured from an opaque bottle of Stevenson's ginger beer before discovering in the remainder of the contents when poured out the remnants of a decomposing snail; that this had caused her gastro-enteritis and nervous shock; and that the presence of the snail in the ginger beer was due to a failure of the manufacturer to take reasonable care in the preparation and bottling of the ginger beer. Since the defender owed to her a duty to take reasonable care in these processes, and since she had suffered harm through his want of care, she was entitled to damages in reparation of the physical harm and nervous shock she had suffered.

No statute covered (or covers) civil liability for such harm; and at the time at which her appeal came up from the Court of Session to the House of Lords there was no binding precedent which settled the issue conclusively one way or the other, although (as we shall in due course see) there was a good number of precedents sufficiently analogous to have some persuasive weight on each side of the case.

In such a case, the question, as the Scots form of pleading puts it, is whether the pursuer's averments are 'relevant' in law to the conclusion for which she moves the court. Is there any reason in law why, if the facts which she states could be proven, she ought to be granted the remedy for which she concludes?

If the question be answered in her favour (as in fact it was), the logic of justification entails, as will be argued in the next chapter, that the 'reason in law' why she ought to get her remedy cannot be individual and particular. If there is some reason which justifies her being granted a remedy for this injury caused in that way, then that reason must be likewise a good reason why anyone injured in the like way ought to be granted a like remedy.

It further follows that the justification of a decision in this pursuer's favour must involve in some sense a decision to assert some general proposition as a sufficient legal warrant[24] for a decision in her favour; and that the justification of a decision against her would require the negation of any such general proposition.

To justify deciding for the pursuer one must be prepared to say: 'Because the facts as averred occurred, she ought to have this remedy': But that can be sustained as a justifying proposition in law only by someone who assents to the proposition 'If ever such facts as here averred occur, the pursuer ought to have this remedy.' But that in turn is a proposition which precisely fits the *if p then q* formula which we have been working with throughout this discussion.

Further argument is required to show why this should be so; for the moment we have said enough to establish a way of stating the general form of this type of problem which may arise in law and whose resolution inevitably transcends deductive argumentation and which goes beyond the bounds even of the 'problem of interpretation'. The problem is, in effect, whether it is justifiable in law to assert, or to negate, some proposition *if p then q* for any *p* which covers the facts of the instant case and any *q* which covers the particular remedy sought.

For reasons of convenience, albeit in slight violation of the technical usage of Scots law, I shall hereinafter call that type of problem 'the problem of relevancy'.

---

[24] My use of the notion of 'warrant' here and elsewhere derives from Stephen Toulmin, *The Uses of Argument* (Cambridge 1958). See pp. 98 f.

Professor D.M. Walker in his discussion of the 'theory of relevancy'[25] in Scots law gives the following description of the Scottish system of pleading:

Reduced to its essentials, the Scottish system of pleading involves stating conclusions, or general requests for the particular form of legal remedy desired by the pursuer, and supporting these by a condescendence or statement of those facts of the particular case which the pursuer believes to be and offers to prove true, and which, he thinks, justify him in asking for the remedy. Among these statements of fact by the pursuer are interpolated the defender's answers thereto; the whole is completed by pleas in law for each party requesting the Court's action in the ways concluded for with special reference to the facts of the case, such as granting or refusing a decree sought or rejecting the conclusions for the opposite party.

What that system of pleading makes pellucidly clear is that, as Walker sums it up, 'to make a relevant case, the pleader is trying to construct a valid legal syllogism.'[26] And by that he intends not merely a logically, but a legally, valid syllogism; Not merely must it be formally valid in structure; it must disclose in the plea in law a *legally valid* major premiss; some *If p then q* formula which will be a sufficient *legal* 'warrant' for claiming that conclusion given those averments of fact by way of minor premiss.

Although the Scottish system of pleading is in some respects more rigorous and formalized (in just those respects to which Walker's remarks draw attention) than that which currently prevails in England and Wales, our earlier discussion of 'the validity thesis' gives us some reason to suppose (and further reasons will in due course be given for supposing) that what it reveals in explicit form is necessarily implicit in any system of pleading. Whoever makes a statement of claim that he ought to be granted remedy R because facts F_1, F_2, $F_3 \ldots F_n$ have occurred implicitly asserts there is some legal warrant for granting that remedy given those facts, and that warrant must be some actual or putative legal norm assigning a given legal consequence to a set of generally specified factual conditions. And any such norm can be recast in our canonical form 'If p (i.e. if facts F_1, F_2, $F_3 \ldots F_n$ occur),

[25] D.M. Walker, 'The Theory of Relevancy' (1951) 63 *Juridical Review* 1, at p. 3.
[26] Ibid. at p. 14.

then q (i.e. the legal consequence C ought to follow)'.

Here again, although it is trivially true that once the necessary 'legal warrant' is established, the given conclusion can be justified by simple deduction therefrom, it is equally obvious that by the hypothesis the argument which justifies establishment of that 'legal warrant' cannot in turn be similarly deductive in form. Here again the limits of deductive justification are surpassed, and we must look to other modes of argumentation to discover a complete justification of decisions which involve consideration of the 'problem of relevancy'.

The argument of this chapter therefore demonstrates that on any view of law and in any type of legal system which involves the use of 'valid rules', the problem of interpretation must on occasion arise; and that at least in some contexts the problem of relevancy may also arise. Our further study of reason in law must therefore concentrate upon those problems and the forms of argument appropriate to solving them. But in proceeding to that question, I shall have to meet a possible objection which could be put in relation to the thesis as stated so far: namely, that it cooks the books or begs the question in assuming without proof that the posing of either of my problems *necessarily* involves the framing of general norms. '*If p'* then q or *if p"* then q?' in the problem of interpretation; 'Is there any relevant norm *if p then q*?' in the problem of relevancy. The next chapter will advance the thesis by meeting that objection.

IV

THE CONSTRAINT OF FORMAL JUSTICE

(a) *Justice and justification*

The ideas of justification and of justice are closely related ones, not merely at the etymological level. To justify doing *x* is to show that it is right and just to do *x*. But of course it is an intrinsically disputable question what it is just to do in given circumstances, although it is a question which does not arise in a pure abstract form in most legal situations. Judges have to do 'justice according to law', not justice pure and simple. The norms of the legal system supply a concrete conception of justice which is in ordinary circumstances—where deductive justification is sufficient in itself—sufficiently fulfilled by the application of relevant and applicable rules according to their terms.

I follow John Rawls in distinguishing between specific conceptions of justice and the concept of justice.[1] The difference is that the concept of justice is abstract and formal; the requirement of formal justice is that we treat like cases alike, and different cases differently, and give to everyone his due; what various conceptions of justice supply is different sets of principles and/or rules in the light of which to determine when cases are materially similar and when they are materially different, and what is each person's due. Hence the Sale of Goods Act (for example) in laying down that 'sales by description' are to be treated differently from sales of specific goods not identified by any generic description (for the purpose of the implied term as to merchantable quality), can be said to embody (at a pretty low level of specificity) a particular conception of justice in mercantile transactions.

Whether or not that conception of justice is a good or a sound one is a question involving general principles of normative legal or moral philosophy in relation to which

[1] J. Rawls, *A Theory of Justice* (Oxford, 1972), ch. 1. Cf. Hart, *Concept of Law*, pp. 155–9.

an interesting debate could be held. But for the most part it is a debate which does not take place in Courts of Law, because the judges' duty to do justice *according to law* settles the issue for them.

But what of our problems of interpretation and of relevancy? We have already settled the point that decision in cases raising these problems cannot be fully justified simply by showing the deducibility of the conclusion enforced by the Court's judgment from some postulated rule, because at the very least what is in issue is what meaning is to be ascribed to some rule, if not indeed whether there is at all any such norm as would warrant the decision sought by one or other of the parties. Settlement of these issues cannot by the hypothesis be a matter of justice 'according to law', in the particular sense of 'according to the specific provisions of valid legal rules'; we have in such situations run beyond the specific and determinate guidance that the rules can give.

Nevertheless it is at least the case that at this level adherence to the formal concept of justice itself may be determinative of the form of justification of decisions. It is trite learning to observe that formal justice supplies one good reason for following judicial precedents. In *Morelli* v. *Fitch & Gibbons* ([1928] 2 K.B. 636; [1928] All E.R. Rep 610) it was held to constitute a sale by description when a purchaser was supplied with a particular bottle of ginger wine in response to his statement '. . .I want Stone's ginger wine at 2s. 9d.'; in *Daniels* v. *White* ([1938] 4 All E.R. 258) it was agreed by both parties that the plaintiff '. . .asked for R. White's lemonade'. To decide that the latter instance was not an instance of 'sale by description' would plainly involve treating this case differently from the essentially similar precedent. If one case is to be treated as a 'sale by description' so is the other; if one is not, neither is the other—so far as formal justice is concerned. (Of course, if the former decision were on some ground substantively unjust, or undesirable for some other reason, it is at the very least an arguable point whether it is better to perpetuate a substantive injustice as the price of satisfying formal justice, or to secure substantive justice in the instant case at the cost of sacrificing formal justice as between the parties to this and the parties to that case. There is no slick, easy answer to that.)

Trite as it is that the requirements of formal justice establish at least a presumptive reason for following relevant precedents, it is no less true, although less commonly observed, that these requirements impose forward looking as well as backward-looking constraints on the decision of litigated disputes.[2]

The court which today decides a specific case between individual parties ought to take account of its duty, at least its prima-facie duty, to decide the case consistently with prior decisions on the same or similar points. At the least, formal justice requires that it shall not save for strong reasons decide this case in a manner unlike the manner of its prior decisions in like cases. Has the Court not then an equally weighty duty to take account in deciding this case of the precedent which it will be setting for cases yet to arise? That I must treat like cases alike implies that I must decide today's case on grounds which I am willing to adopt for the decision of future similar cases, just as much as it implies that I must today have regard to my earlier decisions in past similar cases. Both implications are implications of adherence to the principle of formal justice; and whoever agrees that judges ought to adhere to the principle of formal justice is committed to both these implications.

In my own right, I should certainly advocate the view that judges ought to adhere to the principle of formal justice, as a minimal requirement of doing justice at all, and a fortiori 'justice according to law'. What is more, I should argue that its forward-looking requirement is yet more stringent than its backward-looking, just because—as we saw—there can genuinely be a conflict between the formal justice of following the precedent and the perceived substantive justice of today's case. That conflict cannot in the nature of the case arise when, unconstrained by unambiguous statute or directly binding precedent, I decide today's case in the knowledge

---

[2] As I have argued before in 'Formal Justice and the Form of Legal Arguments', *Etudes de logique juridique*, vi (ed. Ch. Perelman, Brussels, 1976), 103–18. My point is substantially similar to that made by K.N. Llewellyn in his discussion of 'type situations' in his *Common Law Tradition* (Boston, 1960), esp. at pp. 426–9. But my explanation of the matter differs from his.

that I must thereby commit myself to settling grounds for decision for today's and future similar cases. There is no conflict today, though there will be in the future if today I articulate grounds of decision which turn out to embody some substantive injustice or to be on other grounds inexpedient or undesirable. That is certainly a strong reason for being careful about how I decide today's case.

Quite apart from my own favouring of that position, I also believe it to be in fact true that the judiciary and the legal profession in the present-day systems of the U.K., and in all the other western systems with which I am at all familiar, do also subscribe to the view that the principle of formal justice ought to be observed in precisely the sense and with precisely the implications which I have adumbrated. Their practical observation of those principles in the concrete justificatory arguments which they advance in actual cases is overwhelming evidence of that, as will sufficiently appear in due course.

Thus as an observer of the legal system I infer both that those working within it do for the most part adhere to the operational implications of the norm that like cases ought to be decided in like fashion, and that in doing so they are conforming to basic constraints imposed by acknowledgment of the concept of justice as a purely formal virtue. As a participant (in a modest way) in the system, as a citizen of the state, and indeed as a human being, I also for my own part think that they ought to. I follow Thomas Reid in regarding the choice to observe formal justice in such matters as a choice between the rational and the arbitrary in the conduct of human affairs,[3] and in asserting it as a fundamental principle that human beings ought to be rational rather than arbitrary in the conduct of their public and social affairs (spontaneity and a kind of arbitrariness have a welcome part to play in private activities and relations, but what is private is not itself a private question). To somebody who disputes that principle with me, I can indeed resort only to a Humean argument: our society is either organized according to that value of rationality or it is not, and I cannot

---

[3]   Reid, *Essays* (*cit. sup.*, ch. I n. 1), Essay V, ch. 1 *sub.fin.*

contemplate without revulsion the uncertainty and insecurity of an arbitrarily run society, in which decisions of all kinds are settled on somebody's whim or caprice of the moment, without reference to past or future decision making.

All that indicates how, as I candidly stated at the outset,[4] my thesis is both descriptive of actually operative norms within actual legal systems, and in its own right normative in arguing for what I see as good procedures of decision making and justification. I may be wrong on either or both counts, but I would hope that critics will observe and distinguish between errors of observation and points of normative disagreement. One can be censor as well as expositor without necessarily confusing the two roles.

Be that as it may, the theoretical argument so far stated goes some way to vindicating against a possible objection the manner in which in the preceding chapter I formulated my 'problem of interpretation' and my 'problem of relevancy'. What is more, the theoretical argument can easily be corroborated with practical examples.

In the actual case of *Ealing London Borough Council* v. *Race Relations Board* ([1972] A.C. 342; [1972] 1 All E.R. 105) the very question which I gave earlier as an instance of the 'problem of interpretation' did in fact arise in litigation. The Council had refused to add to its housing list the name of a certain Mr. Zesko, on the ground that he was a Polish citizen and not a British subject (though he was a long-term resident in Britain); in so doing they were applying an administrative rule of their own that only 'British subjects' could be admitted to the housing list. The Race Relations Board having taken up Mr. Zesko's case with them, they raised an action in the High Court seeking a declaration that they were not discriminating unlawfully within the meaning of the 1968 Act. They lost, and appealed to the House of Lords.

As Viscount Dilhorne observed in his speech (in which he, together with the majority of the House of Lords, upheld the Council's interpretation of the Act). 'The question to be decided in this appeal is whether discrimination in favour of

4 Ch. I (b), last two paras. (p. 13).

British subjects within the meaning of the British Nationality
Act 1948 and against aliens is discriminating on the ground
of "national origins" ' ([1972] 1 All E.R. at 111).

Observe that although it was a particular question on
which a declaration was sought, viz. whether *the Council* had
itself committed unlawful discrimination within the terms of
the Act, Lord Dilhorne's question is not that particular
question: he conceives it necessary to decide whether any act
of discrimination by *anyone* against *anyone* on the ground
that he is not a British subject constitutes discrimination on
the ground of 'national origins'. That is not a question about
a particular act of discrimination: it is a logically universal
question.

(It would accord more easily with normal speech to describe such a question as 'general' rather than 'universal';
but, as R.M. Hare points out,[5] 'universal' is a more exact
term to use, and it allows us to use 'general' to refer to a
difference of degree rather than of logical type: thus, 'All
discrimination between persons is prohibited' is a *more
general* norm than 'all discrimination between persons on the
ground of national origins is prohibited'; but both are logically
universal in their prohibitions. Hereinafter I shall observe
that distinction, though with this concession to ordinary
usage that I shall treat 'generic' as being more or less equivalent to 'universal', both being distinguished from 'general'.
A like distinction will be observed at the opposite end of the
two scales, as between 'particular' and 'specific'.)

That Lord Dilhorne conceived it necessary to give a
generic or logically universal ruling on the point whether
any and all acts of discrimination on the ground of a person's
nationality are discrimination on the ground of national
origins, even though the actual decision to be given relates
to this particular Council which is alleged to have discriminated
unlawfully, corroborates my earlier argument. The point is
that the House of Lords cannot consistently with formal
justice decide that this Council is or is not discriminating unlawfully without committing itself to the view that anyone

---

[5] R.M. Hare 'Principles', *Proc Arist. Soc.* 1972–3, p.1 (and cf. *The Language
of Morals* (Oxford, 1952) and *Freedom and Reason* (Oxford, 1963)).

else who discriminates on the same ground, viz. a person's nationality at a given time, is (or, as the case may be, is not) discriminating unlawfully.

The Council asserts that it is not discriminating unlawfully, and gives reasons for its assertions; the Board asserts that the Council is discriminating unlawfully, and in turn gives reasons for its assertion. The Court must decide whose assertion to uphold; but either it can given reasons for so deciding which are good reasons for all such cases, or it can not. If it can, it is at least implicitly deciding on an interpretation of the meaning of 'discrimination on the ground of national origins' which is in principle applicable to *any* such case of alleged discrimination; if it cannot, it has failed to satisfy the forward looking implication of the principle of formal justice. All the better that the Court should make explicit, as Lord Dilhorne (and his brethren) made it explicit, that a *justified* decision of the particular point logically requires a decision of the generic point.

But it is merely putting the question another way to put it (as I earlier put it) in the terms that the Court must choose between two rival versions of the rule, both more specific in terms than the rule as enacted (and both in the logical sense 'universal'), but each incompatible with the other:

'If a person discriminates against another on the ground of national origins (including that person's legal nationality) then he discriminates unlawfully,'
and
'If a person discriminates against another on the ground of national origins (as distinct from that person's legal nationality) then he discriminates unlawfully.'

The only virtue of effecting that translation of the question is that it makes it utterly clear that the court must make—and must justify—a choice between two version of the rule in order to reach a justified decision. And the only virtue of the further translation of the choice into the logical shorthand of *If p' then q* versus *if p" then q* is that (a) it is shorthand, and (b) by resorting to propositional forms rather than specific propositions it is appropriate to signifying the question in any, not just one, instance of the problem interpretation.

Not surprisingly, the same observations *mutatis mutandis*

hold good in relation to decisions on the problem of relevancy. My earlier example was *Donoghue* v. *Stevenson*, and I shall for the moment stick to it. Lord Atkin (who was, of course, one of the majority of three to two who upheld Mrs. Donoghue's pleas as relevant) spoke with characteristic lucidity in the opening sentences of this speech in the Lords:

The sole question of determination in this case is legal: Do the statements made by the pursuer in her pleading, if true, disclose a cause of action? I need not re-state the particular facts. The question is whether the manufacturer of an article of drink sold by him in circumstances which prevent the distributor or the ultimate purchaser or consumer from discovering by inspection any defect is under any legal duty to the ultimate purchaser or consumer to take reasonable care that the article is free from defect likely to cause injury to health. ([1932] A.C. at 578–9 1932 S.C. (H.L.) at 43)

Equally, at the end of his speech he returned to the point:

If your Lordships accept the view that the appellant's pleading discloses a relevant cause of action you will be affirming the proposition that by Scots and English law alike a manufacturer of products which he sells in such a form as to show that he intends them to reach the ultimate consumer in the form in which they left him, with no reasonable possibility of intermediate examination, and with the knowledge that absence of reasonable care in the preparation or putting up of the products will result in injury to the consumer's life or property, owes a duty to the consumer to take that reasonable care. ([1932] A.C. at 599; 1932 S.C. (H.L.) at 57)

Lord Macmillan and Lord Thankerton, who agreed with Lord Atkin, were equally clear in stating the 'propositions' which they were affirming—in markedly similar terms to Lord Atkin's. Just as significant, the dissenting minority, Lords Buckmaster and Tomlin, had no doubt that they wished to deny precisely the proposition whose affirmation the majority favoured.

The whole point is to see that, and to realize why, Lord Atkin treats it as being so natural to move from the actual question in the appeal: are *this* pursuer's averments relevant, do they disclose a cause of action?—which is a particular question about a particular pursuer in a particular case—to the eminently generic question which he next posed, about 'the manufacturer' of 'an article of drink' in relation to the utlimate purchaser or consumer'. He is talking, as his concluding sentence makes utterly clear, about any manufacturer, or about all manufacturers. Lord Tomlin hit the nail on the head in saying at the outset of his speech:

> I think that if the appellant is to succeed it must be on the proposition that *every* manufacturer or repairer of *any* article is under a duty to *everyone* who may *thereafter* legitimately use the article. . .It is logically impossible to stop short of this point. ([1932] A.C. at 599; 1932 S.C. (H.L.) at 57; italics added).

What makes it indeed *logically* impossible to stop short of such a point, is of course that Lord Tomlin is concerned (as every judge should be) not with whether the appellant will in fact succeed, but whether she ought in justice to succeed; the logic is the logic of formal justice whereby if this appellant *because she is a consumer* is owed a duty by this respondent *because he is a manufacturer*, then any person who is a consumer is owed a like duty by whoever manufactured that which is consumed. By assigning the appellant to the class of consumers *vis à vis* manufacturers, one is determining what are criteria of relevant similarity for future cases. Cases are not like or unlike in the abstract, or absolutely. They are like or unlike if they can or cannot be assigned to given determinate classes. To put the case for Mrs. Donoghue against Mr. Stevenson on the ground that she consumed what he manufactured is then in effect to fix the generic question which must be answered in justifying any decision between them: Do manufacturers as such owe a duty of care to whoever consumes their products or do they not?

A justified answer to the particular question requires an answer to the universal question—which answer must in its turn be justified by processes which we shall shortly consider. But answering the universal question one way or the other involves affirming one or other of two rival 'propositions' as Lord Atkin put it. It involves giving a ruling on a point of law enunciating a norm as a justifying norm of the legal system. Just as with the problem of interpretation, the problem of relevancy involves making a choice between two rival norms as acceptable propositions of law. To oversimplify slightly: *either*

Manufacturers of products owe a duty of care to the consumers of their products.

or

It is not the law that manufacturers owe a duty of care to the consumers of their products.

Formulaically: either '*If p then q*' or 'It is not the law that *if p then q*'.

For my purposes, of course, *Donoghue* v. *Stevenson* is a good example because of the very explicit clarity with which the various Lords set out what they were doing, and it might be regarded as only weakly corroborative evidence for my general thesis on the very ground that it was all so clearly expressed. As later chapters will show, however, there are many other examples which display equal or similar clarity.

More to the point, I have given clear reasons for believing that what is made clear and explicit in such a case as *Donoghue* v. *Stevenson* is necessarily implicit in any genuine justification of a decision in a case involving the problem of relevancy. These reasons are derived from analysis of the implications of the principle of formal justice as a principle essentially involved in any justification process.

I do not flatter myself that the foregoing argument says more than what is simple and obvious. Yet there is this merit in a statement of the simple and obvious: it may point us towards answers to questions which have puzzled those who have gone at them in more complicated ways. Most readers of this book will be familiar with the problems within the doctrine of binding precedent about defining and identifying the *ratio decidendi* of cases. When a precedent is said to be binding, it is not every word uttered by the judge or judges in justifying the decision which is transubstantiated into binding law—only the *ratio decidendi*. The trouble is that there is no generally agreed statement either of what a *ratio* is or of how you find the *ratio* of any given case.[6]

The very simple argument of this chapter has led us to the point or realizing that whenever the problem of interpretation of the problem of relevancy arises, the particular decision handed down in the particular case is justifiable only given some ruling as to the 'proper' interpretation of

---

[6] The voluminous literature on the topic is comprehensively referred to and discussed in Rupert Cross, *Precedent in English Law* (2nd edn., Oxford, 1968); and see R.W.M. Dias, *A Bibliography of Jurisprudence* (2nd edn., London, 1970), pp. 33–8.

the applicable rule, or some ruling settling (or negating) some 'proposition' of law covering the particulars of the instant case and any other like case which may in due course arise. Even the small amount of evidence so far adduced demonstrates that *sometimes* clear rulings are explicitly given as part of the justification of the particular decision.

I venture to suggest that these truths might set us well on the track of the elusive *ratio decidendi*: When a Court gives a ruling on a point of law which it conceives to be necessary to its justification of its particular decision, it would seem not unreasonable to regard that ruling as the *ratio* of the case.

Not all decisions, alas, are supported by clear and explicit rulings, though by the logic of formal justice there ought to be at least an implicit ruling in any justifying opinion; worse still, when there is more than one judge in a court, those who concur in the final result may adopt different lines in justifying the decision, so that their rulings whether explicit or implicit may be mutually incompatible wholly or in part. (See for example *Chaplin* v. *Boys* ([1971] A.C. 356; [1969] 2 All E.R. 1085).

That could be an objection to my suggestion—but only if we adhere to the dogma that each precedent must have a single clear *ratio decidendi*. My reply is that such a dogma is mere fiction, and indeed mischievous fiction; it can prompt a converse fallacy, when former believers, discovering that some cases have no single articulable *ratio*, leap to the conclusion that none can have one. The fallacy is self evident.

This chapter has shown that there are strong reasons of principle why judges in deciding particular cases should act only in accordance with some ruling which covers not only the particular case, but all other possible cases which are like cases just because they would be covered by the same ruling.

There is already some and there will shortly be more evidence that judges do argue in justification of their decision in just that way; there are therefore some cases in which an essential element in the justification of a particular decision is a ruling on a generic point of law disputed by the parties. Even in appellate courts of more than one judge, it can and does happen that the majority concur in giving the same ruling on the same point.

When that occurs, it can at least make sense to treat the ruling given as the *ratio decidendi* of the case and to use it as a rule for the future. Even when the judges fail explicitly to formulate an exact question of law or answer to such a question, they may do so implicitly. Suppose in the *Ealing* case a judge had said: 'The statute prohibits discrimination against applicants for houses on the ground of national origins, but the material fact is that the Council only discriminated on the ground of the present legal nationality of Mr. X, without having any regard to his origins; so the appeal must be dismissed.' To treat that statement as a *justifying* reason for dismissal of the appeal is to conceive it as being *universalizable*—even though the statement itself has been cast in purely particular terms. It cannot be 'material' in relation to the question of unlawful discrimination that *this* Council only had regard to an applicant's nationality, without being equally and in the same sense material when any Council or other supplier of housing to let does likewise. In that sense such an opinion discloses a clear implicit ruling on the point at issue, given clarity as to the facts treated as material to justifying the decision; and as to the rule whose interpretation was at stake.

A.L. Goodhart's view[7] that the *ratio* of any case is discoverable by ascertaining what facts were treated by the judge as the material facts of the case, coupling these with the decision given, and generalizing the whole as a rule of law is to that extent perfectly sound; but it is not clear why he does not concede that it is only a *faute de mieux* way of exspiscating an implicit ruling when the court has failed to make an explicit one. And it excludes the possibility, which is a perfectly open one, that the judges or the Court failed to have any clear view as to the generic question or the correct generic answer.

So there is a possibility that some precedents contain relatively clear rulings on fairly sharply defined points of law, and that others contain implicit rulings of similar, but perhaps less, relative clarity. Yet others because of judicial

---

[7] A.L. Goodhart, *Essays in Jurisprudence and the Common Law* (Cambridge, 1931), ch. 1.

disagreement or simple confusion contain none. It is only a dogmatic fiction that the third class has anything which could reasonably be called a *ratio* at all, and the truth is that in relation to that type of case even the most rigid doctrine of binding precedent cannot in practice obligate the judge in a later case to do more than find some 'explanatory' proposition which is consistent with the actual decision of the precedent case and also relevant to the instant case; all the better if his 'explanatory' proposition squares in some degree with some at least of what was said in the confused or conflicting opinion or opinions given in the precedent.

It should be remarked also that even where an express ruling is given encapsulating the kind of 'proposition' wherewith Lord Atkin concluded his speech in *Donoghue*, the doctrine of precedent even in its English form leaves the subsequent court with a significant 'explanative' discretion: it is at best the proposition, not the particular words in which it was couched, that is binding. Therefore the later Court is free to *re-express* the proposition, together with further conditions or qualifications which may be deemed appropriate to novel types of circumstance as revealed by the later case. That the norms of the system leave its operators with that discretion gives interpreters of the system a problem which has sometimes been mistakenly supposed to be more than a problem of words: in *Donoghue* v. *Stevenson* a certain 'proposition' was laid down about the manufacturer's duty to consumers of his products; in *Haseldine* v. *Daw* ([1941] 2 K.B. 343; [1941] 3 All E.R. 156) for example, the negligent repair of a defective lift was brought within the doctrine and the repairers held liable to those injured in its collapse (observe that the dissents of Lords Tomlin and Buckmaster had dealt with the case of repairers, though none of the affirming majority did); is the 'ratio' of *Donoghue* v. *Stevenson* the explicit ruling as given by the judges in *Donoghue* itself, or that ruling as re-expressed and extended in *Haseldine*?

The only observation I wish to make is that answering that question does not add to our knowledge of the real world at all. All that it does is to stipulate a particular usage for the technical term *ratio*, which is in fact somewhat ambiguous in its ordinary use, precisely because it is variably used in practice. Sometimes it is used as referring to the proposition as actually laid down in the original decision of a case, sometimes to that proposition as explained reinterpreted qualified or whatever in later cases.

There is not the least probability of any stipulation by me determining usage, so I offer none; I only observe that among judges and practitioners the predominant operational usage of the term *ratio* seems to be as referring to express statements of propositions of law made by judges in their justifying opinion in recorded cases, and (if my opinion matters) that seems to be the least confusing usage available for the term. (This topic is resumed in Chapter VIII (c) below).

All in all, even by reference to such a simple outline account as this, it seems that appreciation of the necessary universality of justifying reasons for the decision of particular cases can enable us clearly to explain otherwise puzzling features of the doctrine of precedent. It does so by focusing on the way in which, quite apart from any doctrine of precedent in any official or binding sense, the constraints of formal justice obligate a court to attend to the need for generic rulings on points of law, and their acceptability as generic rulings, as essential to the justification of particular decisions. That the theory advanced has this explanatory power gives it further plausibility in its descriptive aspect.

(b) *'Decisions on the Facts'*

But it may again be objected that I am concentrating only on types of problem which happen to fit my own hypotheses, and failing to account for other equally important problems answers to which have to be reasoned out in Courts of Law. In particular, it might well be said that I am simply concentrating on cases in which there are arguments over and decisions about 'points of law', and ignoring entirely the equally, or more, important cases which are decided 'on their facts'. There are some points worth picking up here, but it will be best to deal with them in terms of a distinction between two types of decisions 'on the facts'.

(i) *Problems of proof*

We have already noted that all litigation involves the supposition that we can establish present truths about past facts. Sometimes, as in the *Daniels* case, it can be made easier by the fact that everyone now agrees about what happened then. Both Mr. Daniels and Mrs. Tarbard gave concurring accounts as to what passed between them when he bought the bottle of White's lemonade in her pub. So too in the *Ealing* case everyone agreed as to the facts of the matter of Mr. Zesko's application to be put on the Borough Council's housing list and the reason why he was refused. That we are in principle able to establish what happened in the past is obviously a supposition necessarily involved in the whole idea of 'applying' legal rules in Courts, Since the logic of applying rules is revealed by the form.

If p then q

p

$\therefore q$.

Application is possible only given that we consider it always in principle and sometimes in practice possible to prove whether p is or is not true in relation to some given past incident.

The process of legal proof—even when based on parties' admissions—is obviously not guaranteed always to establish the truth. The memories and perceptions of honest people can be false. It has often been shown how unreliable the adversary process of presenting and testing evidence can be, and the exclusionary rules of the law of evidence have often been criticized from the point of view of at least ostensibly respectable 'scientific' positions.[8] Particularly in the case of criminal convictions based on eyewitnesses' evidence of identity, some horrifying mistakes seem on occasion to have been made (though we can only be *sure* that a mistake *was* made if we think we have found some *unquestionably* reliable way of establishing present truths about past states of affairs; and sometimes those who have least confidence of the law's methods seem to have remarkable faith in their own).

[8] See e.g. L.R.C. Haward, 'A Psychologist's Contribution to Legal Procedure' (1964) 27 Mod.L.R., 656; Paton, *A Text-book of Jurisprudence* (4th edn. by G.W. Paton and D.P. Derham, Oxford, 1972), pp. 603–5.

The justification of any present statement about the past must depend upon the kinds of inference we are entitled to make from propositions of whose truth we are presently aware. Disputes about the past must depend on disputes either about what is presently the case, or about what inferences can be drawn from that, or both. Such disputes have an obvious and unavoidable importance in law. People who do not dispute that there is a law *If p then q* nor what is its proper interpretation may well dispute over whether or not *p* has happened. If anyone kills another with malice aforethought, his act constitutes murder. Not many even of the most hotly contested murder trials have cast doubt on the rule defining murder or its meaning: the more common dispute is centred on the prosecution's assertion and the accused's denial that it was he who killed the victim, and that (if he did) he did so with malice aforethought.

For quite arbitrary reasons of space and time I have chosen to exclude from this book any extended consideration of the process of proof, the processes of reasoning from evidence, of justifying conclusions inferred from evidence, and of justifying the rules which determine what constitutes evidence and what is excluded as inadmissible. That is worthy of a book in itself, a book which would both draw on and contribute to the philosophy of science and the philosophy of history.

For the moment, I should like only to pass a few brief and sketchy remarks about the subject. First, for reasons which we touched on earlier, it is unavoidably necessary to have some rule or rules as to burdens of proof. If we are going to base present actions on beliefs about past events, somebody must take responsibility for attempting to prove that the relevant events occurred.

But what then is 'proving'? That is the second and fundamental point. Proving depends on the adduction of evidence. 'Evidence is something which enables us (a) to hold as true propositions about the present; and (b) to infer from these, propositions about the past. Evidence is admissible if (a) it is relevant to making an inference of or concerning a fact in issue in the case; and (b) it is not excluded by some rule founded on the supposition that it is of a kind of evidence which, if admitted, would either be unreliable or unfair. But how can we make 'inferences'?

To take an example: witnesses in a case give testimony to the effect that on a certain date the dismembered trunk of a female body was found in a parcel in Regent Square, and that attached to the parcel was a piece of paper with the words 'Bladie Belgiam' written upon it. That gives me reason to believe that such a thing was found there on that date, only if, in addition to hearing a witness making the relevant statements, I believe (a) that the witness is *honestly* making a statement of that which he remembers; (b) that he is *accurately* stating what he remembers; and (c) that his memory is *reliable*. To the extent that one doubts a witness's honesty, accuracy or reliability, to that extent one has reason to doubt the truth of what he says. All that I *know* is that the witness said what he said.

If witnesses also testify that while the accused was in a police station on a given day he was asked to write on a piece of paper the words 'Bloody Belgian', that he said he had no objection to doing so, and that he then wrote the words 'Bladie Belgiam', it is only subject to similar conditions that one has reason to believe the truth of what is said. Judge or juror may certainly examine directly by their own senses two pieces of paper each bearing the words 'Bladie Belgiam' to decide whether the handwriting is the same, and so on. But they are entirely dependent on testimonial evidence to assure them that the one piece of paper is that which was found with the body, the other that which was written by the accused in the police station—all this subject to the caution that for judge and jury it is no more than probable inference that there was a body, was a piece of paper with it, was a piece of paper written by the accused in the station, and so on.

Even if, as in the case of *R.* v. *Voisin* ([1918] 1 K.B. 531) from which this example is drawn, there is also testimony to the effect that the rooms occupied by the accused and the rooms occupied by the victim both contained traces of human blood; even though there was testimony to the effect that the victim's severed head and hands were in the accused's cellar, that the accused and a woman called Roche had keys to the victim's flat, that at the time of his arrest the appellant had the key of his cellar in his pocket—even though there was all that testimonial evidence, it is not impossible to believe that the facts as recited never actually occurred. Witnesses may be honest but inaccurate, or they may have mistaken memories or they may be lying. And even if (which we could never know for certain) all they say is true, its truth is logically consistent with the possibility that Louis-Marie Joseph Voisin did not kill Émilienne Gérard. It could all be pure coincidence; it could be some amazingly well contrived frame up.

But I do not think so. It is hard to think of a more convincing prosecution case. Why then is it convincing?

The answer is that the story is plausible because it is coherent. It is like a jigsaw whose pieces fit together. The piece which we do not have in the 'evidence' is the proposition that 'Louis Voisin killed Émilienne Gérard'. But that piece fits with all the other pieces, and does so better than 'possibly X who is not Louis Voisin killed Émilienne Gérard'; not that the latter is logically inconsistent with the whole body of the evidence—it is as we saw already logically possible that somebody else did kill Émilienne. But in the absence of any conflicting evidence (and Voisin chose not to testify), there is nothing here which raises that logical possibility to the status of a 'reasonable doubt'.

I suggest that the only type of test which we have available to us for verifying contested assertions about the past is this test of 'coherence'; taking all that has been presented to us in the way of real or testimonial evidence we work out a story that hangs together, which makes sense as a coherent whole. And of course, this involves interpreting the directly visible, audible, performances of witnesses, appearance of productions, and such-like within a web of general assumptions, beliefs, and theories—no doubt rather inexact and unscientific theories.

The best kind of reason we can ever have for believing some proposition about the past to be true is that it is more coherent than any other with our general beliefs about cause and effect and the motivation of human actions, and with a series of other particular propositions of fact which are themselves coherent inter se, and which include some propositions founded on present sensory perceptions. And no such reason can ever be conclusive.

Observe that the fact that that is our only available approach to verifying beliefs about the past has nothing to do with the meaning of the term 'true'; in terms of the old dispute between 'correspondence' and 'coherence' theories of truth,[9] it seems far more satisfactory to *define* true statements as being those which correspond with a reality whose existence is independent of the statement. Of course, only in the case of particular present tense statements can we verify by checking to see whether there is such correspondence, e.g. whether the cat is on the mat. In other instances we are left to the less conclusive test provided by the search for a coherent story some of whose parts can be directly verified by correspondence with present particular realities. Then indeed the force of 'correspondence' is reversed: we do not believe the statement 'Voisin killed Gerard' because there is a now perceptible reality to which it corresponds. *Per contra*, we believe that there was once a perceptible reality which corresponded to that statement, and we so believe because we think we have sufficiently good grounds for regarding the statement as true.

No very exact definition of 'coherence' will be offered here. At least a reasonably clear idea can be conveyed by scrutinizing more closely a particular element in the example of the Voisin case. That Voisin, being asked to write 'Bloody Belgian', wrote 'Bladie Belgiam', and that a note with the words 'Bladie Belgiam' on it was attached to the parcelled up corpse seems strongly to suggest an association between him and at least the note attached to the corpse. But why? Because there is a coherence between the propositions: '*x* who wrote the label on the corpse wrote "Bladie Belgiam" '; 'Voisin who is in the Police station writes "Bladie Belgiam" when meaning to write "Bloody Belgian" '; 'Voisin and *x* could be the same person' 'the number of people who would write "Bladie Belgiam" must be quite small'; 'Voisin must be one of a relatively small number of people who could have

---

[9] For a contemporary discussion of the topic, see Nicholas Rescher, *The Coherence Theory of Truth* (Oxford, 1973), esp. pp. 1–24.

written the note attached to the corpse.' Taking all the evidence all together gives one cumulatively a complete 'story' whose parts are coherent in the way in which the above propositions are coherent.

When there is a conflict of evidence in a case, the effect may be the construction of two rival coherent versions of the past, one of which (say) includes performance by the accused of the *actus reus*, the other of which excludes it—e.g. alibi evidence. When that happens, a key question becomes the opinion formed by the judges of fact as to the credibility of the direct and immediate evidence available to them. The accused and two friends swear that he was out on a yacht with them on the day in question; the Crown's case is that he was robbing the bank on that day. Both stories comprise a set of propositions which are (a) non-self-contradictory; and (b) consistent with general causal and motivational propositions; that is (c) coherent. If one story depends at crucial points on evidence given by a witness who seems to the judge or jury unreliable or untrustworthy or of a poor memory, then that weakens the credibility of the whole story. That one proposition p is coherent with another set of propositions q, r, s gives reason to believe p only so long as there is reason to believe that q, r, s, are true.

Finally, be it noted that the whole point of examination-in-chief and cross-examination is to enable the witness without prompting to set out a coherent set of relevant propositions which is then, by cross examination, tested for internal consistency and tested as to the reliability to trustworthiness of the witness. Nothing could make more obvious the key role of the notion of coherence in the process of legal proof.

Space permits no further development of this account; certainly, in so far as litigation turns on disputed facts rather than disputed law, it raises no problem of interpretation or relevancy—and therefore the universalizability of justificatory rulings is not engaged in such litigation. The problem of proof is a problem about establishing minor premises which are *particular* in character, not major premises which are universal. It is, however, true that there would be no rational way of going about the selection of assertions of fact to be set forward as provable if the logical structure of legal argumentation were not, in general, such as has been adumbrated in Chapters II–IV so far. There would be no way of choosing factual assertions to put in pleadings unless there were legal rules determining the facts proof of which will justify a desired legal conclusion.

(ii) *'Secondary fact' problems*

Sometimes, even after conflicts of evidence have been resolved by the decision of disputed issues of fact, and even if the parties are agreed as to what actually happened, there may remain problems concerning 'the facts'.

For example, in *Maclennan* v. *Maclennan* (1958 S.C. 105) Mr. M. brought an action in the Court of Session for a divorce from his wife on the ground of her adultery, averring *inter alia* that she had borne a child more than one year after their most recent meeting. In her defence, the wife admitted these facts, but condescended that the child had been conceived by means of artificial insemination by a donor, no adulterous act of sexual intercourse having taken place. The husband pled in law that the defence was irrelevant and concluded for a decree of divorce.

A debate was conducted before Lord Wheatley on the question whether the· wife's conduct amounted to adultery, assuming her averments to be provable. Looked at from one point of view, this is a simple example of what I call a 'problem of interpretation'. What does 'adultery' for the purposes of Scots divorce law mean? But from another point of view it might be argued that the key problem here is not so much an issue of interpreting the law as of appreciating the facts. Supposing that this woman had herself impregnated by a process of artificial insemination, does that amount to, count as, or constitute adultery? Certain 'primary facts' have been proven, or assumed as if proved for the purposes of debate: do these primary facts count as an instance of the required 'secondary fact'—adultery—in order to found a claim to a divorce?

Certainly, that is a common way of looking at certain kinds of problem in law. There is a rule which provides that if certain events occur, a certain legal consequence is to follow—*if p then q*. On the evidence in the case *r, s, t*, can be proved: but do these factual propositions amount to or count as an instance of *p* so as to bring the rule into operation?

Is this then a problem of a kind which has so far been ignored? It has in effect been covered already, though it will be advisable to say a few more words.

When we look to the opinion of Lord Wheatley in *Maclennan* v. *Maclennan* we find a clear and characteristic instance of an explicit ruling on a disputed point of law: Having reviewed the authorities on the legal conception of adultery, he proceeded to say

It accordingly follows, in my opinion, that artificial insemination by a donor does not constitute adultery according to our law. . .That it constitutes a grievous marital offence against a non-consenting husband, I have no doubt. The law, however, lays down certain grounds upon which divorce may be granted, one of which is adultery. . .If it be that science has created a *casus improvisus*, the remedy is not to be found in fitting such a case into one of the existing grounds of divorce on arguments which cannot logically or physiologically be supported. (1958 S.C. at 114)

In truth, the constraint of formal justice is as exacting if you pose the question 'Does *r, s, t* count as an instance of *p*?' as if you pose the question 'Should *if p then q* be interpreted as meaning *if p' then q* or *if p" then q*?' Lord Wheatley can justify holding that *this* defendant's conception of a child through A.I.D. does not count as adultery only if he is willing to hold that *any* defendant's indulging in A.I.D. would not count as adultery.

Speaking from the standpoint of pure logic, there is in fact no difference between the two ways of raising the issue:

(1) Should the rule that divorce may be granted on grounds of adultery be interpreted as meaning 'divorce may be granted on grounds of adultery (which includes impregnation by A.I.D.)'?

(2) For the purpose of applying the rule that divorce may be granted on grounds of adultery, does impregnation of a woman by A.I.D. count as an instance of 'adultery'?

And there is therefore a temptation to treat this second type of problem, the problem whether or not to classify the proven primary facts as belonging within some 'secondary fact' category which constitutes the 'operative facts' for a given rule, as identical with the problem of interpretation explained already.

But there may be special legal reasons for treating the 'problem of classification' (to give it a name) as being different from, albeit closely related to, the problem of interpretation. So we shall treat the question 'Is r, s, t an instance of p for the purposes of applying *if p then q*?' as the standard form of that problem, and treat it as different from the standard form of the problem of interpretation even though the one is logically equivalent to the other.

The legal reason for doing so is that in a variety of legal contexts it is held to make a difference whether a problem is posed as a problem of classification or of interpretation. For example when there is an appeal from one tribunal to another and the appeal is restricted to questions of law, it may be held that 'questions of classification' (as characterized here) are questions of fact, not law, and are hence unappealable. As much as anything else, the decision to draw the line at that point may be simply a way of protecting the higher court against a flood of appeals, or of preventing rulings below a certain level of detail acquiring the status of rulings on points of law. The line adopted by the French Cour de Cassation concerning the *pouvoir souverain du juge du fond* is an interesting instance.[10] That Court's function is to restrain inferior jurisdictions from violating the law in their decisions, and it is accordingly not concerned to correct their appreciation of the facts of any given affair.

By and large this means that when a ruling has been given in a form appropriate to our 'problem of interpretation' the Cour de Cassation regards it as plainly within its jurisdiction to correct any errors therein; but when the problem has been formulated as one of 'classification' in our sense, the Cour de Cassation does not normally interfere. On the other hand, just because there is not any genuine *logical* distinction between the two types of problem, the Court can decide to treat a problem of classification in the form of a problem of interpretation in order to assert its jurisdiction and take the opportunity of giving its own ruling on the point.

Equally, in other legal systems, where appeals are restricted

---

[10] See O. Kahn-Freund, C. Levy, and B. Rudden, *A Source-Book on French Law* (Oxford, 1973), pp. 81–2, 256–7, 437–40.

to matters of law, it is possible to exercise a 'leeway' of choice at the same point.[11]

Again, for the purposes of a doctrine of precedent, it may be convenient to treat some 'classification' decisions as being purely 'factual' just so that binding precedents should not be established. In *Qualcast (Wolverhampton) Ltd.* v. *Haynes* ([1959] A.C. 743; [1959] 2 All E.R. 38) which concerned the question whether an employer had taken reasonable care for his employee's safety in the way of providing suitable protective clothing and a safe system of work, the House of Lords ruled that that question is a 'question of fact'.[12] As Lord Denning said

What did reasonable care demand of the employers in the case? That is not a question of law at all but a question of fact. To solve it, the tribunal of fact. . .can take into account any proposition of good sense that is relevant in the circumstances, but it must beware not to treat it as a proposition of law. . .((1959) A.C. at 759)

In the present case the county court judge had treated certain precedents as establishing what counts as reasonable care in such accidents as the one involved in the case before him; said Lord Denning, 'I can well see how. . .he made this mistake. He was presented with a number of cases in which judges of the High Court had given reasons for coming to their conclusions of fact. And those reasons seemed to him to be so expressed as to be rulings in point of law; whereas they were, in truth, nothing more than propositions of good sense.' ([1959] A.C. at 762)

Lord Denning gave two reasons why such matters should not be regarded as 'rulings in point of law': that, if they were, the law would be 'crushed under the weight of our own reports'; and that 'What is 'a proper system of work' is a matter for evidence, not for law books. It changes as the conditions of work change: The standard goes up as men become wiser. It does not stand still as the law sometimes does.'

In short, there may well be good reasons for refusing to treat decisions on what actual conduct counts as 'reasonable' —or, one might add, 'fair', 'proper', 'unconscionable', and so

[11] Provision for such appeals is common in U.K. administrative law. Cf. J.F. Garner, *Administrative Law* (3rd edn., London, 1970), pp. 163–4, and cases there cited.
[12] Of course, evaluating whether or not conduct was 'reasonable' is not a matter of conducting a factual inquiry; but the question is one 'of fact' in the sense that it is a type of question left to a jury to decide in jury trials, on the basis of *their* sense of reasonableness, not some legal rule as to what is reasonable.

forth—as involving rulings which constitute binding precedent. In that sense, evaluative decisions applying criteria such as 'reasonableness', 'fairness', and so forth, are treated within the law as involving only reflection upon 'the particular facts' of the case. But what is good policy for the purpose of the doctrine of precedent has nothing to do with the fundamental logic of justification. He who decides what counts as 'reasonable care' in this case must be committed to treating the same degree of care as reasonable in any case in which the surrounding circumstances are the same. The requirement of universalizability is as much intrinsic to the justification of decisions here as it is elsewhere.[13]

Again, it is because of a perfectly intelligible—indeed sensible—legal distinction, not because of any fundamental logical distinction (Lord Denning in effect admitted as much), that it is proper to treat 'classification' problems as being different for some purposes from 'interpretation' problems.

Sufficient has been said to indicate however that the practical significance of the distinction in no way conflicts with the general argument of the thesis developed so far.

(c) A Final Objection: 'Equity'

To conclude this chapter, it is necessary to review and reply to one further possible objection to the argument advanced. It might perhaps be objected that the view stated in this chapter leaves out of account the possibility of decisions in accordance with equity rather than strict justice. It is sometimes said that equity is a matter of deciding each case on its own special merits without regard to general rules or principles. It seems to me that that view is pure nonsense. I cannot for the life of me understand how there can be such a thing as a good reason for deciding any single case which is not a good generic reason for deciding cases of the particular type in view, that is to say, the 'merits' of any individual case are the merits of the type of case to which the individual case belongs.

What is true is that a system of enacted positive law may

---

[13] I do not mean to say that standards of reasonableness cannot or should not change over time.

be enacted in terms which are of such considerable generality that the application of a given enacted rule to a particular dispute situation may appear to be unjust, unjust because the categories envisaged in the rule are insufficiently subtle. In such a circumstance it is obvious enough that there are good reasons for not applying the rule literally to the instant case, and that an exception ought to be made. For example, a statute providing for divorce on the ground of desertion over a three-year period may specify that desertion continues for three years only if the initially deserted spouse remains willing throughout the triennium to adhere to the deserting spouse if he or she should return or offer to return to cohabitation. But can it conceivably be just to apply that rule if in some given case the deserting spouse's conduct after desertion has been so unconscionable that it would be quite unreasonable to expect the deserted spouse to resume cohabitation even if it were offered?[14] It seems that the answer to that question might well be in the negative. But if that is so, would it be fair to hold someone seeking divorce in those circumstances to the strict terms of the law? Evidently not. But notice: to say that there is a good reason in this case in which these circumstances have been realized for departing from the strict statutory provisions, is necessarily to say that in any case in which a deserting spouse has behaved unconscionably the same decision should hold good. To say, as can truly be said, that in some cases strict application of existing rules of positive law would be contrary to the merits of the case should not lead us to believe in some mysterious concept of equity under which individual cases are conceived as having their individual unique and particular merits. Equity cannot be understood, I would suggest, as something particular by contrast to the universalizability of justice. The contrast can rather and rightly be set as between law and equity, and only then in the sense that formal rules of positive law may work injustice in their application, which may justify the creation of exceptions

---

[14] The problem was a live one in Scots law at one time; see *Borland* v. *Borland* 1947 S.C. 432; but the judges declined to relax the requirement of 'willingness to adhere', and left it to Parliament to remedy the situation. See Divorce (Scotland) Act 1964.

to the law for classes of situations to which for good reason the previously declared or enacted law ought not to be applied. But as that in itself says, equity is as much a matter of what is universalizable as is justice. The thesis here argued is therefore a clear and straightforward one. It is that the notion of formal justice requires that the justification of decisions in individual cases be always on the basis of universal propositions to which the judge is prepared to adhere as a basis for determining other like cases and deciding them in the like manner to the present one.

V

SECOND-ORDER JUSTIFICATION

To recapitulate on the argument so far:

It is sometimes possible to justify legal decisions by deductive arguments whose premises are valid rules of law and propositions of 'proven' fact. Given certain presuppositions about the nature of legal systems and the obligations of legal officials such justifications are conclusive. But we can run out of rules without running out of the need for legal decisions—because rules are unclear, or because the proper classification of relevant facts is disputable, or even because there is dispute whether there is or is not any legal ground at all for some claim or decision at law. The really interesting question about legal argumentation is: how can it proceed when in this sense we do 'run out of rules'?

So far, we have made only a formal point: that any justification of a decision in such areas of dispute must involve the making of a 'ruling' which is (in the strict logical sense) 'universal', or 'generic', even though the parties' own dispute and its facts are irreducibly individual and particular, as must be the order or orders issued to them in termination of the dispute. One can appeal to the concept of formal justice to argue that it is right that decisions be so founded; one can cite judicial adherence to the value of formal justice as a ground for predicting that (a) they will tend to justify their decisions in such terms, and (b) that they will (normatively) expect it of counsel and other judges that arguments be couched in such 'principled' terms. It is gratifying to find that such predictions are not falsified, and to be able to cite a plethora of corroborative instances.

But to have made the formal point has only pushed the inquiry back one stage further. How can we justify making the rulings by reference to which we justify the particular and concrete decisions? If it were to turn out that such rulings could only be arbitrarily made, the idea of 'justification' involved would be a pretty thin one, and any notion of rationality as guiding the process would be fatuous. But in fact the process is not arbitrary.

Following a pattern set in previous chapters, I shall briefly set out some general points which (a) seem to me show good reasons why argument should proceed in certain ways, and (b) suggest that such procedures or argumentation probably are received as normative within the system; then I shall adduce examples which are at least illustrative of my general points, and also, I claim, corroborative of aspect (b) of those general points.

For reasons which are, I hope, obvious, I shall refer to the type of argument now under scrutiny as concerning 'second order justification'.

(a) Second-Order Justification

If it is true that justifying the particular decision involves assertion of some 'universal' ruling relevant to the particular point, then it logically follows that second-order justification is concerned with a choice between such rulings. The *Donoghue* ruling was adopted in competition against the negation of that ruling; the *Ealing* case must involve a ruling either that 'national origins' includes 'nationality' or that it does not. The *Maclennan* case must involve a ruling whether or not A.I.D. counts as adultery. The character of our various types of 'problem' case is precisely determined by the fact that they involve rival possibilities—to assert or not assert a given ruling, to interpret a given provision this way or that way, to treat facts F_1, F_2, F_3 as amounting or not amounting to instances of p.

Second-order justification must therefore involve justifying choices; choices between rival possible rulings. And these are choices to be made within the specific context of a functioning legal system; that context imposes some obvious constraints on the process.

There is a profitable analogy to be drawn here with the Popperian theory of scientific justification:[1] for Sir Karl Popper, the logical element in scientific discovery is the logic of testing. The scientist frames an explanation of a certain range of phenomena, which is in rivalry with other

[1] See Works of Popper, Medawar, and Lessnoff, *cit.sup.*, Ch. I n. 16.

possible explanations of the same phenomena. The process of experimentation is a process of testing two rival hypotheses as explanations; for a relevant experiment is such that it can falsify one or other of the predictions about its outcome which the scientist derives from the two rival hypotheses. No theory can ever be conclusively proved true by such a procedure; but if one theory is corroborated while a rival is falsified by such experimentation, we are justified in adhering to the former rather than the latter.

So one element in testing concerns what happens in the world: what is the empirical evidence? But there is another, for the interpretation of the evidence necessarily involves the use of assumptions which themselves belong to scientific theory.[2] A low-level example: to test the hypothesis that kitchen salt dissolves in water, I put some salt in a glass test-tube, add water, and shake. The salt dissolves, but I can interpret that as corroborative evidence for my hypothesis only if I take it for granted that the use of a glass test-tube is irrelevant—how do I know that it isn't immersion in a liquid *within a glass container* that causes salt to dissolve? To be technical about it, testing always involves reliance on 'auxiliary hypotheses' which are themselves, in a given experiment, taken for granted; though they can themselves be direct objects of experimentation also—in which case other auxiliary hypotheses will be involved.

So we are never testing out scientific hypotheses simply *in vacuo*; we are always and necessarily testing them in the context of a body of theory with which they are compatible, and taken together with which they make sense. What is more, with the possible exception of revolutionary discoveries on the grand scale of a Newton or an Einstein, the making of 'discoveries'—the flash of insight which reveals a new explanatory hypotheses—takes place within a body of scientific knowledge.[2a]

Why, after all, should you or I not have hit on the idea that the shape of the DNA molecule is a double helix before Crick and Watson did? Speaking for myself, I can only say

---

[2]   See Lessnoff, op.cit., pp. 18–19.

[2a]   Cf. T.S. Kuhn, *The Structure of Scientific Revolutions* (2nd ed. Chicago and London, 1970). Kuhn's thesis in my view adds little to Popper's.

that at the material time I did not even know there was a problem about the shape of the thing, far less did I know the whole theoretical context which made the question of its shape an issue of importance, and which in a sense determined the shape of the 'slot' in the relevant branches of knowledge into which the explanation had to fit. You have to know a lot before you even know what sort of thing you're looking for—and your existing knowledge to that extent gives you 'leads' in various directions which are worth thinking out and trying out. To *that* extent, even the most striking and brilliantly creative discoveries do necessarily involve extrapolation from what is already known, along lines determined by the body of existing theoretical knowledge.

A legal system is not, and is in important ways fundamentally different from, a natural science. But from the point of view of the logic of justification there are two points of contact: that legal decisions deal with the 'real world' as do scientific hypotheses, and that they do so not *in vacuo* but in the context of a whole body of 'knowledge'—in this case, the whole corpus of the normative legal system, rather than a corpus of descriptive and explanatory theory.

To put it crudely, legal decisions must make sense in the world and they must also make sense in the context of the legal system. In our problem cases, they must be based on rulings which make sense in the context of the legal system. And just as scientific justification involves testing one hypothesis against another, and rejecting that which fails relevant tests, so (I shall argue) second-order justification in the law involves testing rival possible rulings against each other and rejecting those which do not satisfy relevant tests—the relevant tests being concerned with what makes sense in the world, and with what makes sense in the context of the system.

Of course we are not here using the idea of 'making sense' with any descriptive connotation. It cannot be in issue whether legal rulings describe the world accurately or ground true predictions about natural events. They do not describe it at all, nor are they predictions.

Legal rulings are normative—they do not report, they *set* patterns of behaviour; they do not discover the consequences of given conditions, they ordain what consequences *are to* follow upon given conditions. They do not present a model *of* the world, they present a model *for* it.

That in turn means that choosing between rival possible rulings in a given case involves choosing between what are to be conceived as rival models for, rival patterns of, human conduct in this society. Either manufacturers of consumer goods ought to take reasonable care in preparing and packaging them, and ought to be made liable in damages to anyone injured by their failure in that respect; or they are not required by law to take such care and not made by law liable for failure therein. To take that disjunction seriously as posing a real choice in a real society one must then ask what is the difference; and the answer is that the difference is determined by the differences which would follow from adopting and applying the one or the other of these rival rulings in an actual social situation.

Lord Macmillan in his speech in *Donoghue* v. *Stevenson* asked the question

suppose that a baker through carelessness allows a large quantity of arsenic to be mixed with a batch of his bread, with the result that those who subsequently eat it are poisoned, could he be heard to say that he owed no duty to the consumers of his bread to take care that it was free from poison, and that, as he did not know that any poison had got into it, his only liability was for breach of warranty under his contract of sale to those who actually bought the poisoned bread from him? ([1932] A.C. at 620; 1932 S.C. (H.L.) at 71)

But what made that a relevant or significant question at all in a case involving the less desperate misfortune of one snail in one ginger-beer bottle? What made it relevant is precisely that the Lords had to test one against the other of two rival possible rulings on the question of manufacturer's liability versus manufacturers non-liability on grounds of negligence apart from contract.

If it is *unacceptable*[3] that the baker whose carelessly made bread poisons those who eat it should be free from all liabilities save those arising from contract with some consumers, that is a ground for refusing to adopt a ruling whose

---

[3] The same idea of what is 'acceptable' or not is used by J. Esser in *Vorverständnis und Methodenwahl in der Rechtsfindung* (Frankfurt, 1970), and in Perelman's *Logique juridique*' ¶¶ 43–4.

application would yield that conclusion of non-liability in the event of an actual baker doing that actual deed. That means: a ground for refusing to rule—as the respondent's counsel urged—that a manufacturer of goods for consumption owes no duty to the ultimate consumer to take care in the process of manufacture.

Observe three points:

(i) This is a *consequentialist* mode of argument, albeit in a somewhat restricted sense. It considers the consequences of making a ruling one way or the other, to the extent at least of examining the types of decision which would have to be given in other hypothetical cases which might occur and which would come within the terms of the ruling.

(ii) It is intrinsically *evaluative*, in that it asks about the acceptability or unacceptability of such consequences. There is however no reason to assume that it involves evaluation in terms of a single scale, such as the Benthamite scale of supposedly measurable aggregates of pleasures and pains. Judges characteristically refer to criteria such as 'justice', 'common sense', 'public policy', and 'convenience' or 'expediency' in weighing the case for and against given rulings.[4] It should not be assumed without proof that these really all boil down to the same thing. For that reason, we should be chary of calling it 'utilitarian' argumentation, although there is a marked resemblance to what is sometimes called 'ideal rule utilitarianism'.[5]

(iii) It is in part at least *subjective*. Judges evaluating consequences of rival possible rulings may give different weight to different criteria of evaluation, differ as to the degree of perceived injustice, or of predicted inconvenience which will arise from adoption or rejection of a given ruling. Not surprisingly, they differ, sometimes sharply and even passionately in relation to their final judgement of the acceptability or unacceptability all things considered of a ruling under scrutiny. At this point we reach the bedrock

---

[4] Cf. Lord Reid, 'The Judge as Law Maker', (1972) 12 J.S.P.T.L. (N.S.), 22.
[5] But usage here is very confusing. See Lyons, *Forms and Limits of Utilitarianism* (Oxford, 1965), p. 173, on the notion of 'ideal utilitarianism'. What Lyons calls 'Ideal Rule-Utilitarianism' is different again. I find it best to eschew use of the term 'utilitarianism' altogether, in the present context.

of the value preferences which inform our reasoning but which are not demonstrable by it. At this level there can simply be irresoluble differences of opinion between people of goodwill and reason.

Taking these three points together, I suggest that second-order justification is concerned with 'what makes sense in the world' in that it involves *consequentialist* arguments which are essentially *evaluative* and therefore in some degree *subjective*. That is the first essential element of second-order justification; the second I described earlier as concerning 'what makes sense in the system?' A few brief words will suffice by way of preliminary explanation of that notion.

The basic idea is of the legal system as a consistent and coherent body of norms whose observance secures certain valued goals which can intelligibly be pursued all together.

The idea of a 'consistent' body of norms I use in a strict sense: however desirable on consequentialist grounds a given ruling might be, it may not be adopted if it is contradictory of some valid and binding rule of the system. Of course, an ostensibly contradictory precedent may be 'explained' and 'distinguished' to avoid such a contradiction, or an ostensibly conflicting statute interpreted in a way which avoids such contradiction. But if such devices for reconciliation fail, the requirement of consistency would require rejection of an otherwise attractive ruling on the ground of its irresoluble conflict with (contradiction of) established valid rules.

'Coherence' is intended in a looser sense. One can imagine a random set of norms none of which contradict each other but which taken together involve the pursuit of no intelligible value or policy. A trivial example: a rule that all yellow motor cars must observe a maximum speed limit of 20 m.p.h. does not contradict or logically conflict with a rule that all red, green, or blue motor cars must observe a minimum speed limit of 25 m.p.h. and a maximum of 70 m.p.h. But on the face of it, no principled reason can be given for such a difference. If the goal of road safety is desired, and the speed restriction on yellow cars represented as essential to it, it is prima facie absurd to have a different rule for red, blue, and green cars. There appears to be no rational principle which could explain or justify differential treatment of two cases so essentially similar from a road-safety point of view.

The 'validity thesis' presents law as comprising or at least including a set of valid rules for the conduct of affairs: such rules must satisfy the requirement of consistency, at least by including procedures for resolving conflict. But rules can be consistent without the system being coherent as a means of social ordering, if 'order' involves organization in relation to intelligible and mutually compatible values. To the extent however that the rules are, or are treated as being, instances of more general principles the system acquires a degree of coherence. When problems of relevancy or of interpretation or of classification arise within the system, the requirement of coherence is satisfied only to the extent that novel rulings given can be brought within the ambit of the existing body of general legal principle.

Among reasons why this is a requirement of legal justification is that there are limits to the ambit of legitimate judicial activity: judges are to do justice according to law, not to legislate for what seems to them an ideally just form of society. Although this does not and cannot mean that they are only to give decisions directly authorized by deduction from established and valid rules of law, it does and must mean that in some sense and in some degree every decision, however acceptable or desirable on consequentialist grounds, must also be warranted by the law as it is. To the extent that the existing detailed rules are or can be rationalized in terms of more general principles, principles whose tenor goes beyond the ambit of already settled rules, a sufficient and sufficiently legal warrant exists to justify as a *legal* decision some novel ruling and the particular decision governed by it.

So much by way of introductory outline: second-order justification involves two elements, consequentialist argument and argument testing proposed rulings for consistency and coherence with the existing legal system. Because consequentialist argument is intrinsically evaluative, and because coherence as explained above involves reflection on the values of the system, the two interact and overlap as will appear; but they are not identical. That must appear in due course, for more than enough already has been said at the abstractly analytical level: to make sense of what has gone before, it is necessary to look in detail at an illustrative (and thus corroborative) example. Since the problem of relevancy is intrinsically a more far-reaching problem than the problems of interpretation and of classification, it will be best to take an example of that problem; it will accordingly be most economical to pursue further the running example of *Donoghue* v. *Stevenson*.

(b) *Consequentialist Arguments Exemplified*

Let us first consider key passages from the speeches of Lords Atkin, Macmillan, and Thankerton; the majority group in the House of Lords whose votes carried the day in favour of Mrs. Donoghue's appeal.

Lord Atkin said this:

In English law there must be, and is, some general conception of relations giving rise to a duty of care of which the particular cases found in the books are but instances...There will no doubt arise cases where it will be difficult to determine whether the contemplated relationship is so close that the duty arises. But in the class of case now before the Court I cannot conceive any difficulty to arise. A manufacturer puts up an article of food in a container which he knows will be opened by the actual consumer. There can be no inspection by any purchaser and no reasonable preliminary inspection by the consumer. Negligently, in the course of preparation, he allows the contents to be mixed with poison. It is said that the law of England and Scotland is that the poisoned consumer has no remedy against the negligent manufacturer. If this was the result of the authorities I should consider the result a grave defect in the law, and so contrary to principle that I should hesitate long before following any decision to that effect which had not the authority of this House. I would point out that, in the assumed state of the authorities, not only would the consumer have no remedy against the manufacturer, he would have none against anyone else, for in the circumstances alleged there would be no evidence of negligence against anyone other than the manufacturer; and, except in the case of a consumer who was also a purchaser, [which as we have seen Mrs. Donoghue was not], no contract and no warranty of fitness, and in the case of a purchaser of a specific article under its patent or its trade name, which might well be the case in the purchase of some article of food or drink, no warranty protecting even the purchaser-consumer. There are other instances than that of articles of food and drink where goods are sold intended to be used immediately by the consumer, such as many forms of goods sold for cleansing purposes, where the same liability may exist. The doctrine supported by the decision below would not only deny a remedy to the consumer who was injured by consuming bottled beer or chocolates poisoned by the negligence of the manufacturer, but also to the user of what should be a harmless proprietary medicine, an ointment, a soap, a cleaning fluid or cleansing powder. I confine myself to articles of common household use where everyone, including the manufacturer, knows that the articles will be used by persons other than the ultimate purchaser—namely, by members of his family and his servants, and in some cases his guests. I do not think so ill of our jurisprudence as to suppose that its principles are so remote from the ordinary needs of civilised society and the ordinary claims it makes upon its members as to deny a legal remedy where there is so obviously a social wrong. ([1932] A.C. 562 at 580−3; 1932 S.C. (H.L.) at 44−6)

Lord Macmillan's speech contains a markedly similar argument, part of which has been quoted already:

In the present case the respondent, when he manufactured his ginger beer, had directly in contemplation that it would be consumed by members of the public. Can it be said that he could not be expected as a reasonable man to foresee that if he conducted his process of manufacture carelessly he might injure those whom he expected and desired to consume his ginger beer? The possibility of injury so arising seems to me in no sense so remote as to excuse him from foreseeing it. Suppose that a baker through carelessness allows a large quantity of arsenic to be mixed with a batch of his bread, with the result that those who subsequently eat it are poisoned, could he be heard to say that he owed no duty to the consumers of his bread to take care that it was free from poison, and that, as he did not know that any poison had got into it, his only liability was for breach of warranty under his contract of sale to those who actually bought the poisoned bread from him?. . .I cannot believe, and I do not believe, that neither in the law of England nor in the law of Scotland is there redress for such a case. . .Yet the principle of the decision appealed from is that the manufacturer of food products intended by him for human consumption does not owe to the consumers whom he has in view any duty of care, not even the duty to take care that he does not poison them. . .I am happy to think . . .that the principles [of Scots and English law] are sufficiently consonant with justice and common sense to admit of the claim which the appellant seeks to establish. ([1932] A.C. at 620−1; 1932 S.C. (H.L.) 71−2)

A similar point was taken by Lord Thankerton when he contrasted with the instant case the earlier decision in *Gordon* v. *M'Hardy* ((1903) 6.F. 210) where the Court of Session had dismissed as irrelevant an action by a pursuer who averred that his son had died of ptomaine poisoning caused by eating a tin of salmon purchased from the defender, a grocer; he averred that the tin was dented when sold, but not that the grocer had actually pierced the tin or damaged its contents. The ground for the dismissal of the action was that the grocer could not have examined the tin of salmon 'without destroying the very condition which the manufacturer had established in order to preserve the contents' (ibid. at p. 212, *per* Lord J.-C. Kingsburgh)

Apparently in that case [said Lord Thankerton] the manufacturer's label was off the tin when sold, and they had not been identified. I should be sorry to think that the meticulous care of the manufacturer to exclude interference or inspection by the grocer in that case should relieve the grocer of any responsibility to the consumer without any corresponding assumption of duty by the manufacturer. ([1932] A.C. at p. 604; 1932 S.C. (H.L.) at p. 60)

These three extended quotations show the Lords of the majority arguing why the consequences entailed by a ruling against the pursuer are (in their view) unacceptable, and therefore the ruling ought to be that manufacturers do owe to consumers the relevant duty of care. It is worth stressing again that such arguments would be utterly pointless if the contest were not envisaged *by them* as involving the need for a generic ruling on manufacturers' liability or non-liability (hence they corroborate the point made in Chapter IV). It is also vital to note that these must be seen as the clinching arguments which justified the ruling given, for, as we shall see, there were arguments 'on the authorities' for *both* sides, and arguments of general legal principle on *both* sides of the case. The case being on these points open either way, it is only the consequentialist argument which can bring it to a conclusion. Lord Atkin in effect said this explicitly when he said: 'if [these consequences were] the result of the authorities I should consider the result a grave defect in the law, and so contrary to principle that I should hesitate long before following any decision to that effect which had not the authority of this House.'

But why a 'grave defect', why 'so contrary to principle'? The three passages quoted have an almost intuitionistic quality, as though it is enough simply to contemplate these consequences in order immediately to perceive their unacceptability—and perhaps it is. But perhaps one can detect three grounds of evaluation which cumulatively lead to that conclusion of utter unacceptability.

There are, as Lord Atkin put it, 'the needs of civilised society': a general public interest in securing that those activities which are capable of causing harm to other people be conducted in a way which minimizes such harm. Precisely what a manufacturer of products intends and desires is that they shall be consumed or used by others well beyond the range of any contractual nexus with him; he can secure, as no one else can, that they are safe for consumption and use. To secure that they are safe is in the interest of people at large and therefore a proper goal of public policy.

Secondly, there is the matter of principle, of 'justice' as Lord Macmillan put it. Clearly all three of their Lordships adhere to that conception of corrective justice according to which he who suffers harm ought to be compensated for that harm if somebody else was responsible for it: responsible in the sense that he could reasonably have foreseen it as a direct outcome of what he intended to do (in this type of case, the relevant intention is to put goods on the market in conditions excluding inspection by intermediate sellers of users); and in the sense that he could reasonably have prevented it by taking greater care than actually he took.

Thirdly, as Lord Macmillan said expressly, there is a matter of 'common sense' as well as of justice. This I believe depends on an appeal to contemporary positive morality as understood by the judge. People at large, 'right minded' people, so the judge thinks, would assent to the view that it is wrong for a manufacturer by carelessness to cause injury to others, and absurd to leave him free of all liability if he does not take reasonable care and harm ensues.

There would be little profit in a more elaborate analysis. It seems clear that these are distinguishable though interlocking grounds of evaluation, and clear why somebody who adheres to them should come to the conclusion of 'unacceptability' to which all the judges came.

It is also evident how closely in particular the conception of justice involved is a reflection of the legal order within which the judges work. It is not some daring or radical new venture into an original theory of justice: it is rather a matter of taking seriously the conception of corrective justice which the existing body of law however imperfectly embodies; the principle which Lord Kames (or any Scots lawyer) could uncomplicatedly regard as a principle of equity: 'That for every wrong there ought to be a remedy.'[6] It was mentioned earlier that there is a necessary inter-relationship between consequentialist arguments and the type of argument dictated by the requirement of 'coherence'; we can now see why. The conception of justice applied in the evaluation of consequences may be in effect a reflection of the conception of justice embodied in received principles of law—indeed, I think it usually is. And also, of course, a lawyer's view of what is 'common sense' must be heavily coloured by the whole set of attitudes which belong to him as a lawyer.

We must not, however, press this to the point of arguing that there is some single standard shared judicial conception of 'public interest', 'justice', or 'common sense': nor, *a fortiori* that the concluded evaluations made by different judges could or should always be identical or objectively conclusive. I repeat the point that such evaluative judgments are not a matter of objective measuring or 'weighing' (The latter term is altogether too commonly used by legal writers in a way which trades on the connotation of the exact and objective measurements of the honest butcher's scales.)[7] Such judgments are at least in part irreducibly subjective. Lords Buckmaster and Tomlin, after all, produced arguments which, though replicating the *form* of the majority's arguments, reversed the content.

Lord Buckmaster had this to say:

The principle contended for must be this—that the manufacturer, or, indeed, the repairer of any article, apart entirely from contract, owes a duty to any person by whom the article is lawfully used to see that it has been carefully constructed. . .Nor can the doctrine be confined to cases where inspection is difficult or impossible to introduce. This conception is simply to misapply to tort doctrines applicable to sale and purchase.

---

[6] Henry Home, Lord Kames, *Principles of Equity* (1st edn., Edinburgh, 1760).

[7] See, e.g., Ronald Dworkin's frequent use of it in *Taking Rights Seriously* (London, 1977), also that of Twining and Miers in *How to Do Things with Rules*, e.g. at p. 212.

The principle of tort lies completely outside the region where such considerations apply, and the duty, if it exists, must extend to every person who, in lawful circumstances, uses the article made. There can be no special duty attaching to the manufacture of food, apart from those implied by contract or imposed by statute. If such a duty exists it seems to me it must cover the construction of every article, and I cannot see why it should not apply to a house. If one step, why not fifty? Yet if a house be, as it sometimes is, negligently built, and in consequence of that negligence the ceiling falls and injures the occupier or anyone else, no action against the builder exists according to the English law, although I believe such a right did exist according to the laws of Babylon. . .

In *Mullen* v. *Barr and Co.*, *McGowan* v. *Barr and Co.* (1929 S.C. 461) a case indistinguishable from the present, except upon the ground that a mouse is not a snail. . .Lord Anderson says this:

'In a case like the present, where the goods of the defenders are widely distributed throughout Scotland, it would seem little short of outrageous to make them responsible to members of the public for the condition of the contents of every bottle which issues from their works. It is obvious that, if such responsibility attached to the defenders, they might be called upon to meet claims of damages which they could not possibly investigate or answer.'

In agreeing, as I do, with the judgment of Lord Anderson, I desire to add that I find it hard to dissent from the emphatic nature of the language in which his judgment is clothed. . .([1932] A.C. at 577−8; 1932 S.C. (H.L.) at 42−3)

In similar vein Lord Tomlin adopted an argument used by counsel for the defendant in *Winterbottom* v. *Wright*, ((1842) 10 M. & W. 109) to illustrate the 'alarming consequences' of the principle at stake: 'For example, every one of the sufferers by such an accident as that which recently happened on the Versailles Railway might have his action against the manufacturers of the defective axle.' ([1932] A.C. at 600; 1932 S.C. (H.L.) at 57.)

I have said that the judgments involved are 'in part' subjective, which leaves open the possibility that in some degree disagreements must be capable of objective resolution. The point can well be made in relation to Lord Buckmaster's and Lord Anderson's reason for thinking it 'outrageous' to hold manufacturers liable. It is not in fact *true* that manufacturers are called on 'to meet claims of damages which they cannot . . .investigate or answer' under the majority's ruling; because (a) the pursuer in such a case bears the burden of proving harm, causation of the harm, and failure of reasonable care on the manufacturer's part; and (b) as *Daniels* showed, it remains open to a manufacturer to show what care he did take and argue that that amounted to taking all *reasonable* precautions. In so far as that was not obvious at the time of the *Donoghue* decision, experience has confirmed that it is in fact so.

So although Lords Buckmaster and Anderson applying *their* conception of justice concluded that it would be unjust to impose such liability on manufacturers, their argument is beside the point—beside the point because of a false factual opinion about the outcome of the ruling in favour of manufacturers' liability. *Non sequitur* however that even if they were to admit the error of fact, they would necessarily agree that it is just to impose such liability.

Apart from the justice argument, there is the fall-back position supplied by Lord Tomlin's 'alarming consequences', equally evident in Lord Buckmaster's 'If one step, why not fifty'. It is not at all uncommon to find judges treating it as a *reductio ad absurdum* of some proposed ruling that it must give rise to a vast crop of actions which will flood the courts with unmeritorious claimants and which will spell commercial ruin for those exposed to the claims. The manufacture of railway axles will not be worth the risk if the manufacturer may be exposed to claims from all those injured when it turns out defective (what is not explained by such reasoning, however, is why manufacturers of that kind who fail to take reasonable care ought to be kept in business at all).

This criterion of evaluation I call 'expediency' or 'convenience'; it is a form of the public-interest argument, and is advanced as showing that a claim which might be meritorious on grounds of corrective justice ought not to be admitted if the admission of the whole class of such claims would generate gross inconvenience, or be wholly inexpedient in the general interest. I do not claim that *I* know how to calculate such matters. But I observe that judges rely on such an argument sufficiently often to indicate that they think it possible.

'Inconvenience' as a criterion of evaluation is certainly a distinct notion from 'injustice', indeed judges on occasion make it clear that the 'convenience/inconvenience' scale of valuing has to be applied in competition with the 'justice/

injustice' scale. For example, in *London Street Tramways* v. *L.C.C.* ([1898] A.C. 375) the House of Lords was invited to hold that it could on occasion reverse its own precedents. The house decided not to, and set a rule which stood until 1966 (see [1966] 1 W.L.R. 1234) that all House of Lords decisions were binding as precedents even upon the House itself. Lord Halsbury's speech reveals the central justification for that view in the following terms:

I do not deny that cases of individual hardship may arise, and there may be a current of opinion in the profession that such and such a judgment was erroneous; but what is that occasional interference with what is perhaps abstract justice compared with the inconvenience —the disastrous inconvenience—of having each question subject to being re-argued and the dealings of mankind rendered doubtful by reason of different decisions, so that in truth and in fact there can be no final court of appeal. (Ibid., p. 380)

There we see an explicit recognition of the possibility of a collision between the demands of justice and of convenience, with the latter on this occasion being given priority.

The point of stressing that possibility of collision is that it reveals why it could be misleading to regard consequentialist arguments in law as simply utilitarian; consequentialist argument is indeed concerned to establish that a preferred ruling is the best all things considered; but that conclusion as to the 'best' is not determined by reference to a single scale of evaluation (e.g. the pleasure–pain scale as in the hedonistic utilitarianism of a Bentham); it is a final judgment passed in summation of the cumulating or competing results of evaluation by reference to a number of criteria of value, including 'justice' and 'common sense' as well as 'public benefit' and 'convenience'. Some versions of 'ideal utilitarianism' as against 'hedonistic utilitarianism' allow for complex rather than simple criteria of 'the best', and on that ground consequentialist justification in law could be regarded as involving a form of ideal utilitarianism.[8]

But again it must be pointed out that since the focus of such justifications is on the consequences of rival rulings (in the form of universal propositions of law), not on the consequences for the particular parties of the particular decision, the utilitarianism involved is 'rule utilitarianism' not 'act

[8] See Lyons, loc.cit.

utilitarianism'—hence, as I remarked earlier, we should have to resort to the somewhat cumbersome ethical terminology of 'ideal rule utilitarianism' if we wanted to use the idea of utilitarianism in this context at all.

These remarks involve more than a fruitless excursion into the taxonomy of ethical theories; there has been controversy over the question whether a 'rule-utilitarian justification procedure' could be desirable at all. In his brilliant pioneering study R.A. Wasserstrom argued[9] for what he called a 'Two-level Justification Procedure' as a good procedure for justifying legal decisions, and by that he meant a procedure whereby particular decisions were justified as deducible from rules adopted by judges as having better consequences than any possible alternative rule which could also cover the decision. That is, in short, a rule-utilitarian justification procedure. Against that, D.H. Hodgson has argued most persuasively[10] that adoption of such a procedure would (by an apparent paradox) have disutilitarian consequences; for no one could ever have rational grounds for predicting how a judge would decide a particular case if he knew that the judge would follow Wasserstrom's procedure. Hence there would be precisely the kind of recourse to litigation *ad infinitum* which Lord Halsbury apprehended occuring if House of Lords precedents were not treated as binding for all purposes.

Since there is an obvious parallel between the Wasserstrom 'Two-Level Procedure of Justification' as a rule-utilitarian procedure, and consequentialist argumentation as analysed here in the context of second-order justification, it is on that ground alone important to stress that we are here concerned with an 'ideal' version of rule utilitarianism if with utilitarianism at all.

But even at that, if the theory were that consequentialist argumentation proceeded *in vacuo* as a sole sufficient element of second-order justification, it might yet be open to the objection raised by Hodgson. It could be open also to a further and not unrelated objection, namely that there is on

---

[9] Wasserstrom, op.cit. *supra*, Ch. I n. 15.

[10] Hodgson, op.cit. *supra*, Ch. I n. 15, (cc. 4–6).

the face of it no limit to the number of varying possible 'universals' which could be constructed as potential rulings to cover a particular decision and to determine the range of 'like cases' to be tested by consequentialist arguments.

In a slightly different context, Julius Stone has made just this point, that in relation to *Donoghue* v. *Stevenson* the 'facts' can be treated at any of many possible 'levels of generalisation'. His argument is that Goodhart's theory of the *ratio decidendi* yields wholly indeterminate results because the 'principle' derivable from a case by the Goodhart method of 'material facts plus decision' (to put it in an unfairly crude and encapsulated formula) is entirely dependent on the level of generality at which one chooses to describe the facts. Stone makes the following remarks:[11]

Donoghue v. *Stevenson*, standing alone, could yield logically a range of propositions (quite apart from the diverse reasoning of the speeches) concerned at least with any or any combination of the following facts:

1) *the presence* of dead snails *or* any snails *or* any unpleasant foreign body, *or* any foreign body *or* any unexpected quality.

2) *in* opaque bottles of beverage *or* in any bottles of beverage *or* in any chattels for human consumption *or* in any chattels for human use, *or* in any objects whatsoever (including land or buildings),

3) *Caused by the negligence of the defendant* who is a manufacturer whose goods are distributed to a wide and dispersed public by retailers, *or* of any manufacturer, *or* of any person working on the object for reward, *or* of any person working on the object *or* of anyone dealing with the object,

4) *provided* the object may reasonably be expected to be rendered dangerous by such negligence *or* whether or not this is the case,

5) *if* it results in physical injury to the plaintiff *or* nervous or physical injury to the plaintiff *or* any injury whatsoever to the plaintiff.

6) The plaintiff being (a) a Scots widow, *or* a Scotswoman, *or* a woman, *or* any adult *or* any human being *or* any legal person who (b) received the object directly from a purchaser for value from a retailer who bought directly from the defendant, *or* from a purchaser for value from such, *or* from a purchaser for value from anyone, *or* is a person related to such purchaser *or* any person into whose hands the object rightfully comes, *or* into whose hands it comes at all,

7) *Provided that* no intermediate party (a) could physically inspect and discover the defect without destroying the saleability of the commodity,

[11] J. Stone, *The Province and Function of Law* (London, 1947), pp. 187–8. Substantially the same point is made in *Legal System and Lawyers' Reasonings* (London, 1964), at pp. 269–70.

or (b) had any duty to inspect and discover the defect *or* (c) could reasonably be expected by the defendant to inspect and discover the defect *or* (d) could reasonably be expected by the court or jury to do so,

8) *and provided that* the facts complained of occurred in 1932 *or* any time before 1932 *or* after 1932 *or* at any time,

9) will render the Defendant liable to the Plaintiff in damages.

Most of these alternatives and any combination of them were, logically speaking, possible elements in any principle framed on the facts and speeches of *Donoghue* v. *Stevenson* alone.

Not too much can be made of that argument as indicating the total indeterminacy of the *ratio* of *Donoghue*, because as was pointed out in Chapter IV the Lords of the majority in that case took some care to indicate what ruling they had in mind, at what level of generality. But if one thinks of it as of the time *before* the case was decided the problem seems more acute. It is all very well to say that the principle of formal justice requires the judge expressly or implicitly to formulate and to test some possible ruling for the case and for like cases in order to justify a decision in the case. But (as the distinction earlier drawn between 'universality' and generality indicates) a suitably 'universal' ruling could be hit upon at any of Stone's 'levels of generality'.

What is more, all that deals only with differing levels of generality in terms of one possible 'line of argument' about the case. But it could perhaps have been taken on a wholly different track. For example, since it was a Scots case, and since Scots law recognizes the possibility of enforceable third-party rights arising from contracts (the doctrine of *jus quaesitum tertio*),[12] might it not have been tried out as an action by Mrs. D. against the cafe proprietor who sold the ginger beer to her friend? Alternatively, might one not have looked at it in terms of an implied promise by the manufacturer to any ultimate consumer that his products are sound and fit from consumption? (There being no doctrine of consideration in Scots law, no difficulty need have arisen on that head—not that English lawyers would necessarily

---

[12] See, e.g., D.M. Walker, *Principles of Scottish Private Law* (2nd edn., Oxford, 1975) pp. 627–30 (vol. i); Scottish Law Commission Memorandum No. 38 (*Constitution and Proof of Voluntary Obligations: Stipulations in Favour of Third Parties*), 1977.

find it too difficult to invent some 'consideration moving
from the promisee' in such a context as this.) The former of
these alternatives is indeed the one which French law uses
to deal with problems analogous to Mrs. Donoghue's,[13] and
the latter in some form has found favour in many U.S.
jurisdictions.[14] Nor need ingenuity be thought confined to a
mere three possibilities.

So even if consequentialist argumentation can show
rational grounds for choosing between possible rulings in
the case, is there any rational or even reasonable ground for
choosing what ruling at what level of generality to test by
that procedure? If not, again we must conclude that an
ostensibly rational process is at bottom no more than arbitrary.
We face the question: what, if any, limits can govern the
judicial choice of rulings to test, and how, in any event, can
judges begin to frame any ruling appropriate to fit the
concrete case when so vast a range of possibilities is open?

(c) *Arguments of Coherence and Consistency*
Explained and Exemplified

The answer to the second of these questions leads us to
an answer to the first, and is relatively simple: the judges are
presented with potential rulings by counsel. It is the task of
the pursuer's or the defender's counsel to state and frame the
case in pleadings and to argue it before the Court in the
manner which represents his client's case in the most favourable light (as he sees it) which can be put upon the case.
Our system of administering justice in civil affairs proceeds on the
footing that each side, working at arm's length, selects its own evidence.
Each side's selection of its own evidence may, for various reasons,
be partial in every sense of the term. . .It is on the basis of two carefully selected versions that the judge is finally called upon to adjudicate.[15]
And the basis on which an advocate selects his evidence is his
view of the generalizations he can profitably make on behalf
of his client with a view to winning the case.

---

[13] See Kahn-Freund, Levy, and Rudden, op.cit. *supra*, Ch. IV n. 10, at
pp. 437–40. Delictal remedies are of course also possible.

[14] See, e.g., J.J. White and R.S. Summers, *Handbook on the Uniform Commercial Code* (St. Paul, Minn., 1972), pp. 329–32.

[15] *Thompson* v. *Glasgow Corporation* 1962 S.C. (H.L.) 36, *per* Lord J.-C.
Thomson at p. 52.

When some established valid rule appears straightforwardly applicable, the process of selection will simply be governed by the need to prove the operative facts in question. When none is immediately applicable, how can we tell what line of argument may be profitable? It is a necessary condition, obviously enough, that some good consequentialist argument can be put in favour of a potential ruling capable of covering the pursuer's situation, or some aspects of it; but it is not of itself a sufficient condition. Counsel who advanced an argument *solely* based on the reason and justice of some novel principle in favour of his client would rightly be told that a Court is the wrong place for such arguments. There must also be some basis for the decision he seeks in the legal system as it already stands. *Ex hypothesi* that basis need not be an established valid rule directly applicable to the instant case. But, perhaps it will be sufficient if there exists some convincing analogy with some existing established rule, or if some relevant general principle of the law exists or can be framed—all the better if dicta of judges formulating and appealing to such general principles can be found. The closer the analogy and the more authoritative the statement of principle, the stronger the argument; but such arguments can never have compelling force, as can the argument that the facts one has proven count clearly and unequivocally as the operative facts of some mandatory legal rule.

The point rather is to show that the decision contended for is thoroughly consistent with the body of existing legal rules, and is a rational extrapolation from them, in the sense that the immediate policies and purposes which existing similar rules are conceived as being aimed at would be *pro tanto* controverted and subjected to irrational exceptions if the instant case were not decided analogously with them.

Thus the need to find, in default of some directly applicable rule, some supporting analogy or principle of law, is a requirement which guides the lawyer in framing his case. A further guide is his need to show that his case is consistent with the law as it exists, in the still stronger sense that a ruling for the decision can be framed which is not directly contradictory of any existing mandatory rule. The area within which counsel chose to argue Mrs. Donoghue's case was the delictal, presumably on the supposition that nothing could be made of any contractual point, despite the doctrine in Scots law of the *ius quaesitum tertio*. Within the area of delictal liability, it was necessary to show that House of Lords cases such as *Cameron* v. *Young* ([1908] A.C. 176; 1908 S.C. (H.L.) 7) or *Cavalier* v. *Pope* ([1906] A.C. 428) could be distinguished, and that the considerable line of prima facie adverse authorities, albeit of lesser weight, were capable of being 'explained' and 'distinguished' so as to square with the asserted principle of manufacturers' liability.

Moreover, the form of the argument was necessarily settled by the previously settled principle governing delictal liability for negligence, that there can be no such liability save where the defender owes the pursuer a duty to take care. For consistency with that principle it was necessary to adduce and argue some reason why the defender should be held to have owed a duty to the pursuer. The clinching argument from consequences can make no headway unless it can be shown that there is some general principle rationalizing all the situations in which one person is legally required to take care for the safety of another, and that that principle covers the ruling which the consequentialist argument in this case favours.

Thus the requirement upon a litigant's lawyers to frame his case as a *legal* claim or defence imposes, in wide terms, two limits on the formulation of the case: first, it must be so formulated as to avoid conflict with existing rules—here the possibility of 'explaining' and 'distinguishing' unfavourable precedents, and of 'literally' or 'liberally' interpreting statutes (depending on the needs of the case) must be borne in mind; and secondly, it must be formulated in such a way that it can be shown to be supported by analogies from existing case law (or, more rarely, statute law) or by 'general principles' of the law, preferably authoritatively stated by judges in *obiter dicta*, or by institutional or at least respectable legal writers, or *faute de mieux* newly minted by counsel as explaining and rationalizing some relevant group of acknowledged legal rules.

Of course, this is in no sense a mechanical or easy task, nor is it an exact science; it calls for imagination, understanding of the 'feel' of the system, a good knowledge of the law, and expertise in following up useful 'leads' in precedents and textbooks, and for a slightly odd combination of intellectual boldness and sound judgment. The precise choice how to do it depends upon the legal acumen and experience, and indeed the creative imagination, of the good lawyer. Academics (like the present writer) and law students mainly look at leading cases *after* they have been decided and all looks obvious and easy. From this perspective it is all too easy to miss the boldness, resourcefulness, and imagination which must go into the formulation and arguing of a difficult case, as that case presents itself to lawyers *before* the matter gets into court, and *before* the Court pronounces judgment. The skill in doing that can only be learned by doing, cannot be learned from books, and anyway can only be learned by those endowed by nature with the necessary mental gifts.

So the answer to the question how the judges come upon the generalization of the fact situation essential to the evaluative justification of decisions is indeed the simple one that they are presented to them by counsel. And the elaboration of that answer solves the other problem about the limits upon the judicial choice of relevant potential rulings. For judges work within the same normative constraints as do lawyers. What is more, the constraints upon lawyers operate merely as technical rules—there is for a lawyer no point in advancing an argument wholly unsupported by even the smallest fragment of an analogy or the thinnest shadow of a colourable principle; but the technical rules exist for the lawyers precisely because of the acknowledged obligations of judges—there is no point in so arguing because, or to the extent that, the judges recognize an obligation to work within the framework of existing laws; because they recognize an obligation to keep their legislation 'interstitial'. Of course this cannot and should not be taken as denying the degree of imagination wisdom resourcefulness boldness or skill involved in the judge's any more than in the advocate's function; all the more of these is required in that the judge has the task of deciding which side has the better case, whereas the conclusion towards which counsel must argue is fixed for him by his duty to do his best to put his client's case in the most favourable way possible (consistently with the ethics of honest advocacy). What it does show is that we can rule out simple caprice or arbitrariness in the judicial formulation of potential rulings in law.[16]

That skilled lawyers are instructed on either side to make the best available case for each party tends to secure, at least it ought to secure, that the Courts do not overlook any useful possibility one way or the other. That both judges and counsel operate within the limits of the existing law and the analogies and principles available therein makes possible the formulation of potential rulings and eliminates the possibility of arbitrary or capricious generalizations as the starting-point of second-order justification. At least, it does so if the persons exercising these functions are up to their jobs and honourable in conforming to their proper duties. The area within which it is possible to formulate new potential rulings in the justification of decisions in cases of first impression must be a tolerably well-defined one if it is bounded on the one hand by the need not to contradict or controvert established valid rules, and on the other hand by the need to find some supporting analogy or principle or other legal warrant for the decision. There is here no unfettered discretion.

All this may tend to cast some doubt upon ethical theories (such as those of Kant[17] or Hare[18]) which insist on the absolute autonomy of the moral agent, coupled with a requirement of universalizability of moral judgment (theories which are to a marked extent paralleled by the present theory of legal justification). For although in law there are a number of factors which tend towards limiting and defining the area within which and the terms in which novel generalized principles of decision can be framed so that they may be evaluated and tested, these factors follow precisely from the public and institutionalized character of the processes of decision and justification in law. It is accordingly hard to see any similar factors in the moral predicament as

---

[16] Dr. Paterson's thesis (*cit.sup.*, Ch. I n. 13) shows that the House of Lords makes a firm practice of abstaining from ruling on points not argued by counsel.

[17] See Kant, *Groundwork* (*cit.cup.*, Ch. I n. 10).

[18] See R.M. Hare, *The Language of Morals* and *Freedom and Reason*.

envisaged by advocates of pure autonomy which might tolerably narrow the range of 'maxims of action' which in any given case we might universalize so as to test a resultant moral principle for action in universal form. Unless one were fairly arbitrary about it, and to that extent non-rational, one would linger at least a year over every moral decision. Surely the truth is that our moral, like our legal, life has a necessary social setting, which provides us with a basis of rules and principles in the context of which we can frame and test new principles of action in new or difficult circumstances. Autonomy is real, but only against a back-cloth of heteronomy, a point taken up again in Chapter X.

Be that as it may, there remains the little matter of concretely exemplifying from *Donoghue* v. *Stevenson* precisely the kinds of argument from coherency and consistency which the foregoing explanation suggests as being essential within second-order justification. Again it is not hard to cull from the speeches plain and evident examples of what has already been described.

We have already quoted Lord Atkin's remark that '[T]here must be and is some general conception of relations giving rise to a duty of care, of which the particular cases found in the books are but instances. . .' But why 'must' this be so? It is at least open to us to conceive of the law's being a 'codeless myriad of precedents' and a wilderness of single instances' unified by no underlying rationalizing principle. But such was not Lord Atkin's view. The immediately preceding paragraph reads:

It is remarkable how difficult it is to find in the English authorities statements of general application defining the relations between parties that give rise to the duty [of care]. The courts are concerned with the particular relations which come before them in actual litigation, and it is sufficient to say whether the duty exists in those circumstances. The result is that the courts have been engaged upon an elaborate classification of duties as they exist in respect of property, whether real or personal, with further divisions as to ownership, occupation or control, and distinctions based on the particular relations of the one side to the other, whether manufacturer, salesman or landlord, customer, tenant, stranger, and so on. In this way it can be ascertained at any time whether the law recognises a duty, but only where the case can be referred to some particular species which has been examined and classified. And yet the duty which is common to all the cases where liability is established *must logically* be based upon some element common to the cases where it is found to exist. To assert a complete logical definition of the general principle is probably to go beyond the function of the judge, for the more general the definition, the more likely it is to omit essentials or introduce non-essentials. The attempt was made by Lord Esher in *Heaven* v. *Pender* ([1883] 11 Q.B.D. 503) in a definition to which I shall refer later. As framed it was demonstrably too wide, though it appears to me, if properly limited, to be capable of affording a valuable practical guide. ([1932] A.C. at 579–80; 1932 S.C. H.L. at 44. Italics added.)

If we are to take seriously (and why should we not?) Lord Atkin's claim that the duty must logically be based on some element common to the established cases, we can only do so by presupposing that Lord Atkin holds, as his 'tacit major premiss', a view of the law as a rational teleological enterprise. The ascription of rational purposes to the established rules is a necessary condition of asserting that the specific cases giving rise to a duty of care must be instances of a single general conception. Then by formulating the 'general conception' of which the individual cases are deemed to be instances so as to reveal the ascribed underlying purpose is *eo ipso* to state the 'general principle' of the law whose rules are now perceived, or at least capable of being perceived, as instances of the general principle.

That is, of course, precisely what Lord Atkin went on to do in formulating his famous 'neighbour principle' in the following terms:

The rule that you are to love your neighbour becomes in law: You must not injure your neighbour, and the lawyer's question: Who is my neighbour? receives a restricted reply. You must take reasonable care to avoid acts or omissions which you can reasonably foresee would be likely to injure. . .persons who are so closely affected by [your] act that [you] ought reasonably to have them in contemplation as being so affected when you are directing your mind to the acts or omissions which are called in question. ([1932] A.C. at 580; 1932 S.C. (H.L.) at 44)

In doing so, he was, as we have just seen him acknowledge, building upon Lord Esher's previous attempt made in *Heaven* v. *Pender* ([1883] 11 Q.B.D. 503 at 509), as he subsequently qualified it, by introducing a notion of 'proximity', in *Le Lievre* v. *Gould* ([1893] 1 Q.B. 491). But of course, such a wide statement was in no sense binding upon him, and in no way made a decision in favour of Mrs. Donoghue mandatory upon him. (Lord Buckmaster, indeed thought it 'better that [these dicta] should be buried so securely that their perturbed spirits shall no longer vex the law'.[19]) Rather, it supported him, and guided him in his own formulation.

The formulation of a 'general principle' of this kind calls for a real effort of the creative imagination. The importance of the process cannot be overemphasized, yet it is vital not to misunderstand it. A judge, by formulating a general principle as expressing the underlying common purpose of a set of specific rules[20] at once rationalizes the existing law so as to reveal it in the light of a new understanding, and provides a sufficient ground for justifying a new development in the relevant field. He does not thereby show that the decision must be as he proposes to give it in the instant case; only that it may legitimately be so given. He does not simply find and state the rationale of the rules; to a greater or less degree, he makes them rational by stating a principle capable of embracing them, and he uses that as a necessary jumping-off point for a novel decision, which can now be represented as one already 'covered' by 'existing' law.

That this process should be possible depends in itself on the existence of analogous authorities brought before the Court through the researches and ingenuity of counsel. This is a point which need not be elaborated here. It is also essential that there should not be flatly contradictory authorities of binding character. Let us skim through the rest of Lord Atkin's speech to make the point. Immediately after his critical evaluation of the question, liability or no liability of manufacturers to injured consumers, he says:

It will be found, I think, on examination that there is no case in which the circumstances have been such as I have just suggested where the liability has been negatived. There are numerous cases where the relations were much more remote where the duty has been held not to exist. There are also dicta in such cases which go further than was necessary for the determination of the particular issues, which have caused the difficulty experienced by the Courts below. . .

In my opinion, several decided cases support the view that in such

---

[19]   [1932] A.C. 562 at p. 576, 1932 S.C. (H.L.) 31 at p. 42.
[20]   Cf. MacCormick ' "Principles" of law' 1974 *Juridical Review* 217, and see Chapter VII below.

a case as the present the manufacturer owes the consumer a duty to be careful. . .([1932] A.C. at 583 −4; f 932 S.C. (H.L.) at 46 −7.)

His Lordship then reviewed *George* v. *Skivington* ((1869) L.R. 5 Exch. 1) *Hawkins* v. *Smith* ((1896) 12 TLR 532), *Elliott* v. *Hall or Nailstone Colliery Co.* ((1885) 15 Q.B.D. 315), *Chapman* v. *Sadler and Co.* ([1929] A.C. 584), and *Grote* v. *Chester and Holyhead Rail Co.* ((1848) 2 Exch. 251).

It now becomes necessary to consider the cases which have been referred to in the Courts below as laying down the proposition that no duty to take care is owed to the consumer in such a case as this. . . (Ibid at 587 and 49 respectively)

His Lordship then proceeded to 'explain' and/or 'distinguish' the following cases: *Dixon* v. *Bell* ((1816) 5 M. & S. 198); *Langridge* v. *Levy* ((1838) 4 M. & W. 337); *Winterbottom* v. *Wright* ((1842) 10 M. & W. 109; *Longmeid* v. *Holliday* ((1851) 6 Exch. 761); *Earl* v. *Lubbock* ([1905] 1 K.B. 253); *Blacker* v. *Lake & Elliott* ((1912) 106 L.T. 533); *Bates & anor.* v. *Batey & Co. Ltd.* ([1913] 3 K.B. 351).

Again, we must insist that the citation of supporting authorities, whether more or less closely analogous (and only *George* v. *Skivington* was directly in point), and the distinguishing of hostile authorities cannot be seen as compelling the decision in the instant case. Nor can they even be represented as the decisive element in Lord Atkin's justification; they are decisive in showing that a decision in favour of Mrs. Donoghue is *legally justifiable*; without them the decision would lack any distinctively *legal* warrant; but to show that the decision is justified as well as justifiable, we must look to the 'consequentialist' argument, to the argument evaluating and testing the proposed principle of decision and its alternatives. The proof of the pudding is Lord Buckmaster's speech, in which the same set of authorities are— quite legitimately—used as supporting the opposite conclusion, and Lord Atkin's favourable authorities distinguished or overruled (*George* v. *Skivington* and the dicta of Lord Esher in *Heaven* v. *Pender*).

As Lord MacMillan said,

[I]n the discussion of the topic which now engages your Lordships' attention two rival principles of the law find a meeting place where each has contended for supremacy. On the one hand, there is the well-established principle that no one other than a party to a contract can complain of a breach of that contract. On the other hand, there is the equally well-established doctrine that negligence, apart from contract, gives a right of action to the party injured by that negligence— and here I use the term negligence of course, in its technical legal sense, implying a duty owed and neglected. ([1932] A.C. at 609−10; 1932 S.C. (H.L.) at 64)

In such a contention for supremacy, it is plain that neither principle of itself can determine its own victory; it is up to the Court to evaluate which ought to win. As Lord Macmillan himself said earlier, with respect to certain dicta of Lord Ormidale in *Mullen's* case,

The truth, as I hope to show, is that there is in the English reports no such 'unbroken and consistent current of decisions' as would justify the aspersion that the law of England has committed itself irrevocably to what is neither reasonable nor equitable, or require a Scottish judge in following them to do violence to his conscience. (ibid at 608 and 63 respectively)

It is the perceived 'reason and equity' of the matter which justify the ultimate result; they can only justify it given the existence of the principle of negligence, and given that the authorities are not compelling against the application of the principle in the manufacturer/consumer context. The argument is exactly an argument (a) of consequences; (b) of coherence; and (c) of consistency.

VI

CONSEQUENTIALIST ARGUMENTS

There are good reasons for supposing that judges ought to consider and evaluate the consequences of various alternative rulings open to them in vases involving the 'problem of relevancy' or of 'interpretation' or of 'classification.' *Donoghue* v. *Stevenson* as analyzed in the last chapter gives one very clear instance in which Lords of Appeal did so, and gives some corroboration of the claim that judges do in fact recognize that they ought to take account of such matters. The claim is, of course, by no means a new one. In the 37th of his *Lectures on Jurisprudence*[1] John Austin said:

A law made judicially is made on the occasion of a judicial decision. The direct or proper purpose of its immediate Author is, the decision of the specific case to which the rule is applied, and not the establishment of the rule. In as much as the grounds of the decision may serve as grounds of decision in future and similar cases, its Author legislates substantially or in effect: And his decision is commonly determined by a consideration of the effect which the grounds of his decision may produce as a general law or rule. . .

Is Austin right and am I right in thinking that decisions are 'commonly determined' by such considerations? The answer must be Yes; to dip into the Law Reports is to be confronted at every turn with such arguments. It is however right and proper that one should produce evidence by way of examples of this; which shall be the function of the present chapter.

(a) *Constitutional Problems*

There is perhaps no more striking example of the kind of argument at present in view than that used by Marshall C.J. in *Marbury* v. *Madison* ((1803) 1 Cranch 137) when he and the Supreme Court gave their celebrated and fundamentally important ruling that the Supreme Court of the U.S.A. must apply enactments even of the U.S. Congress only if they are satisfied that they do not contravene the provisions of the

---

[1] Op.cit. *supra*, Ch. III n. 10.

Constitution. Consider the following words of his:

If. . .the Courts are to regard the constitution, and the constitution is superior to any ordinary act of the legislature, the constitution, and not such ordinary act, must govern the case to which they both apply.

Those then, who controvert the principle that the constitution is to be considered, in court, as a permanent law, are reduced to the necessity of maintaining that courts must close their eyes to the constitution, and see only the law.

The doctrine would subvert the very foundation of all written constitutions. It would declare that an act which, according to the principles and theory of our government, is entirely void, is yet, in practice, completely obligatory. It would declare that if the legislature should do what is expressly forbidden, such act, notwithstanding the express prohibition, is in reality effectual. It would be giving to the legislature a practical and real omnipotence, with the same breath which professes to restrict their powers within narrow limits. It is prescribing limits, and declaring that those limits may be passed at pleasure. (Ibid. at p. 178)

Observe particularly the words 'The doctrine would subvert the very foundation of all written constitutions'; elsewhere in his opinion he develops more fully a doctrine of the 'written constitution' of the U.S.A. The 'sovereign people' having set up a constitution, and a legislature whose powers are defined thereby, the question is whether that legislature is to be able to override the terms of its establishment or not. It would be unacceptable to adopt any doctrine of judicial review which would involve the Court in conniving at subversion of the constitutional definition of the range of legislative power.

Since the United Kingdom of Great Britain was, like the United States of America, first established by adoption of a particular set constituent provisions (the Articles of Union of 1707, adopted by enabling legislation of each of the previously separate Scottish and English Parliaments) it ought not to be surprising that similar questions have been raised here as to the powers of the U.K. Parliament in respect of these constituent provisions. On that point, in *MacCormick* v. *Lord Advocate* (1953 S.C. 396) Lord Cooper made the following observations:

The principle of the unlimited sovereignty of Parliament is a distinctively English principle which has no counterpart in Scottish constitutional law. It derives its origin from Coke and Blackstone, and was widely popularised during the nineteenth century by Bagehot and Dicey, the latter having stated the doctrine in its classic form in his Law of the Constitution. Considering that the Union legislation extinguished the Parliaments of Scotland and England and replaced them by a new Parliament, I have difficulty in seeing why it should have been supposed that the new Parliament of Great Britain must inherit all the peculiar characteristics of the English Parliament but none of the Scottish Parliament, as if all that happened in 1707 was that Scottish representatives were admitted to the Parliament of England. That is not what was done. Further, the Treaty and the associated legislation, by which the Parliament of Great Britain was brought into being as the successor of the separate Parliaments of Scotland and England, contain some clauses which expressly reserve to the Parliament of Great Britain powers of subsequent modification, and other clauses which either contain no such power or emphatically exclude subsequent alteration by declarations that the provision shall be fundamental and unalterable in all time coming, or declarations of a like effect. I have never been able to understand how it is possible to reconcile with elementary canons of construction the adoption by the English constitutional theorists of the same attitude to these markedly different types of provisions. (Ibid. at p. 411)

The particular issue in the case was whether or not the ascription to Queen Elizabeth of the style and title 'Elizabeth II' involved a breach of the first of the Articles of Union, there having been no previous monarch *of the United Kingdom* (as distinct from England) who bore the name Elizabeth; in so far as this was authorized by the Royal Style and Titles Act 1953, was that Act then valid as law? The First Division held that the Act did not authorize the 'numeral', but the choice of a monarch's name and numeral did not require statutory authority in any event, hence the question of the validity of the Act was not relevant to the issue in the case.

Further, Lord Cooper doubted whether a justiciable issue could arise in Scottish Courts on the question of purported laws concerning 'public right', as distinct from matters of 'private right' or of the guaranteed continuity of the Court of Session itself. Finally, on title to sue, he made the following significant remark:

I agree with the Lord Ordinary on title to sue. . .It is true that we in Scotland recognise within certain limits the *actio popularis*, in which any member of the public may be entitled as such to vindicate certain forms of public right. But the device has never been extended to such a case as this. *I cannot see how we could admit the title and interest of the present petitioners to raise the point in issue before the Court of Session without conceding a similar right to almost any opponent*

of almost any political action to which public opposition has arisen.
(Ibid. at p. 413, italics added)

The italicized passage indicates clearly a fundamental consequentialist element in the justification of the dismissal of the petitioners' case. But observe how the whole argument takes place within the framework of an attempt to tease out and explicate constitutional principles, and principles defining the right of the citizen to raise and of the Court to determine the extent of its own power to settle the limits of Parliament's power, standing the existence of the articles of Union as 'fundamental law' (*per* Lord Cooper, 1953 S.C. at p. 412). The parallel with Marshall C.J.'s testing out of rival principles against the basic American conception of a written constitution is as striking as the differences; for both, there is a key point of differentiation between questions of the rights of citizens and questions essentially political.

The Courts in England have of course taken a different view again; a clear statement of the basic justification of their attitude was given by Willes J. in the case of *Lee* v. *Bude and Torrington Railway Co.* ((1871) L.R. 6 C.P. at 576) a decision recently upheld by the House of Lords in *British Railways Board* v. *Pickin* ([1974] A.C. 765); when it was argued that a Private Act of Parliament ought to be set aside on the ground that it had been procured by fraud on the part of its promoters, a round and robust answer was forthcoming:

If an Act of Parliament has been obtained improperly, it is for the legislature to correct it by repealing it; but, so long as it exists as law, the courts are bound to obey it. *The proceedings here are judicial, not autocratic, which they would be if we could make laws instead of administering them.* ((1871) L.R. 6 C.P. at 582, italics added)

Again, we see an example of consequentialist argument; again, we see that the rejection of one possible ruling as unconstitutional is dependent not on any straightforward hedonistic utilitarianism, but on perceived constitutional values concerning the proper limits on judicial as distinct from legislative functions. The theme, together with the recurrence of a 'political question' doctrine recurs in Salmon L.J.'s short opinion in *Blackburn* v. *Attorney-General* ([1971] 2 All E.R. 1380 at 1383).

When Mr. Blackburn sought to challenge the competency

of the Crown to ratify the Treaty whereby the U.K. acceded to the European Economic Community, his action was dismissed. Salmon L.J. gave the following reasons:

Whilst I recognise the undoubted sincerity of Mr. Blackburn's views, I deprecate litigation the purpose of which is to influence political decisions. Such decisions, have nothing to do with these courts. These courts are concerned only with the effect of such decisions if and when they have been implemented by legislation. Nor have the courts any power to interfere with the treaty-making power of the Sovereign. As to Parliament, in the present state of the law, it can enact, amend and repeal any legislation it pleases. The sole power of the courts is to decide and enforce what is the law and not what it should be—now, or in the future. I agree that this appeal should be dismissed.

The foregoing examples show clearly how at the level of fundamental questions concerning the scope and limits of the 'rule of recognition' within legal systems, consequentialist arguments necessarily come into play. But the process of evaluation of consequences depends heavily on their scrutiny in the light of what are taken to be fundamental constitutional principles.

On this ground one must agree with R. Sartorius's remarks[2] concerning Hart's doctrine of the ultimate rule of recognition; the existence of the constitution cannot be regarded simply as a matter of plain fact, from the point of view at least of those who have to decide questions about it (but see Lord Denning's remarks in Blackburn's case, *cit.sup.*, at p. 1383). How we decide matters about the constitution depends, says Sartorius, on our view of constitutional theory, itself derived from constitutional practice. I should put it in the terms that possible alternative rulings on fundamental constitutional points must be evaluated in terms of constitutional values as understood by the judges and as expressed in principles concerning the right basis of authority and allocation of authority in the state. Which is probably no more than a different way of saying the same thing. But it is not clear that this falsifies Hart's thesis; Hart could fairly say that what we are doing is unpacking what he calls 'the internal point of view'.

In any event, the 'rule of recognition' concerns also the

[2] R. Sartorius, 'Hart's Concept of Law', (1966) 51 ARSP 161; also in *More Essays in Legal Philosophy*, ed. R.S. Summers (Oxford, 1971), p. 131.

authority of precedents; there too the question may arise for the Courts: which precedents are to be binding, and why? Lord Halsbury's strongly consequentialist justification of the ruling that House of Lords precedents ought to bind all courts and to be reversible only by Parliament was noted in the previous chapter. But the consequences of adhering to that ruling have in turn been found sufficiently unsatisfactory for the House of Lords to have reversed itself on that point, which it did in a Practice Statement issued by the Lord Chancellor on behalf of the House in 1966 (see [1966] 1 W.L.R. 1234).

The first instance in which (at least arguably) the House exercized its reasserted power of reviewing its own previous decisions concerned judicial power, this time power *vis à vis* the Executive. The case illustrated the possibility that experience of the operation of a rule initially justified on grounds of utility may provide good evidence as to the fallibility of the original justifying argument. In *Conway* v. *Rimmer* ([1968] A.C. 910) the House of Lords was called upon to rule upon the question whether the Courts had power to order discovery of documents in litigation if a Minister of the Crown certified in an affidavit that they were documents of a class whose disclosure would be injurious to the public interest and adverse to the efficient working of the public service. Lord Simon L.C. had laid down in the single speech in *Duncan* v. *Cammell Laird* ([1942] A.C. 624) that in cases of national security or of such a class of documents, the Minister's affidavit was conclusive of the question and could not be overridden by the Courts. *Duncan's* case itself came under the 'national security' heading, since there the documents withheld ·were the plans of a new type of submarine, the prototype of which had been lost with all hands during trials. The consequentialist considerations telling in favour of such a ruling especially in time of war hardly need quotation or recital.

In the post-war period, however, the most regular application of the ruling was in 'class' cases, many of which gave rise to serious judicial concern and criticism.[3] In *Conway's* case

---

[3] Critically discussed and reviewed in S.A. de Smith, *Constitutional and Administrative Law* (2nd edn., Harmondsworth, 1973), pp. 618–23.

Lord Reid, proposing the assertion of a rule in English law equivalent to that prevailing in Scots law,[4] passed this remark:

In my judgment, in considering what it is 'proper' for a Court to do, we must have regard to the need shown by twenty five years' experience since *Duncan's* case that the Courts should balance the public interest in the proper administration of justice against the public interest in withholding any evidence which a Minister considers ought to be withheld. I would therefore propose that the House ought now to decide that the Courts have a power and duty to hold [that balance]. (Ibid. at pp. 951–2)

Part of the 'twenty five years experience' was the strong dissatisfaction expressed by lawyers over the non-disclosure of documents sought by the defence in criminal cases, in response to which Lord Kilmuir (then Lord Chancellor) had made a Ministerial statement on 6 June 1956 stating a new government policy that 'if medical documents, or indeed other documents are relevant to the defence in criminal proceedings, Crown privilege should not be claimed.' But as Lord Reid pointed out, this in effect drove a coach and four through the original policy justification of the rule in *Duncan's* case: '[We] have the curious result that "freedom and candour of communication" is supposed not to be inhibited by the knowledge of the writer that his report may be disclosed in a criminal case, but would still be supposed to be inhibited if he thought that his report might be disclosed in a civil case' (ibid. at p. 942).

Here we have seen a clear instance of the conflict of justice-based evaluations and 'expediency' or 'public interest' evaluations. We also see that the process of evaluating a ruling at law is as appropriate, perhaps even more appropriate, to a reassessment of a precedent ruling as to the justificatory testing of a ruling at first impression. The defect, it may well be said, of a system which treats even a single precedent as irremovably binding is that it forecloses this possibility of using experience to confirm or disconfirm consequentialist grounds of justification of prior decisions.

Lord Abinger's notorious decision in the case of *Priestley* v. *Fowler* ((1837) 3 M. and W. 1) provides an awful warning

---

[4] *Glasgow Corporation* v. *Central Land Board* 1956 S.C. (H.L.) 1.

about the demerits of any such foreclosure. The action was raised by a servant against his master for damages for the negligence of the driver of a van which caused it to crash and injure the plaintiff. The driver was fellow servant of the same master.

Lord Abinger had no doubt what kinds of factor he should take into account: 'It is admitted that there is no precedent for the present action by a servant against a master. We are therefore at liberty to decide the question upon general principles, and in so doing we are at liberty to look at the consequences of a decision one way or the other' (ibid. at p. 5).

The action was dismissed, and Lord Abinger's justification of the dismissal of the injured servant's action is a good example of a bad consequentialist argument.

If the master be liable to the servant on this action, the principle of that liability will be found to carry us to an alarming extent...The footman who rides behind the carriage may have an action against his master for the defect in the carriage owing to the negligence of the coachmaker or for a defect in the harness owing to the negligence of the harness maker, or for drunkenness neglect or want of skill in the coachman; nor is there any reason why the principle should not, if applicable in this class of cases, extend to many others. The master, for example, would be liable to the servant for the negligence of [a long list, including both fellow servants and independent contractors, concluding with] the builder, for a defect in the foundation of the house, whereby it fell, and injured both the master and the servant by the ruins.

The inconvenience, not to say the absurdity of these consequences, affords a sufficient argument against the application of the principle in the present case.

The argument is a bad one because the 'absurdity' and 'inconvenience' of making a master liable to a servant for the negligence of an independent contractor is irrelevent to the question whether a master ought to be vicariously liable to one servant for another servant's negligence; it is easier for the master to control a drunken coachman than to supervise a careless builder, for one thing. So the case which was the *fons et origo* of the notorious 'common employment' doctrine (not finally interred until the passage of the Law Reform (Personal Injuries) Act 1948) was itself based on a most questionable justificatory argument. This observation suggests that there is a radical weakness in a doctrine of precedent according to which the binding authority of a decided case is entirely independent of the strength or validity of the justifying arguments employed in the case (though it must be added that, as Lord Reid has recently pointed out,[5] the 'common employment' doctrine despite resistance in the Inner House of the Court of Session, was widely regarded during the nineteenth century as being based on reasonableness and common sense—at any rate, among the economically dominant classes). The abandonment of the *London Street Tramways* doctrine has, however, opened the road to such reconsiderations, as *Conway* v. *Rimmer* indeed shows. And it is worth observing that the Scottish Courts have all along taken the view that one ground for departing from an otherwise authoritative precedent is an error of argument in the justifying opinion stated by the prior court, as when in *Macdonald* v. *Glasgow Western Hospitals* (1954 S.C. 453) Lord Carmont gave it as a ground for not following *Reidford* v. *Magistrates of Aberdeen* (1935 S.C. 276) that in *Reidford* the Court had proceeded upon a false application of the distinction between *locatio conductio operis faciendi* and *locatio conductio operarum*. That doctrine can be coupled with the principle that an authoritative precedent should not be followed if it is based upon principles enshrining social or economic conceptions which have been legislatively abandoned or otherwise by-passed, as laid down by Lord Cooper and the First Division in *Beith's Trustees* v. *Beith* (1950 S.C. 66). The two taken together would provide a basis for the consequentialist revaluation of precedents and lines of authority of which the original justifications were either unsound or have ceased to be appropriate to contemporary social conditions. In *Beith* for example, the Court justified its departing from the rule laid down by seven judges in *Menzies* v. *Murray* ((1875) 2 R. 507) restricting variation of antenuptial settlements on the ground that the original reason of the rule was the need to protect married women by restricting their, and their husbands', access to trust capital. The force of that reason was now wholly spent, as a result of changed social conceptions of the relationship

---

[5] 'The Judge as Law Maker' (*cit.sup.*, Ch. V n. 4), at p. 26.

between wife and husband, mirrored by the legal changes wrought by married women's property legislation.

That such an approach to the criticism of existing precedents would be a sound one seems to be a justifiable conclusion in the whole context of the present argument. It has to be said, however, that the House of Lords has not unequivocally taken that line in its discussions so far of the question how it ought to exercise its self-conferred power to depart from its own precedents.[6] On that ground it may be objected that the present thesis fails to be faithful to the actuality of current practice in the House of Lords if not the Court of Session. But I should reply to that, with all due respect, that the House of Lords has failed as yet to articulate a clear and satisfactory set of justifying criteria for departing from precedents, and that its doing so would have to be on the basis of some more general theory of legal argumentation and justification. In this context, and given a general faithfulness to the actuality of legal reasoning in our Courts, the present thesis has a critical function—I hope a constructively critical one.

At this stage in the exposition, I can turn to redeeming a pledge made earlier.[7] In looking at consequentialist elements in arguments concerning the powers of legislatures and the binding nature of precedents we are discussing how the judges reach conclusions on the actual application of 'criteria of recognition' for 'valid rules of law' within the system. That judges actually have and apply such criteria of recognition is, as we saw earlier, an essential tenet of legal positivism and an accepted and important truth for many natural lawyers—probably all contemporary ones. But it was pointed out that judges may have, and may on occasions have to articulate, 'underpinning reasons' which justify (a) the acceptance of particular criteria of recognition and (b) their rulings as to the proper application of such criteria in controverted cases.

What the foregoing discussion in this section of this chapter shows is that these underpinning reasons are indeed

---

[6] But see *Miliangos* v. *George Frank (Textiles) Ltd.* [1976] A.C. 443, with which the present thesis is fully compatible.

[7] In Chapter III above, at p. 65.

articulated in terms of arguments based on the consequences of rival possible rulings about validity or bindingness in certain generic contexts; the evaluation of relevant consequences depends on criteria of 'justice' and of 'common sense' and above all on reference to basic constitutional principles which draw in turn on fundamental assumptions about political philosophy and the proper distribution of authority among the superior organs of the state.

That puts an important qualification on the findings of Chapter II. It is certainly the case that deductive reasoning from established legal rules and premisses of fact takes place in law; and certainly the case that such arguments are treated as giving conclusive reasons for decisions. But we can now see that what gives these reasons conclusiveness *as justifications* is the tacit presupposition of the obligatory character of respect for criteria of recognition, which in turn rests upon considerations of the kind more recently reviewed—considerations which only have to be articulated in problem cases. Deductive justifications do not expound, but they take place within, a framework of values which supplies the ground for treating them as conclusive.

From the point of view of general legal theory, that is a finding which must be important for any account of law which accords centrality to the 'validity thesis'. Not all jurisprudents who give such accounts would necessarily disagree. Hart, whose theory of the 'rule of recognition' has been here treated as a central example of the 'validity thesis' does indeed assert that the existence of a rule of recognition is *from the point of view of an observer* a matter of 'social fact', albeit complex. *Non sequitur* that in its 'internal aspect' as confronted by those for whom the rule has normative force as agents within the legal system, 'social fact' is all that there is to it. Elsewhere[8] I have suggested that Hart's brilliant elucidation of the 'internal aspect' of conduct under rules needs to be in various ways elaborated beyond the confines of his analysis in *Concept of Law*.[9] The present argument reinforces that suggestion. What must be essential to the 'internal aspect' of the rule of recognition

[8] See Appendix to this book.
[9] Hart, *Concept of Law*, pp. 55–6. 86–8, 96, 99–100, etc.

is some conscious commitment to pursuing the political values which are perceived as underpinning it, and to sustaining in concrete form the political principles deemed inherent in the constituted order of the society in question. Whether or not that is correct in itself, it is not inconsistent with Hart's thesis, though it involves taking it further than anything said by Hart himself would authorize.

(b) *Consequentialism at Random*

The cases considered in the preceding section were chosen deliberately as illustrating a given theme, the settlement of problem cases concerning criteria of recognition. Even if I have succeeded in demonstrating in such cases as well as in *Donoghue* v. *Stevenson* the relevant operation of consequentialist arguments (as well as arguments from principle) it might fairly be said that these also belong to a rather special class of case. Are these modes of arguing as general as I claim or as my general theory suggests they ought to be?

By giving a number of examples chosen at random from my own case reading I can at least refute the view that such reasoning is special to front rank leading cases and constitutional decisions. To conclude the chapter I shall do just that, looking promiscuously at cases involving problems of relevancy, of interpretation and of classification, and, no less promiscuously, different branches of law from different jurisdictions.

A problem which has considerably agitated British Courts in recent years concerns the extent of liability for negligent conduct. If by a careless act A creates a situation in which B suffers economic loss, without any form of physical injury to person or property, can B competently sue A for damages for such loss? For example, the facts in *Dynamco Ltd.* v. *Holland & Hannen & Cubitts (Scotland) Ltd.* (1971 S.C. 257) were that the pursuers' factory had had its electric power cut off on two occasions in 1969 when employees of the defender (illegally by fault and negligence) severed cables belonging to the South of Scotland Electricity Board; and that thereby the pursuers suffered loss of production and of profits. Similar accidents have led to similar litigation in England. The concluding passage of Lord Kissen's opinion in *Dynamco* captures a theme to be found in all the judgments on the topic:

My opinion is, to summarise, that by the law of Scotland the pursuers cannot competently sue for the financial loss on which their case is based, in that physical damage to property owned or possessed by them was not the cause of the loss. Whether the law should be extended to cover economic loss in cases of negligence where there has been no damage to the property of the person claiming the loss is another matter.

There are many judicial observations in the cases which I have mentioned, including *Reavis* v. *Clan Line Steamers*, (1925 S.C. 725), on the multiplicity of litigations which could follow one act of negligence if the law was as the pursuers stated it, and on the practical necessity for limitations. . .If the pursuers are correct in their submissions, the results would be 'startling' to use the word of Lord President Clyde in *Reavis*, at p 740. Every company or person who uses electricity for business could have a claim for loss of profit and other pecuniary loss if a cable was damaged by negligence and electricity was cut off. There could be no distinction between owners or occupiers of factories with machinery, of shops, of offices, of hotels, of restaurants, of mines, of quarries, and, in some cases, of houses. . .(Ibid. at 263)

Earlier in his opinion, in considering the scope of 'reasonable foreseeability' of damage arising from a negligent act, Lord Kissen had concluded that existing legal principles did not support the pursuer's case. 'A negligent wrongdoer is not to be held bound to have surmised purely financial or economic loss to persons other than the owners or possessors of damaged property' (ibid at 261).

It seems obvious that this is not simply a matter of what is foreseeable in the sense of 'capable of being foreseen'. It is obvious that the key point is in the 'not *to be* held bound to have surmised. . .'. The catastrophic range of losses which could arise from careless severing of electric cables is such that nobody would be an insurable risk against liability for it; to hold even a large firm liable on such an account would simply bankrupt it, to the actual benefit of nobody. Those who are dependent on electricity supplies ought to insure themselves against loss arising from losses or power. So, at any rate, the point has been argued by judges in the 'economic loss' cases.

It is characteristic of the Scots lawyer's approach to such arguments that in *Dynamco* Lord Kissen advanced the argument quoted only after elucidating what he took to be the relevant principle of Scots law, by way, as it were, of cross-checking, or further justifying the argument from principle; yet even in that tradition, it would be hard to deny the considerable importance of consequentialist arguments. A further instance is available in, for example, Lord Hunter's judgment in *Henderson* v. *John Stuart (Farms) Ltd.* (1963 S.C. 245)

The pursuers were the widow and daughter of a farm hand who had been gored to death by a Friesian dairy bull while cleaning out its loose-box. Their claim was based on the averment that Mr. Henderson's death had been caused by the defender's negligence, specifically his failure to provide a safe system of work. The defender averred however that the bull in question had never previously evinced dangerous propensities, and accordingly that the pursuers had failed to make a relevant case since there could be no liability for harm done by domesticated animals unless they were known from previous actions to have vicious propensities, along the lines of the English '*scienter* action'

Lord Hunter rejected that argument; the authorities on which it relied, in part dependent on English case law, in part on Stair I. ix.5., he considered as relating to the duty to confine effectually animals known to be vicious. But he saw no reason of principle why the existence of that duty ought to be conceived as contradicting or eliding general principles of liability for reparation of wrongs, and he advanced consequentialist arguments which to his mind demonstrated the undesirability of giving any such interpretation to the established body of case law:

the proposition that a master cannot be liable in reparation upon any ground, including that of negligence, for loss and damage resulting from the act of his servant, in the absence of proof that the servant was to his actual foreknowledge outrageous and pernicious is plainly unstatable. I do not see any reason in principle why this negative proposition should become stateable when related to a beast. I realise that the foregoing observations bear some resemblance to one of the passages in the opinion of Lord Cockburn, who was one of the majority in *Fleeming* v. *Orr* (1853) 15 D. 486, whose decision was afterwards reversed by the House of Lords; but this consideration does not, in my respectful opinion, make it impossible to hold such views. Otherwise one would have to accept, inter alia, the proposition that a man might intentionally and with malice set his dog upon another, and defend himself successfully by maintaining that it had not attacked anyone before, or that a farmer could knowingly release a bull of breed notoriously unreliable into a field of ladies wearing scarlet coats, and, when as a result of this incautious act the inevitable happened, be heard to assert that the animal had never previously gored a single person, male or female. In any event, I am of opinion that the passage from Stair (Inst I. ix 5) has no such meaning or effect. . .(Ibid. at 249).

These considerations Lord Hunter in effect resumed when towards the end of his opinion he said:

Counsel for the defender was constrained more than once during the debate to concede that the practical results of his argument might seem in certain respects unjust and even weird. . .I freely confess that I have no enthusiasm for arriving at weird results, particularly when these seem to conflict with well known principles of Scots law. But to apply an existing and accepted principle to a new set of facts is not to usurp the function of the legislature [contrary to the suggestion of counsel for the defender]. (Ibid. at 255)

It should not be thought that arguments such as these are only available in matters of common law. That is far from being the case, for argument in very similar terms may be equally apposite in interpreting an admitted rule of statute law.

In *Anisminic* v. *Foreign Compensation Commission* ([1969] 2 A.C. 197) the Courts had to consider the effect of s 4(4) of the Foreign Compensation Act 1950: 'The determination by the Commission of any application made to them under this Act shall not be called in question in any Court of Law.' Despite that provision, the House of Lords declared null and void a decision of the F.C.C. in a matter arising out of the Suez affair. One of the justifying factors appealed to in the House of Lords for construing the section as leaving untrammelled the Courts' power to set aside purported determinations which were 'nullities' was the consideration that otherwise the limited competence confered by Parliament on the Commission might be plainly exceeded without possibility of correction. And that would defeat Parliament's intention that the Commission should stick within the bounds of an expressly limited jurisdiction. The argument for treating as fundamental the particular 'mistake' made by the Commission in applying the relevant Order in Council so as to reject Anisminic's application, was itself an argument from justice and expediency. To construe the Order as the Commission did was to yield the result that an

original owner deprived of Egyptian property after the
Suez affair received no compensation if he had succeeded in
bringing sufficient pressure to bear on the Egyptian Government to obtain partial compensation for his loss, an unjust
and inexpedient consequence. The House of Lords argued
that the process whereby this was done could be classified
as taking into account an 'irrelevant consideration,' and thus
excess of jurisdiction. Accordingly, the 'purported determination' could justifiably be set aside, notwithstanding s.
4(4) of the 1950 Act. Thus in a double way argument from
evaluation of possible competing interpretations of the Act
and the delegated legislation made under it justified the
Court's assertion of power to review the decision, and the
actual exercise of that power.

That is, in terms of our current distinction, a case involving
a 'problem of interpretation' of statute law. But the interpretation of common-law doctrine can also be problematic,
e.g. in relation to the common-law doctrine of frustration
of contracts.

On 3 January 1937, the *S.S. Kingswood* was lying at
anchor off Port Pirie when she was severely damaged by a
violent explosion in her boilers, so delaying her as to frustrate
a contract of charter whereby she was to have collected
a cargo from Port Pirie on the following day. The charterers
of the ship claimed damages, and on arbitration the arbitrator
found it impossible to establish the true cause of the explosion.
The law was clearly settled that it is a defence to a claim
for damages under a contract that the contract has been
rendered impossible of performance as a commercial venture
('frustrated') by events subsequent to its formation, but
that if the defendant's own act had brought about the
frustrating event he could not rely on that defence. In the
instant case, *Joseph Constantine Steamship Line Ltd.* v.
Imperial Smelting Corporation Ltd. ([1942] A.C. 154)
the charterers (the respondents) contended that the burden
of proving that the frustrating event had not been caused by
the wilful or negligent actions of the shipowners or their
servants lay upon the appellant shipowners, and the shipowners asserted the contradictory of that. Atkinson J.
decided in favour of the latter view, but the Court of Appeal

reversed him and was in turn reversed by the House of Lords.

A decisive element in their Lordships' reasoning was put thus by Lord Wright:

It is clear that the rule which the Court of Appeal has laid down would in many cases work serious injustice and nullify the beneficial operations of the doctrine of frustration which has been somewhat empirically evolved with the object of doing what is reasonable and fair, as I have already explained. That the rule adopted by the Court of Appeal is inconvenient seems to me obvious. . . .(I)f a ship is lost with all hands in a cyclone, must the shipowners establish affirmatively that the master did not receive and ignore warnings of the danger area? There may be many maritime losses in which evidence how they happened is impossible to find. If a ship is torpedoed with all hands, must the shipowner prove affirmatively absence of fault, such as that a light was not shown on the ship or that the ship obeyed the convoy regulations? (Ibid. at p. 193)

Lord Simon L.C. in like vein pointed out that '[If the Court of Appeal's ruling] were correct, there must be many cases in which, although in truth frustration is complete and unavoidable, the defendant will be held liable because of his inability to prove a negative—in some cases, indeed, a whole series of negatives' (ibid at p. 161). And he proceeded to figure a series of testing examples akin to Lord Wright's. Lord Simon added a further argument to the effect that the matter could be stated as based on an implied term in the contract, analogous to an express 'perils of the seas' clause, whereupon the burden would fall on the charterer of rebutting the application of that exception, under the principle of *The Glendarroch* ([1894] P. 264).

Professor Stone[10] has contended that this latter argument was treated as the essential argument justifying the decision; so he says that, because the distinction between an exception to a rule and a qualification of the rule is meaningless, the case was decided by reference to a 'legal category of meaningless reference', one of the 'Categories of Illusory Reference' which he says are used by courts to disguise the policy choices they necessarily make. But the passages cited from the speeches of Lords Wright and Simon expressly explain the adverse consequences which they conceive as flowing from

[10] J. Stone, *Legal System and Lawyers' Reasonings* (London, 1964) pp. 244–6.

the alternative rule to the one they adopted. The consequentialist argument is clearly stated and quite explicit. It is true that for Lord Simon, one way in which the matter 'can be stated' is by spelling out implied terms of the contract; but it must be the explicit policy argument which justifies his particular choice as to the manner of explicating the implied terms. To that end, it is surely obvious that the citation of *The Glendarroch* is by way of a supporting analogy, ultimately justifiable itself on the same policy ground. In this instance at least it appears that Stone's thesis misses its mark by failing to perceive the difference between the function of a supportive analogy (which can never be of itself a compelling justification of a decision, going merely to its permissibility and coherence with settled law) and that of an argument which constitutes of itself a positive justification. What is more, if one accepts Lord Wright's opinion that the result is also required by extrapolation from the underlying principle and policy of the frustration rule as already developed, the analogy, though it adds weight to the justification, is essentially supererogatory.

Illegality of contracts is a topic not unrelated to frustration, in that the illegality of a contract may prevent a plaintiff from relying upon it to found a claim in Court. But here, too, problems may arise as to the application of the rule against enforcement of illegal contracts in particular novel situations. In *St. John Shipping Corporation* v. *Joseph Rank Ltd.* ([1957] 1 Q.B. 267) the defendants had refused to pay part of the freight on a load of grain delivered to Birkenhead in the plaintiffs' ship, which had crossed the Atlantic overloaded well beyond the maximum permitted limit, thereby committing a criminal offence. Before Devlin J. they argued that they were entitled to withhold payment, to which the plaintiff had no right since he had been guilty of criminal misconduct in carrying out his side of the contract. The penetrating wit with which Devlin J. dealt with that contention justifies a somewhat extensive quotation (which clearly examplifies the point of the present thesis):

The defendants cannot succeed unless they claim the right to retain the whole freight and to keep it whether the offence was accidental or deliberate, serious or trivial. The application of this principle to a case such as this is bound to lead to startling results. Mr. Wilmers does not seek to avert his gaze from the wide consequences. A shipowner who accidentally overloads by a fraction of an inch will not be able to recover from any of the shippers or consignees a penny of the freight. There are numerous other illegalities which a ship might commit in the course of the voyage which would have the same effect Mr. Roskill has referred me by way of example to section 24 of the Merchant Shipping (Safety Conventions) Act, 1949, which makes it an offence to send a ship to sea laden with grain if all necessary and reasonable precautions have not been taken to prevent the grain from shifting. He has referred me also to the detailed regulations for the carriage of timber—similar in character to regulations under the Factories Acts— which must be complied with if an offence is not to be committed under section 61 of the Act of 1932. If Mr. Wilmers is right, the consequences to shipowners of a breach of the Act of 1932 would be as serious as if owners of factories were unable to recover from their customers the cost of any articles manufactured in a factory which did not in all respects comply with the Acts. Carriers by land are in no better position; again Mr. Wilmers does not shrink from saying that the owner of a lorry could not recover against the consignees the cost of goods transported in it if in the course of the journey it was driven a mile an hour over its permitted speed. If this is really the law, it is very unenterprising of cargo owners and consignees to wait until a criminal conviction has been secured before denying their liabilities. A service of trained observers on all our main roads would soon pay for itself. An effective patrol of the high seas would probably prove too expensive, but the maintenance of a corps of vigilantes in all principal ports would be well worth while when one considers that the smallest infringement of the statute or a regulation made thereunder would relieve all the cargo owners on the ship from all liability for freight.

Of course, as Mr. Wilmers says, one must not be deterred from enunciating the correct principle of law because it may have startling or even calamitous results. But I confess that I approach the investigation of a legal proposition which has results of this character with a prejudice in favour of the idea that there may be a flaw in the argument somewhere. (Ibid. at pp. 281−2)

It would be unsatisfactory to conclude without some reference to the two cases which I introduced earlier as exemplars of the 'problem of classification' (*Maclennan* v. *Maclennan* (1958 S.C. 105) and of the problem of interpretation (the *Ealing London Borough Council* case ([1972] A.C. 342). In the former, Lord Wheatley held that A.I.D. did not constitute adultery for the purpose of divorce law; his main argument was founded on an elucidation of the concept of adultery expounded in the case law; but a strong subsidiary argument concerned the apparent absurdity of extending the notion of adultery to include A.I.D. His Lordship pointed out that under the alternative ruling it would be possible that a wife might be found to have committed adultery with a dead man—constructive necrophilia, as it were—a conclusion which seemed to him unacceptably absurd.

In the *Ealing* case, the Lords of the majority were concerned that the Race Relations Acts also used the phrase 'discrimination on the ground of . . . national origins' in certain criminal provisions. They considered it unacceptable that the criminal law be extended by implication, and on that and other grounds excluded 'nationality' from the ambit of national origins. But Lord Kilbrandon in his dissenting speech was even more outright in his reliance on consequentialist argument:

> The practical consequences of excluding discrimination on the ground of nationality from the scope of national origins are striking. . .If 'national origins' is not wide enough to include 'nationality', then exclusion of persons (from places of public resort) by a notice which read, for example, 'No Poles admitted' would have been of debatable legality. . .'No foreigners' would have been safer, since the word 'foreigners' properly describes a foreign national rather than a British subject of foreign origin; while, as counsel for the council conceded, a notice 'British subjects only' outside a public house would have been unexceptionable. . .The arguments in favour of either interpretation are finely balanced. I would not accept the view that there is some presumption here in favour of freedom from liability; the race relations code does, of course, contain some criminal sanctions, and it restricts liberty, but, on the other hand, it is conceived as a measure of social reform and relief of distress. Not much help is to be got from presumptions either for freedom or in favour of benevolent interpretation. ([1972] A.C. at pp. 268–9)

It seems fair to say that sufficient examples have been cited to justify the assertion that the pattern of testing the generalized principle of a decision which we detected in *Donoghue* v. *Stevenson* is by no means uncommon. If a great judge's extra-judicial testimony is admissible, there is a recent remark of Lord Reid's which supports the thesis by summarizing it, from experience of doing rather than merely of reflecting upon what others do:

> One often says to oneself when some proposition is put forward: 'That just can't be right' and then one looks to see why it cannot be right. Sometimes it offends against common sense, sometimes against one's

sense of justice, but more often it just will not stand with legal principles, though it may seem to be supported by some judicial observations read apart from their context.[11]

Although the mere adduction of examples cannot constitute proof that the consequentialist evaluation of general propositions as possible rulings in law is an essential element of legal justification whenever the two limiting problems of deductive justification arise, the examples at least indicate that any theory must take some account of this sort of evaluation. Lord Reid suggests that the process of testing must take into account 'common sense' 'one's sense of justice', 'legal principles'—and elsewhere in his article he adds to that the test of 'public policy'. That is another way of stating the types of value which were earlier suggested as being operative in the testing of the rival propositions of law in *Donoghue's* case. What it seems to come down to—and the further examples confirm this—is that laws must be conceived of as having rational objectives concerned with securing social goods or averting social evils in a manner consistent with justice between individuals; and the pursuit of these values should exhibit a sort of rational consistency, in that the consequences of a particular decision should be consonant with the purposes ascribed to related principles of law, as shown by Lord Wright's appeal in the *Constantine* case to the self-defeating effects of adding to the principle of frustration the requirement that the defendant prove that the frustrating event was not due to his fault. 'Common sense' has a dual role to play, as implying the sort of rough contemporary consensus on social values to which judges conceive of themselves as giving effect, and as covering the test for consistency of two possible objectives, to decide what makes pursuing one 'self-defeating' in the context of pursuit of the other. Lord Kilbrandon's adversion to the possibility of 'No foreigners' notices on pubs as being lawful, on the majority view, in the *Ealing* case is another instance.

Given that laws are conceived of in that rational purposive way, it does indeed seem essential that the justification of any decision in an area not governed by an express mandatory

[11] Op.cit.*supra*, p. 137 no. 5, at p. 26.

rule, or when such a rule is ambiguous or incomplete, should proceed by testing the decisions proposed in the light of their consequences. But because the justification proceeds by way of showing why such a decision *ought* to go one way rather than the other, the relevant consequences are those of the generic ruling involved in deciding one way or the other, not just the specific effects of the specific decision on the individual parties. In Lord Reid's way of putting it, one is looking at rival 'propositions' as covering the decision. The citation of examples now puts us on stronger ground in pressing again the suggestion that this mode of proceeding is necessarily demanded by the prospective element in the principle of justice in adjudication—to treat like cases alike, and therefore to treat this case in a way in which it will be justifiable to treat future like cases.

It could not be asserted as true that in every case courts succeed in clearly explicating the justifying grounds for decisions given on difficult problems. But the present thesis is concerned to establish how—according to the standards observed by judges and lawyers—decisions *ought* to be justified. So it will not be decisive against the thesis to show that sometimes no clear procedure of testing a generic ruling is to be found in any of the judgments in a case of first impression. What will be decisive is whether such instances are taken to be all right, to be satisfactory justifications. So far as one can see, they are not.

In *Scruttons Ltd.* v. *Midland Silicones Ltd.* ([1962] A.C. 446) which concerned the question whether a third party could take advantage of a clause in the contract between the two principal parties limiting damages for damage done to chemical drums in carriage under English law, the third parties appealed to the decision of the House of Lords in *Elder Dempster & Co. Ltd.* v. *Paterson, Zochonis & Co. Ltd.* ([1924] A.C. 552) in which a third party to a contract had successfully claimed such elision of liability. But of that case Lord Reid said:

Lord Finlay said that a decision against the shipowner would be absurd and the other noble Lords probably thought the same. They must have thought that they were merely applying an established principle to the facts of the particular case.

But when I look for such a principle, I cannot find it, and the extensive and able arguments of counsel in this case have failed to find it. (Ibid. at 477)

So it was fatal to the subsequent applicability of *Elder Dempster* that no viable justifying principle of decision had been explicated in Lord Finlay's speech; just to say that a particular decision in a particular case would be 'absurd' was not a proper justification, in view of the fact that the case could not be represented as 'merely applying an established principle'. Another illustration of such adverse criticism of failure to explicate a coherent justificatory principle of a decision is to be found in Lord Dunedin's well-known animadversions upon the decision in *River Wear Commissioners* v. *Adamson* ((1877) 2 App. Cas. 743) expressed in his speech in *The Mostyn* ([1928] A.C. 57, at p. 73).

The fact of these critical animadversions further supports the claim that it is a received requirement of justification that judges ought to make clear the ruling on law upon which they are acting in deciding a case, and ought to test it by the application of appropriate criteria of evaluation, such as 'common sense', 'justice', 'consistency with legal principles', and 'public policy'. Equally, therefore, counsel must press such considerations before the Court to establish a winning case. If it is also correct to claim that such a requirement necessarily follows from the principle of justice in adjudication, it is difficult to see how the present thesis could be more convincingly put, and the case may rest here.

VII

THE REQUIREMENT OF 'COHERENCE': PRINCIPLES AND ANALOGIES

The function of this chapter is to give more extended consideration to the place of arguments from general principles of law in legal reasoning. It has earlier been suggested that the place of such arguments depends on a postulated requirement of 'coherence' in the law; 'coherence' in the sense that the multitudinous rules of a developed legal system should 'make sense' when taken together. Sets of rules may be such that they are all consistent with some more general norm, and may therefore be regarded as more specific or 'concrete' manifestations of it. If that more general norm is regarded by someone as a sound and sensible, or just and desirable, norm for the guidance of affairs, then that person may properly treat that norm as a 'principle' which both explains and justifies all or any of the more specific rules in question.

As for justification: if some norm n is valued in itself or as a means to a valued end, then to show that a specific rule can be subsumed under it is to show that it is a good rule to have. As for explanation: when we are in doubt about the proper meaning of the rule in a given context, reference to the principle may help us to explain how it is to be understood; also, trivially, we can explain why the rule is considered to be worth adhering to. To call a norm 'a principle' is thus to imply that it is both relatively general, and of positive value.

To say that someone else observes a certain principle is not to imply that one does oneself ascribe positive value to the norm in question, but to imply that the other person does regard it as having positive value and thus having the kind of justificatory and explanatory relationship to particular decisions and rules which was mentioned above.

The same, it seems, applies to principles of law. If I seek to ascertain the principles of a given legal system, I ought to search for those general norms which the functionaries of the system regard as having, on the ground of their generality and positive value, the relevant justificatory and explanatory function in relation to the valid rules of the system. If I were to say that it is a principle of contemporary South African law that the black and white races ought to be discouraged from mingling socially or sexually, I believe that what I say would be true. But it remains open to me vigorously to dispute the value of, and indeed to condemn, adherence to that norm as a principle whether of individual action or of law.

Of course, from the 'insider' point of view, the matter is different. Working out the principles of a legal system to which one is committed involves an attempt to give it coherence in terms of a set of general norms which express justifying and explanatory values of the system. This engages one both in trying to understand the values which legislation and case law rules in the intendment of legislators and judges are supposed to serve, and in imposing what to oneself appears an acceptable value basis for the rules. There is a mixture of adopting received values and of adding to, extrapolating from, or modifying, them in one's own right.

It will be suggested in what follows that 'arguing by analogy' in law has to be understood in essentially similar terms. Here again, what is at stake is an attempt to secure a value-coherence within the legal system. The requirement of coherence can then be further understood as delimiting the field within which judicial law-making is legitimate.

All this takes one into a field of lively current controversy in jurisprudence. Professor R.M. Dworkin[1] has mounted a challenge, or a series of challenges, to positivistic jurisprudence on the basis of an appreciation of the significance of arguments from legal principle in 'hard cases'. He claims thereby to have subverted the theory of judicial discretion to which positivists such as H.L.A. Hart are committed.[2] His argument deserves perhaps to be of particular interest to Scots lawyers, who have traditionally made much of the reliance of their system since the days of Stair (and under his

---

[1] Ronald Dworkin, *Taking Rights Seriously* (London, 1977), cc. 1–4, 12, 13, brings together the series of essays, in which this challenge is stated.

[2] See especially Dworkin, op.cit., cc. 2 and 3.

influence) more on principles than on precedents.

Certainly, in development of ideas which I first developed in published form in 1966,[3] I do wish to advance a theory which ascribes considerable importance to the place of general principles in legal argumentation. Yet for my part I do not consider this theory to be subversive of as much as complementary to arguments such as Hart's. The crucial point, which has been made already, is that, just as much in relation to principles as to rules, one can describe a legal system without approving it or the values which it favours.

What is more, just as the rules of a system can be changed, so can its principles. One way to change them is to enact new laws. Lord Morris of Borth-y-Gest made some very relevant remarks in *Charter* v. *Race Relations Board* ([1973] A.C. 868; [1973] 1 All E.R. 512), the relevance of his remarks being in no way diminished by the fact that he dissented from his brethren as to the actual decision in that case:

My Lords, by enacting the Race Relations Acts 1965 and 1968 Parliament introduced into the law of England a new guiding principle of fundamental and far-reaching importance. It is one that affects and must influence action and behaviour in this country within a wide-ranging sweep of human activities and personal relationships. In the terms decreed by Parliament, but subject to the exceptions permitted by Parliament, discrimination against a person on the ground of colour, race or ethnic or national origins has become unlawful by the law of England. In one sense there results for some people a limitation on what could be called their freedom: they may no longer treat certain people, because of their colour race or ethnic or national origins, less favourably than they would treat others. But in the same cause of freedom, although differently viewed, Parliament has, in statutory terms now calling for consideration, proscribed discrimination (on the stated grounds) as being unlawful. ([1973] A.C. at 889; [1973] 1 All E.R. at 518)

If one asks how Parliament introduced this 'new guiding principle of fundamental and far-reaching importance' the answer is simple: by enacting the Race Relations Acts. The set of relatively detailed rules of law comprised in the sections of the Acts are valid rules of English (and, for that matter, Scots) law on precisely the grounds which the 'validity thesis' adduces. They are, taken together, a means of giving

---

[3] MacCormick, 'Can *Stare Decisis* be Abolished' 1966 Jur.Rev. 197; cf. also ' "Principles" of Law' 1974 *Jur.Rev.* 217.

the 'new principle' concrete legal embodiment; but for the adoption of such means, the principle, however admirable on moral or political grounds, would not be a principle *of these legal systems*. Alternatively it could be introduced less dramatically by a gradual accretion of relevant judicial decisions.

Such observations suggest that the processes of change are not radically different as between the 'valid rules' and the principles of a legal system; the principles can indeed be changed by changing the rules. So far as concerns 'criteria of recognition' there is a similar relationship. The principles of a legal system are the conceptualized general norms whereby its functionaries rationalize the rules which belong to the system in virtue of criteria internally observed. Of course that involves controversial questions of the ascription of values to 'the law'—what the 'true' values are is an essentially contestable question, and of course at this level of generality there is much in the way of inherent flexibility and open texture. But that is hardly an observation which is embarrassing to positivistic elucidations of law.

Dworkin has also asserted[4] that rules characteristically have 'all or nothing' applicability to contested cases—either they are valid and applicable to a given case, in which case they determine the outcome, or they are invalid or otherwise inapplicable and so contribute nothing to the decision. Principles, by contrast, have (he says) a 'dimension of weight'; principles can conflict in given fact-situations without either being invalid—rather, it has to be determined which has the greater weight for the given situation. The one which is 'outweighed' is not thereby invalidated.

Again, the difference is exaggerated. The whole point of argument by analogy in law is that a rule can contribute to a decision on facts to which it is not directly applicable; cases of 'competing analogies' involve rules pulling in different directions over debatable land between. What is more the notion of 'weight', as suggested before, is a metaphorical notion which can mislead precisely in the way in which it appeals to a quality of material objects which is objectively

---

[4] Op.cit., pp. 24–7.

measurable. In second-order justification in hard cases there
is a complex interplay between considerations of principle,
consequentialist arguments, and disputable points of interpretation of established valid rules. All this will sufficiently
appear from a consideration of the role of arguments from
principle and from analogy as these actually manifest themselves in the cases. Let me restate what I believe we mean
when we speak of 'principles of law' as distinct from rules
of law. My opinion is that legal rules (let me for this purpose
call them 'mandatory legal rules'), singly, or much more
commonly, in related groups may be conceived of as tending
to secure, or being aimed at securing, some end conceived as
valuable, or some general mode of conduct conceived to be
desirable: to express the policy of achieving that end, or the
desirability of that general mode of conduct, in a general
normative statement, is, then, to state 'the principle of the
law' underlying the rule or rules in question.

Thus, it is a rule of law in the U.K. that vehicles must
be driven on the left-hand side of the road: there is no special
reason why we should choose the left rather than the right,
but there is a compelling reason, safety, why we should
fix on one or the other. The principle is that safety on the
roads ought to be secured by specifying codes of conduct
for drivers, or that people ought to drive in a way which will
minimize danger to other road users. These principles (or,
that principle alternatively stated) are the underlying reason
for, the whole body of Road Traffic laws, not merely of the
'keep left' rule. There may of course be other principles,
such as that the free and speedy movement of traffic on the
roads ought to be fostered, which laws imposing parking
restrictions and prohibiting obstruction are seen as embody-
ing. So even in this simple, and almost banal case, we can
identify at least two principles underlying the rules of one
branch of law, which principles are obviously capable of
coming into conflict with each other. The free and speedy
movement of traffic is not always consonant with safety. All
this is, I hope, uncontroversial.

The effect of explicating general principles in this way, is
to create the possibility of perceiving the Road Traffic Acts,
not just as a congeries of arbitrary commands prohibitions

and permissions, but as a coherent set of rules directed at securing general ends which at least those who framed the rules conceived to be desirable. In this sense, to explicate the principles is to rationalize the rules.

Let us recall that this is precisely what Lord Atkin did, or purported to do, in relation to the existing body of case law laying down liability for negligence in certain relatively specific fact-situations: 'In English law, there must be and is, some general conception of relations giving rise to a duty of care, of which the particular cases found in the books are but instances', ([1932] A.C. 562 at p. 580; 1932 S.C. (H.L.) 31 at p. 44). And then he went on to specify that general conception in his now celebrated formulation of the 'neighbour principle', under which one has a general duty to take reasonable care to avoid causing foreseeable harm by one's acts or omissions to those whose relationship to one is such that their suffering harm as a result of lack of care in carrying out the act or omission in question, is a foreseeable risk.

As every law student knows, the 'neighbour principle' is not 'binding'; it is *obiter dictum*, not *ratio*; a Court is perfectly free to say of any generic act or omission not covered by a mandatory rule, that the careless performance of that act is not a ground of liability even though its careless performance may cause foreseeable harm. Everybody knows that a lawyer's carelessness in the preparation of pleadings or the conduct of litigation in Court may produce the most disastrous consequences for his client. Yet in *Rondel* v. *Worsley* ([1969] 1 A.C. 191) it was authoritatively laid down after careful and anxious consideration that a barrister is not liable to his client for any defect in the presentation of a case in court. Among the reasons advanced against the recognition of such liability were: (1) that a barrister or advocate—and, perhaps, a solicitor acting as an advocate in courts—is acting as an officer of the court, to see justice done, and is not merely acting in his client's interest alone; an advocate must not mislead the Court, and must present the issues and the law relating to them fairly and honestly to the court, albeit in a way which makes the strongest case which can legitimately be made for his client; and (2) that the admission of liability of counsel would open the possibility of infinite regress of litigation by disgruntled litigants; anyone who lost a case he thought he should have won, after exhausting all appeals, could simply set about reopening the question by suing his lawyer for negligence in failing to win a case which should have been won.

But let us take a counter-example: in *Home Office* v. *Dorset Yacht Co. Ltd.* ([1970] A.C. 1004), the question was whether or not the Home Office owed any duty of care to members of the public to prevent the escape of boys from an open borstal. A party of boys from a borstal who were working under the supervision and control of three borstal officers on Brownsea Island in Poole Harbour escaped during one night and did extensive damage to two yachts anchored in the harbour, one of which belonged to the respondents. The respondents sued the Home Office for damages, and plainly an affirmative answer to the question mentioned was an essential precondition of their success. They got their affirmative answer.

A passage from the dissenting speech of Lord Dilhorne is, however, of great interest:

There is no authority for the existence of such a duty under the common law. Lord Denning, M.R. in his judgment in the Court of Appeal, I think, recognised this, for he said: 'It is, I think, at bottom a matter of public policy which we as judges must resolve' and 'What then is the right policy for the judges to adopt?' He went on to say:

'Many, many a time has a prisoner escaped—or been let out on parole—and done damage. But there is never a case in our law books when the prison authorities have been liable for it. No householder who has been burgled, no person who has been wounded by a criminal, has ever recovered damages from the prison authorities; such as to find a place in the reports. The householder has claimed on his insurance company. The injured man can now claim on the compensation fund. None has claimed against the prison authorities. Should we alter all this: I should be reluctant to do so if, by so doing, we should hamper all the good work being done by our prison authorities' ([1969] 2 Q.B. at p. 426)

Where I differ is in thinking that it is not part of the judicial function to 'alter all this'. The facts of a particular case may be a wholly inadequate basis for a far reaching change of the law. We have not to decide what the law should be and then to alter the existing law. That is the function of Parliament. ([1970] A.C. at 1051)

But in saying that, Lord Dilhorne took a different view from his colleagues' of the permissible range of judicial extension of liability for negligence. Lords Reid, Morris of Borth-y-gest, Pearson, and Diplock all took the 'neighbour principle' as being, in view of its subsequent history, a sufficient supporting ground for a decision in the respondents' favour, even in the absence of other directly relevant authority. Of course, as Lord Diplock warned, it is not a 'universal',[5] and would be misused if it were taken as such— that is, as being a norm of 'mandatory' application in the present sense. It was, as Lord Pearson said,

permissible, indeed almost inevitable that one should revert to the statement of basic principle by Lord Atkin in *Donoghue* v. *Stevenson* [though that] principle is a basic and general but not universal principle and does not in law apply to all the situations which are covered by the wide words of the passage. To some extent the decision in this case must be a matter of impression and instinctive judgment as to what is fair and just. It seems to me that this case ought to, and does, come within the *Donoghue* v. *Stevenson* principle unless there is some sufficient reason for not applying the principle to this case. ([1970] A.C. at p. 1054)

Lord Reid, too, drawing a contrast with the early part of the century when torts involving negligence were conceived as a closed list, observed that,

In later years there has been a steady trend towards regarding the law of negligence as depending on principle so that, when a new point emerges, one should ask not whether it is covered by authority but whether recognised principles apply to it. . .I think the time has come when we can and should say that [the neighbour principle] ought to apply unless there is some justification or valid explanation for its exclusion. ([1970] A.C. at pp. 1026–7)

These strong statements by Lords Reid and Pearson are of interest in that they show a shift from the acceptance of the neighbour principle as a general statement which may be applied in recognizing new areas of negligence liability, if supported by strong reasons of policy and closeness of analogy, to one which ought to be applied unless countervailing reasons be shown. The presumption, the onus of argument, has shifted. The reason for that shift is the steady accretion of judicial experience of the development and

---

[5] [1970] A.C. 1004 at p. 1060.

refinement of this branch of law, and therefore of the constant testing of the principle in new cases, and of its steady reinforcement by its adoption—qualified as necessary—in novel situations. Lord Diplock's speech contains a masterly exposition of the methodology of analogical extension of law and in its discussion of the authorities indicates the steady accretion of force to the principle.

It is important to notice the importance of this process of historical development, in the steady accretion of force to a general statement of legal principle. It is by no means confined to the law of negligence, as we shall see—for an immediate example, the post-war development of the law relating to 'natural justice' is no less obvious. The first, or early, attempts to formulate a rationalizing principle covering an area of legal liability, or legal right, or whatever, function in their original context as justifying or legitimating a judicial extension of law which is positively justified on other, evaluative, grounds as being highly desirable; such formulations 'legitimate' the decision by showing it to follow by way of extrapolation from atomic or fragmentary rules already settled. But no one judge or court can by such a formulation conclusively determine the further development of that branch of law, nor should he. That is one virtue of the legal doctrine that a decision can only be authoritative for the relatively narrowly defined category of facts before the Court. Once formulated, such a principle provides a permissive ground for further development of the law, so far as justified by the desirability (in the judges' view) of particular steps of development, on the basis of 'the cumulative experience of the judiciary'. We may borrow Dworkin's metaphor, and say that at each stage, the balance being weighted against innovation, there must be good consequentialist reasons added to the weight of the principle to bring down the balance in favour of an innovative decision; and it may be that the accumulation of judicial experience goes against extended reliance on the principle. If, on the other hand, it passes the test of revaluation in a steady line of authorities, it may come to acquire such weight as to tip the balance by its own movement, unless what are deemed to be sufficient countervailing reasons of policy or principle (as in *Rondel* v. *Worsley*) tell against it. It passes from being simply permissive to being mandatory subject to defeasance; that point was reached in the *Dorset Yacht Club* case.

It remains true that the appeal to a general principle is—as their Lordships said—not of itself conclusive. The need may be for further evaluative argument in favour, without which a sufficient justification for the decision applying the principle will not be made out, or for contrary evaluative reasons and (as it may be) rebuttal thereof. But it is the adduction of such reasons which must be conclusive of the issue. Either way, the principle sets the limits within which judicial decisions fully justified by consequentialist arguments, are legitimate. Its existence makes permissible to a judge a decision which ought otherwise to be left to the legislature.

The function of 'argument by analogy' is similar, indeed no clear line can be drawn between arguments from principle and from analogy. A neat illustration of the latter is provided by *Steel* v. *Glasgow Iron and Steel Co. Ltd.* (1944 S.C. 237) The guard of a shunting train was killed while trying unsuccessfully to avert an imminent collision with a runaway train which had run loose down a converging gradient due to the carelessness of employees of the defender company. If, instead of trying to take action to protect his employer's property, the guard had looked to his own safety he could clearly have escaped unscathed. But he did not. His widow then sued the defenders for damages and solatium on the ground that her husband's death was due to the actionable negligence of their servants.

The question at issue was whether the guard's action in endangering himself to minimise damage from the imminent colliding should be taken as a *novus actus interveniens* breaking the 'chain of causation' between the defenders' careless act at the top of the hill and the accident to the guard at the bottom of it for the purpose of imputing liability to the Company. Was the guard to be treated as the author of his own misfortune who had voluntarily taken on himself a risk he could have avoided? If so, his injury would be too 'remote' from the act which created the situation of risk to involve liability of the defender.

There was no direct authority on the point, but at the

material time it was already settled in Scots law that a
rescuer's act in saving another person endangered by the
wrongful act of a third person is entitled to reparation from
the latter if he suffers injury,[6] and the English Courts had
followed along the same lines, authoritatively expounded in
Haynes v. *Harwood*.[7] The defenders claimed that that rule
operated exclusively in favour of rescuers of life and limb:
but as Lord Justice-Clerk Cooper observed, 'I do not find in
the previous cases any solid basis for the reclaimers' contention that it is only the rescuer who may claim to "intervene"
with impunity, and that rescuer and "salvor" are necessarily
in classes apart. . .' (1944 S.C. at p. 246). And he went on to
conclude that

> Upon this view the difference between intervention to save life and
> intervention to save property becomes a difference in degree and not a
> difference in kind. In both cases there must be imminent danger and
> sufficient justification for the risk which is assumed. Neither the
> rescuer nor the salvor may embark with impunity upon an act of
> intervention which is unduly hazardous or unwarrantably extreme and
> beyond the exigencies of the situation. In both cases it is necessary
> to weigh the degree of risk to which the rescuer or salvor has exposed
> himself against the value which the law attaches to the stake at peril. . .
> Clearly a much higher degree of risk may normally be taken by a
> rescuer than by a salvor, and in weighing the justification for the
> intervention of a salvor it would usually be necessary to consider not
> only the nature and value of the property sought to be protected and
> the measure of the risk run but also the salvor's antecedent relationship
> or duty, if any, to the property. (Ibid., pp. 248–9)

So the analogy between going to save life endangered by a
wrongful act, and going to save property so endangered, is
sufficient to justify the same conclusion in each case, that
neither rescuer nor salvor is precluded by his voluntarily
taking a risk from asserting a right to reparation from the
wrongdoer who created the risk situation; but the difference
in value between life and property justifies differentiating
between the degrees of danger which it is reasonable to incur.
Again, of course, while the analogy supports, it does not
compel, the result in question—as Lord Mackay's dissenting

---

[6] *Woods* v. *Caledonian Rly.* (1886) 13 R 1118, *Wilkinson* v. *Kinneil Cannel &*
Coking Co. (1897) 24 R 1001.
[7] [1935] 1 K.B. 146 Cf. *Brandon* v. *Osborne Garrett & Co.* [1942] 1 K.B.
548 and *Cutler* v. *United Dairies (London) Ltd.* [1933] 2 K.B. 297.

judgment in favour of drawing a line between salvor and rescuer, shows.[8] The analogy is clear in that all the elements of a 'rescuer' situation are present in a 'salvor' situation, save for the difference between the subject to be saved, importing a difference in the moral value of the act of saving it. The majority's decision entails treating that difference as going not to the existence of liability, but to the degree of risk which it is reasonable to take.

But it is vital to see why the similarity counts as a legally relevant analogy. The answer is in fact made explicit by Lord Cooper in his opinion. 'The view' upon which the difference 'becomes' one of degree, not of kind, is a view of the underlying principle of this branch of law. 'The question being. . . an open one, it must be answered by the application of our native principles of the law of reparation; and by following these principles to their logical conclusion I consider that the desired solution can be found' (ibid., at p. 247). But the principle in question was, in words borrowed from Lord Macmillan,[9] that 'The duty to take care is the duty to avoid doing or omitting to do anything the doing or omitting to do which may have as its reasonable and probable consequence injury to others. . .' And, said Lord Cooper,

. . .human conduct, if reasonable in the sense to be defined, may be one of the reasonable and probable consequences, flowing from an act of negligence, which the ordinary reasonable man ought to foresee. Here I find the ultimate explanation in principle both of the 'alternative risk' cases and of the 'rescue' cases.

That was the view on which 'reasonable' attempts to save property fell to be treated as different only in degree from attempts to rescue life. So the relevance of the analogy is dependent upon perceiving a rational principle within which the two items compared can both be contained—together, as it may be, with other related-type situations.

It has been suggested that it is a limiting requirement of legal justification that decisions in cases not covered by mandatory rules must be shown to be supported by some general legal principle or some relevant analogy, or other

---

[8]   1944 S.C. at pp. 252–65, esp. p. 259.
[9]   *Per* Lord Macmillan in *Bourhill* v. *Young* 1942 S.C. (H.L.) 78 at p. 88, [1943] A.C. 92 at p. 104.

'persuasive' legal source. It would be strange indeed if there were no such limiting requirement, for otherwise it would appear that the judges would have an unlimited power of innovation, save in the areas where clear mandatory rules exist and cannot be 'interpreted', 'distinguished', or 'explained' away.

We need not rest, however, upon this mere *a priori* impression of 'strangeness'. It is not hard to find clear instances of judges' refusing to make extensive innovations, grounded upon absence of sufficient legal warrant for such innovation, even when they expressly concede that good reasons of justice or utility can be advanced in favour of the principle of decision proposed to them by counsel. The force of such illustrations will be the greater if we find express statements by judges whose reputations for creativity and boldness is well established. For that reason, a particularly apt example is to be found in the speech of Lord Reid in *Myers* v. *D.P.P.* ([1965] A.C. 1001 at pp. 1021–2).

I have never taken a narrow view of the functions of this house as an appellate tribunal. The common law must be developed to meet changing economic conditions and habits of thought, and I would not be deterred by expressions of opinion in this house in old cases; but there are limits to what we can do. If we are to extend the law it must be by development and application of fundamental principles. We cannot introduce arbitrary conditions or limitations; that must be left to legislation: and if we do in effect change the law, we ought in my opinion only to do that in cases where our decision will produce some finality or certainty. If we disregard technicalities in this case and seek to apply principle and common sense, there are a number of other parts of the existing law of hearsay susceptible of similar treatment, and we shall probably have a series of appeals in cases where the existing technical limitations produce an unjust result—[I] t seems to me to be against public policy to produce uncertainty. The only satisfactory solution is by legislation. . .

Acting upon this view, he held that certain evidence adduced in a criminal trial for theft of motor cars was inadmissible as being 'hearsay evidence', even although its cogency and reliability was not in doubt. (The evidence in question was the manufacturing company's records of the chassis, engine, and cylinder-block numbers of cars made by them; though the records were retained by the company, it was completely impossible in the case of any given car to trace the particular employee who had made the original record.) Lords Morris of Borth-y-gest and Hodson concurred with him in the view that to admit an exception covering such cases would be beyond the legitimate functions of the House, though Lords Pearce and Donovan were prepared to admit it.

Another nice example from the opinion of a 'strong' judge is provided by a passage from Lord Cooper's judgment in *Drummond's J.F.* v. *H.M. Advocate* (1944 S.C. 298). There the question was whether Scots law should recognize the presumption that when two persons die in a common calamity, the younger is deemed to have survived the older for the purposes of succession law. That presumption of survivorship was recognized in Roman law, yet the second division declined to adopt any such presumption as governing the instant case, ruling that the question which person survived the other was one which had to be answered by the adduction of evidence. Lord Cooper said

If the question had arisen for decision. . .in the later seventeenth century, Scotland might conceivably have adopted, as being in accordance with equity and expediency, the Roman solution or some modification of it. But Scotland did not do so, and I have great difficulty in entertaining the suggestion that, in relation to a problem which must have arisen on many past occasions, we should now for the first time adopt from Rome or from any other source an entirely new solution; for such a step would in the circumstances partake of judicial legislation. (Ibid. at p. 301)

These remarks are particularly instructive in view of the fact, adverted to by Lord Cooper, that in Scots law as a 'civilian' system, there was a time when Roman law might be used in Scotland as a self-sufficient source of principles applicable in the solution of novel problems.[10] But in the modern period, in the absence of any analogous Scots authority in the field, it would be inappropriate simply to incorporate a wholly novel Roman solution for the first time. It would not be a development of principles already recognized, but 'judicial legislation'.

Examples are not proofs. But they help to confirm a

[10] Cf. P. Stein, 'The Influence of Roman Law on the Law of Scotland' (1963) *Jur.Rev.* (N.S.) 205; I am indebted to this article for drawing my attention to the passage quoted.

conclusion which is itself derivable from the reason of the case. Judges, let us say it again, must do justice indeed, but 'justice according to law'. That does not, indeed cannot, mean that judges are only to decide cases in a manner justifiable by simple deduction from mandatory legal rules; yet on the other hand, it cannot mean that they are left free to pursue their own intuitions of justice utility and common sense free of all limitations. The area of their freedom, power, and indeed duty to seek solutions justifiable by an evaluation in consequentialist terms of the needs of the generic case, is limited by the requirement that they show some legal warrant for what they do. The 'general principles' which provide this needed guidance on the one hand, but limitation on the other hand, express the underlying reasons for the specific rules which exist. As such, they are not found but made; to give principle p as the 'underlying reason' of rule r, or rules r, r_2, r_3 and so on, is to impute to those who first introduced it some general policy whose introduction it was supposed to promote, or alternatively to state what seems the best contemporary justification for maintaining it. The content of the rules partly determines the possible range of reasons which could conceivably be adduced as explanatory of them. The contemporary standards of received values (what judges call 'common sense') further limit the matter; only what is conceived good or desirable can count as a policy whose furtherance by the introduction or maintenance of legal rules can be propounded as the underlying justification and rationalization of the rules in question. Statements of 'legal principles' are normative expressions of such rationalizing or justifying policies.

Thus it might be said that the ultimate purpose or underlying policy of the law of tort or delict is the provision of just compensation for injuries to person or property. In the explication of 'just' compensation, the judges have found it necessary to refer to a complementary, sometimes conflicting, policy of protecting individuals from incurring legal liability in cases in which they were not to blame for accidents resulting from their acts, at least (in the modern period) if they could not reasonably have been expected to insure against the occurrence of such accidents. Normative expressions of the desirability of attaining these policies are statements of principle: 'There should be no liability without fault'; and, 'Persons should be liable for all damage accruing to others by reason of their fault' are such statements of principle.

Acceptance of these principles plainly supplies a rationalization of, and thus a justifying reason for, many of the detailed case-law and statute-based rules of the law of torts and delict. As such, therefore, they provide a necessary (albeit not sufficient) element of justification for the extension of the law by enunciation of new specific rules of liability in novel type-cases, as we saw in the context of the *Dorset Yacht Club* case.[11] I think it will not be doubted, either that such principles *can* be adduced in rationalizing justification of that branch of law, or that they *are* at present accepted by many judges and lawyers as being the rationalizing principles of the law—both by those who endorse them warmly as a matter of personal conviction, and by those who would rather see them supplemented by doctrines of 'liability for risk'.

As to that, it must at once be said that not the whole law of torts can be subsumed under the single principle of 'No liability without fault' and its converse. As Lord Simonds observed in *Read* v. *J. Lyons & Co. Ltd.* ([1947] A.C. 156 at p. 180): 'Here is an age long conflict of theories which is to be found in every system of law. "A man acts at his peril" says one theory "A man is not liable unless he is to blame" answers the other. It will not suprise the students of English law or of anything English to find that between these theories a middle way, a compromise has been found.'

Read's case itself was a demarcation dispute between the two 'theories' or 'principles'. The appellant, a government inspector in a wartime munitions factory, was injured by an explosion which occurred when shells were being filled with high explosive. She claimed damages from the operators of the factory, without averring negligence on their part. Her contention was that in any case of dangerous substances which escape from control causing injury to persons or property, the party in control of the substance is liable in

---

[11] [1970] A.C. 1004; *supra*, pp. 158–161.

damages for that injury without proof of fault on his part. That is, she founded her claim on 'the principle laid down in *Rylands* v. *Fletcher* ([1868] L.R. 3 H.L. 330)'.[12] He who conducts a highly hazardous activity ought to bear the risk of accidents occurring and causing damage, whether damage to property, or injuries to persons, and whether or not any dangerous thing or substance escapes from the property of the undertaker, it was urged by her counsel.

This contention was unanimously rejected by the House of Lords in its application to the instant facts. Even those who were prepared to concede that strict liability under the *Rylands* v. *Fletcher* rule might exist in cases of personal injuries insisted upon the requirement of escape of the dangerous substance from the defendant's premises or land. 'It was urged. . .', said Lord Porter[13], 'that it would be a strange result to hold the respondents liable if the injured person was just outside their premises but not liable if she was just within them. There is force in the objection, but the liability [sc. for personal injuries under *Rylands* v. *Fletcher*] is an extension of the general rule, and, in my view, *it is undesirable to extend it further*.' The passage italicized explicitly acknowledges that in such a case, where there are competing principles which could provide the necessary legal support for a decision either way, the final choice between them must be based upon an evaluation of which general principle it is desirable to follow in the type of case in question.

The same observation follows from this more extensive passage from Lord Macmillan's speech:

Whatever may have been the law of England in early times I am of opinion that, as the law now stands an allegation of negligence is in general essential to the relevancy of an action of reparation for personal injuries. The gradual development of the law in the matter of civil liability is discussed and traced with ample learning and lucidity in HOLDSWORTH'S HISTORY OF ENGLISH LAW, Vol. 8 pp. 446 et seq., and need not here be rehearsed. Suffice it to say that the process of evolution has been from the principle that every man acts at his peril and is liable for all the consequences of his acts to the principle that a man's freedom of action is subject only to the obligation not to infringe any duty of care which he owes to others. The emphasis formerly was on the injury sustained and the question was whether

---

[12] *Per* Lord Porter [1947] A.C. 156 at p. 175.
[13] Ibid. at pp. 177–8; italics added.

the case fell within one of the accepted classes of common law actions; the emphasis now is on the conduct of the person whose act has occasioned the injury and the question is whether it can be characterised as negligent. I do not overlook the fact that there is at least one instance in the present law in which the primitive rule survives, namely, in the case of animals ferae naturae or animals mansuetae naturae which have shown dangerous proclivities. The owner or keeper of such an animal has an absolute duty to confine or control it so that it shall not do injury to others and no proof of care on his part will absolve him from responsibility but this is probably not so much a vestigial relic of otherwise discarded doctrine as a special rule of practical good sense. At any rate, it is too well established to be challenged. But such an exceptional case as this affords no justification for its extension by analogy. (Ibid. at pp. 170−1)

It is perfectly clear here, as elsewhere in his speech, that Lord Macmillan regards adherence to fault as a condition of liability for personal injury as being a more desirable, because a more just, policy, than the alternative possibility of making undertakers of dangerous activities insurers of the risk of accidents to others occurring even without lapse of care. So although the 'analogy' with animals cases *could* provide relevant legal support for a more generalized doctrine of risk liability covering personal injuries, by extension of the *Rylands* v. *Fletcher* rule, it *should* not be used so as to create such liability. The case of *scienter* liability is 'exceptional' and *ought not* to be 'exten[ded] by analogy'.

There is no difficulty in multiplying such illustrations of conflict of legal doctrines or principles, where there are two (or more) recognized principles each of which is by its own terms applicable to the events in dispute, with the result that a decision either way can be adequately supported at law. The case is thus such that the Court may permissibly and legitimately given a ruling either way; accordingly, although appeal to one or other principle is a necessary, it cannot be a sufficient or conclusive justification of the decision actually given. The Scots case of *White & Carter (Councils) Ltd.* v. *McGregor* ([1962] A.C. 413; 1962 S.C. (H.L.) 1) was one in which the appellants sued the respondent for the price due under an advertising contract, whereby the appellants were to advertise the name of the respondent's garage on litter-bins over a three-year period. The contract was made with the manager of the respondent's garage, but on the very day on which it had been made the respondent repudiated the contract by a letter written as soon as he heard of it. Although the appellants had taken no steps in performance of the contract they refused to accept repudiation, and in due course went ahead with the advertisements as agreed. They then claimed their full price due under the contract, to which the respondent replied that they were entitled only to damages for breach of the contract, calculated on the basis of loss of profit, rather than the full price. By a bare majority, the House of Lords reversed the interlocutor of the Second Division, and upheld the appellants' claim.

The principle to which the majority gave effect in the case was that a contract cannot be revoked by the unilateral repudiation of one party, but is only revoked if the other party accepts the repudiation and elects to sue for damages. 'The general rule cannot be in doubt,' said Lord Reid. '. . .If one party to a contract repudiates it. . .the other party. . .has an option. He may accept that repudiation and sue for damages for breach of contract whether or not the time for performance has come; or he may if he chooses disregard or refuse to accept it and then the contract remains in full effect' (ibid. at p. 427, 11–12, respectively).

As against that, there is an equally well-established 'general rule' or 'principle' that a party who has sustained damage as a result of another's breach of contract must take reasonable steps 'in mitigation of damages', to minimize his own loss and thus to minimize the compensation recoverable. If he fails to take such steps, the party in breach is nevertheless liable only to compensate for such loss as the other would have incurred had he taken reasonable steps to minimize his loss. The only exception to this principle is in cases of contracts for which the remedy of specific implement (*anglice* specific performance) may be granted. To this Lord Morton of Henryton adverted in contending for dismissal of the appeal.

The innocent party is entitled to be compensated by damages for any loss which he has suffered by reason of the breach, and in a limited class of cases the Court will decree specific implement. The law of Scotland provides no other remedy for a breach of contract, and there is no reported case which decides that the innocent party may act as the appellants have acted. The present case is one in which specific implement could not be decreed, since the only obligation of the respondent under the contract was to pay a sum of money for services to be rendered by the appellants. Yet the appellants are claiming a kind of inverted specific implement of the contract. They first insist on performing their part of the contract, against the will of the other party, and then claim that he must perform his part and pay the contract price for unwanted services. In my opinion, my Lords, the appellants' only remedy was damages, and they were bound to take steps to minimise their loss, according to a well-established rule of law. Far from doing this, having incurred no expense at the date of the repudiation, they made no attempt to procure another advertiser, but deliberately went on to incur expense and perform unwanted services with the intention of creating a money debt which did not exist at the date of the repudiation. (Ibid, at pp. 432–3, 16, respectively).

It was neither contested, nor open to doubt, that the respondent in the case was legally in the wrong, that he had broken his contract with the appellants, who were accordingly entitled to *some* remedy. The question was, *what* remedy. Since there were available two 'general rules' or 'well-established rules', or (we might say) 'principles' either of which was applicable to the facts, it is as plain as can be that the bare applicability of one or the other could not provide a decisive justification; what was needed was a choice between them, and the justification of that choice was a matter for evaluative argument. It is of interest to note one of the arguments of counsel for the respondent, which was adopted by the dissentient Lords Morton and Keith, and which gave some embarrassment to the majority.[14] The argument is a neat illustration of our earlier observations about generalization and testing by hypothetical examples as exhibiting the characteristic form of consequentialist argument.

In the majority of cases the innocent party cannot perform the contract without the concurrence of the party repudiating the contract, who must either allow or accept something, and so the refusal of that cooperation results in the innocent party being obliged to restrict his claim to damages. Even where this is not so, it would be contrary to public policy that he should be permitted to do so. An expert employed by a large company to travel abroad for the purpose of drafting an elaborate report should not be allowed to waste thousands of pounds in preparing it if the company has repudiated the contract

[14] See [1962] A.C. 413 at 428–9, 430–1 *per* Lord Reid, p. 445 *per* Lord Hodson.

before anything has been done under it. A far smaller amount of damages would compensate him for his loss, and any other view would only enable him to extort in settlement far more than reasonable compensation.

The contention of the appellant company is unsupported by authority or common sense. It did not take account of the cases where the innocent party is physically unable to perform the contract without invoking the assistance of the Court. But there is no distinction in principle between such cases as those and other cases. For example, a painter employed to paint a portrait, and then told not to do so, could not normally paint it if the subject would not sit for him. But suppose the subject was a public man and the painter could paint him without his consent in public places? Or take the case of the garage owner employed to repair a car. What if the car was left parked in the street where he could get at it? In neither case should the law allow the unwanted services to be rendered because of such accidental circumstances.

Suppose a firm entered into a contract with an advertising agency to advertise a new soap on television and in the newspapers but soon afterwards discovered that it was liable to cause skin disease and took it off the market, cancelling the contract with the advertising agents. The advertising agents would not be entitled to go on with the advertising campaign although the contract was cancelled. (*per* Bennett Q.C. *arguendo* [1962] A.C. at pp. 422–3; cf. 1962 S.C. (H.L.) 8–11)

Having adduced those reasons of policy, justice, and 'common sense', in favour of the respondent's contention counsel proceeded to distinguish the cases on anticipatory breach to show that they did not compel a decision the other way: 'Cases on anticipatory breaches of contract are not relevant here because they go no further than to show that the innocent party has a right not to perform it in the face of repudiation. . .' (ibid at p. 423). Counsel was even prepared to argue the point of disutility on a macroeconomic view:

If it is a matter of public policy that the resources of the nation should not be wasted, it follows that the court will not compel the guilty party who does not want performance to submit to it, although, as here, he derives no benefit from it. It is contrary to public policy that the innocent party should swell his own profits by insisting on going on with performance in rendering services or manufacturing goods which no one wants. The respondent is not seeking to make any inroad into the sanctity of contracts. The appellant company's contentions lead to commerical and economic absurdity with far-reaching and serious consequences. Justice would be done here simply by a claim for damages for breach of contract. (Ibid. at pp. 423–4)

The decision in the case necessarily involved choosing

between the values of keeping parties to the contracts they have made, and protecting the rights of innocent parties to contracts (who may sometimes lose everything by refusing to accept repudiation and waiting for the time of performance[15]) on the one hand and on the other, considerations of the sort urged by counsel in the passages quoted, and adopted by Lords Morton and Keith. The justification of the decision must depend upon the reasoned assessment of the relative, or comparative, desirability and undesirability of the consequences which the decision as a decision of principle will entail. But it can only fall within the judges' rather than the legislature's province to make such evaluations and give effect to them if there exist within the law competing analogies or general rules or principles such that the decision—whichever way made—can be shown to be supported by the existing law even though it be not compelled one way or the other by an unequivocal rule of mandatory character.

It can also happen that a single 'general rule', or 'principle' is clearly recognized, and accepted by the parties to a litigated case as the governing principle covering their dispute, but that there is a contest over the result to which it ought to lead in the particular dispute. That parties claiming damages for breach of contract or for breach of a delictal duty are 'bound to take steps to minimise their loss' is indeed well established. But what if a large company takes over a smaller, and instals its man as managing director, displacing the former managing director in beach of his contract while offering him a subordinate post at the same salary as he previously had? Must the demoted managing director swallow his pride and minimize, or indeed eliminate, his pecuniary loss by accepting?[16] Or what if a dentist who buys himself a new Rover car every second year to be sure of getting to his surgery punctually and dependably has his present car smashed up in an accident caused by another's negligence? Must he, contrary to his invariable previous practice, buy himself a second-hand car at once, or is he entitled, at the defendant's expense, to hire himself a mint-new car while waiting for

---

[15] Cf. *Avery* v. *Bowden* (1855) 5 El. Bl. 714.
[16] *Yetton* v. *Eastwoods Froy Ltd.* [1966] 3 All E.R. 353.

delivery of a new car on sale?[17] In each case, the courts apply the test of reasonableness, and in each case they found that plaintiffs who rejected the job in the first case[18] and who insisted on the new car in the second case[19] had acted reasonably, so the damages need not be reduced as against them. Such conclusions plainly depend on evaluation, and the rulings made yield new concrete rules subsumed under the wide rubric of the overriding principle.

Again, it is trite law that in all claims for civil damages the principle governing assessment of damages is that the plaintiff is to recover full compensation for the loss he has suffered as a result of the other's wrong, but not more than compensation (except in those cases in which English law exceptionally allows aggravated or punitive damages). But how does that principle apply if a very highly paid engineer is seriously injured in a railway accident caused by negligence, so that he can no longer sustain his high level of earnings by work? If £n represents his gross annual earnings, and he is wholly incapacitated from work, and might otherwise have worked m more years, is he entitled to £mn as damages? Should we not take some account of the fact that an annual income of £n is subject to £x income tax and surtax? In that case his damages of £$m(n-x)$ will fully compensate him for his actual loss.

When the problem came before the House of Lords in *B.T.C.* v. *Gourley* ([1956] A.C. 185) the majority favoured this latter aproach, even though in doing so they overruled a fair number of contrary authorities, both Scots and English (none of which had House of Lords'-sanction). Said Lord Reid

It is true that there are several authorities and a long line of practice against taking tax liability into account in assessing damages, but this is not the type of case in which vested interests may have accrued or in which people may have ordered their affairs relying on the validity of existing practice. In my opinion, this is a case in which it is proper for your lordships to consider the question on its merits as one of principle.

The general principle on which damages are assessed is not in doubt. A successful plaintiff is entitled to have awarded to him such

[17] *Moore* v. *D.E.R. Ltd.* [1971] 3 All E.R. 517
[18] *Supra*, n. 16.   [19] *Supra*, n. 17.

a sum as will, so far as possible, make good to him the financial loss which he has suffered and will probably suffer as a result of the wrong done to him for which the defendant is responsible. . .

The real question in this case is whether the liability to pay taxes is something which the law must regard as too remote to be taken into account [the '*res inter alios acta*' principle being irrelevant] . (Ibid. at pp. 216−18)

His Lordship then argued that the law could not, consistently with that general principle treat tax liability as 'too remote' in the assessment of damages. To award a plaintiff a sum to compensate loss of past and future earnings calculated on the basis of gross earnings without any reduction for tax payable on such gross earnings, would be to give the plaintiff a windfall, a greater sum in compensation than he would in fact have obtained had he not been put out of work. Liability to pay tax, whether tax was (as in the case of P.A.Y.E.) deductible before payment of salary to a plaintiff, or assessed and paid in arrears (as in the case of surtax), was a liability arising under the general law of the land, applying to every person as a citizen earning income. It was a necessary and unavoidable charge on income, not a contingent and personal one; thus it was distinguishable from the converse situation of a plaintiff who had as it happened taken out an insurance policy which covered the very sort of injuries he had suffered. This contingent and personal act of prudence, though it might in effect diminish or eliminate pecuniary loss accruing to the plaintiff, was rightly to be regarded as too remote to be taken into account in assessing damages as against the defendant.

A further difficulty for his Lordship's view on the merits of the case concerned the applicability of the rule (laid down in the case) that income net of tax was the measure of damages for loss of earnings to cases of wrongful dismissal from employment. Why, it had been urged, should an employer who wrongfully dismissed an employee thereby reduce his own expenditure? Under the rule contemplated the employer, who would have had to pay the full gross salary if the contract had stood, would find it cheaper to break than to keep the contract since his liability would now be in respect of income net of tax, thereby gaining by his own wrong. To that point his Lordship gave two answers:

first that the proper function of damages, under the received principle, is to compensate the innocent party for his actual loss, not to penalize the wrongdoer; and secondly, that there was in truth no gain to the employer, since he had to employ someone else to do the job of the dismissed man, unless work of the kind performed by him was no longer required by the employer; so the employer either had to pay twice for services he required, or to pay compensation for services which he did not require, and in neither case could he be said to be 'gaining' anything.

Lord Keith of Avonholm, however, came to the opposite conclusion[20] as to the proper application of the general principle of damages-as-compensation-only in the class of case before the Court. If A and B each earn £2,000 per year, and both are badly injured and thus put out of work, it is rightly regarded as irrelevant (because 'too remote') in assessing damages if A (say) happens to have a wealthy wife with a large income, even although in that case A may in fact need less compensation than B. But by taking into account tax liability, you will in effect make A's wife's income relevant to his entitlement to damages, since spouses' incomes were always at that time aggregated for tax purposes. Of the alternative rules available to the courts, 'The first alternative [gross earnings as the basis of damages] provides a simple rule which has been adopted for generations and creates the minimum of trouble. The second alternative must, I think, give rise to serious difficulties and complications' (ibid. at p. 216).

Among such difficulties he mentioned the question of possible liability to foreign tax, which would necessarily be covered by the same rule as British tax, but proof of which would raise formidable complications. Another difficulty, which goes at least as much to justice as to convenience, concerns the question whether the plaintiff would not have been able in future so to arrange his affairs as to reduce his over-all tax liability, by entering into covenants or taking out appropriate insurance policies. It would be unfair to rule out the possibility of the plaintiff's taking such steps legitimately

[20] See especially [1956] A.C. at pp. 216–18.

to diminish his tax liability, but hopelessly speculative for courts to try to take the possibility of such steps into account.

Moreover, there was a constitutional point involved. It is a fundamental principle that Parliament and Parliament alone has authority to impose taxes. The rule favoured by the majority savoured of extra-Parliamentary taxation. 'If there is a case for thinking that assessing damages on a basis of gross earnings in actions for personal injuries or for wrongful dismissal, enables the individual to escape his fair contribution to the national revenue, the position, in my opinion, should be rectified by legislation' (ibid. at p. 218). (It is fair to remark that Parliament's necessary annual concern with taxation in the Finance Act makes such an appeal to Parliament as the proper legislature much more reasonable than when it is resorted to in cases of pure lawyers' law.)

Thus *Gourley's* case nicely illustrates that even when it is tritely true that there is a single well-established and often reiterated principle of law which is accepted by all parties as the governing principle of the branch of law in question, its application to a particular factual problem may well be a matter of reasonable controversy. Acceptance of the principle as the relevant governing norm can only provide guidance as to the relevant evaluative considerations which may legitimately be used in justification of a concrete ruling one way or the other. The principle determines the legitimate range of justifying considerations; it does not, and cannot, be represented as yielding a conclusive answer.

Moreover it is of interest to note the appeal made by Lords Reid and Keith severally to two different principles at decisive points in their arguments. It will be recalled that Lord Reid justified departing from settled authorities and established practice, by pointing out that the decision he proposed involved no disappointment of established expectations nor divestment of vested rights. That is he contended for the inapplicability of the principle that courts should not upset the expectations of parties who have acted in reliance on one view of the law, nor interfere with rights presumptively vested, by laying down novel rules at variance with prior practice. (Alternatively, he applied the converse principle that Courts may innovate where expectations or vested rights are not prejudiced.) Consideration of these principles was plainly ancillary to the main justification offered by Lord Reid for the rule proposed by him.

In like manner, Lord Keith's animadversion to the principle that questions of taxation are within the exclusive competence of Parliament[21] was ancillary to his principal argument. Being persuaded of the greater convenience and justice of the gross-earnings rule, he was able to cite that principle in further support of his argument, as a powerful auxiliary justification.

It may be thought that the discussion so far of the use of general legal principles in legal argument has failed fully to account for their importance. The speeches in the *Dorset Yacht Club* and *Gourley* cases seem to indicate that the principles used in justification played a more important role than merely that of necessary elements in justification. It might well be said that the neighbour principle and the principle of damages as compensation only, were clearly accepted as the norms which ought to govern the decision, and that the other arguments adduced were merely supplementary. In each case, at the very least, the principle in question fell to be applied unless some strong countervailing reason—of principle or of policy—could be advanced against applying it. In such cases, the existence of a well-established —that is, frequently and authoritatively recognized, enunciated, and applied—principle, provides in itself a strong if not compelling and indefeasible reason justifying the decision of the case one way rather than the other. The point could be taken at least as strongly in relation to the modern development of administrative law. At least since the decision in *Ridge* v. *Baldwin* ([1964] A.C. 564), for example, the principle that a person is entitled to a fair hearing before any decision seriously affecting important interests of his is taken by anyone exercising public or quasi-public power, has come to be accepted as being of practically mandatory application in any relevant situation; that the principle is applicable is taken to be a sufficient justification for a decision applying it unless some strong countervailing reason

---

[21] As to which, see e.g., *Attorney General* v. *Wilts United Dairies* (1921) 37 T.L.R. 884, and *Hotel and Catering Industry Training Board* v. *Automobile Proprietary Ltd.* [1969] 2 All E.R. 582, and [1968] 3 All E.R. 399.

can be convincingly put against applying it.[22] It might even be argued that there is no possibility of drawing a real, hard and fast distinction between well-established principles and mandatory legal rules.[23]

There is much truth in this, but it is important not to exaggerate it. First, let it be conceded that consistency and coherence as between related legal rules in similar areas of law is itself an important legal value, being indeed one aspect of justice, of treating like cases alike and refraining from arbitrary differentiation of cases. To return to an earlier example, it would appear irrational to have one rule according to which rescuers of life had a right to compensation for injuries suffered as against those negligently endangering life, and then to lay down a rule that salvors of property had no analogous right. But that proposition holds good only if the former rule is conceived to be a good and beneficial rule. There are after all numerous instances in which judges have declined analogously to extend rules which they conceived to be 'anomalous' or 'exceptional'—as we saw in Read v. Lyons.[24] If we are stuck with one incontrovertible mandatory rule which we conceive to be disadvantageous or unjust, there is a greater rationality in refusing to extend it than in extending it.[25] It is regular judicial practice in such cases to deprecate an excessive regard for 'logic'.[26] So if consistency is only good in the context of consistent extension of and generalization from rules conceived to be good on ground other than that they manifest instances of well-established legal principles, it is hard to avoid the conclusion that the decisive consideration is judges' and lawyers' evaluations and perceptions of desirable lines of legal development. What is more such evaluations and perceptions change through time. Read v. Lyons was perhaps the high-water mark of judicial reverence for 'no liability without fault'. Thus although it is true that at any point in time there exist in a legal system recognized

[22] See, e.g., *Malloch* v. *Aberdeen Corporation* 1971 S.C. (H.L.) 85.
[23] Cf. C.H. Tapper, 'A Note on Principles' (1972) 34 *M.L.R.* 628.
[24] [1947] A.C. 156, *supra*, pp. 167–169.
[25] Cf. *Cassell & Co. Ltd.* v. *Broome* [1972] A.C. 1027 at p. 1086 (*per* Lord Reid).
[26] Cf. p. 40 *supra*.

principles which are conceived as expressing fundamental or at least important values of the system, so that they tend to be regarded as supplying self-sufficient justifications of decisions, in the absence of countervailing considerations, this is so because the values they express are conceived to be overriding. Moreover, the possibility of admitting countervailing considerations indicates that such principles can never be conclusive in the way in which we have so far suggested mandatory rules may be. To this extent at least, we are justified in suggesting that in cases covered by no indistinguishable mandatory rule, the applicability of a general principle, although it is a necessary, is not a conclusive jusitification for acting upon a novel rule.

The same proposition has been suggested as to the legal force of argument by analogy. A neat illustrative example is provided by the case of *R.* v. *Arthur* ([1968] 1 Q.B. 810). One Edward David Arthur was charged at Assizes on an indictment, count one of which charged that he 'at Gravesend in the county of Kent on August 31st 1967 maliciously set fire to a dwelling house, one Edward David Arthur being therein, contrary to s. 2 of the Malicious Damage Act 1861'. That section is in the following terms:

Whoever shall unlawfully and maliciously set fire to any dwelling house, any person being therein, shall be guilty of felony.

The Statute makes this an aggravated form of arson, as against setting fire to an empty dwelling house, for which the penalties are lesser.

For the defendant, Abdela Q.C. moved to quash this count of the indictment on the ground that the statute should not be construed as contemplating the situation in which the accused was the only person in the dwelling house at the time of the act of arson. It would be absurd to treat differently someone who set fire to his own house before leaving it, and someone who threw a lighted match in the window after leaving home. Although judicial dicta[27] and Archbold supported the view that such an indictment was valid, the act ought to be construed as applying only to the case in which the accused was alleged to have set fire to a dwelling house,

---

[27] *R.* v. *Pardoe* (1897) 17 Cox C.C. 715 *per* Coleridge C.J.

some other person being inside it. In support of this proposition, he drew Howard J.'s attention to the terms of s.18 of the Offences against the Person Act 1861:

Whosoever shall unlawfully and maliciously by any means whatsoever wound or cause any grievous bodily harm to any person. . .

That section, he pointed out, had never been and could not reasonably be interpreted as applying to cases of self-inflicted wounds. Since both the statutes were enacted in the same year by Parliament, the rational conclusion was to take 'any person' in the same sense in each case, as applying only to persons other than the accused.

Notwithstanding the Crown's argument that the analogy was inapposite, because s.18 could apply to cases of self-mutilation and because, in any event, suicide was a crime at time of the enactment, Howard J. was persuaded by the defendant's argument, though not without some evident reluctance. The problem, in his view, was that the defence case in effect depended on reading into the act a word not included by Parliament, as though s.2 had said 'any *other* person being therein'. 'I think that would be really a matter for Parliament, and this court would be legislating, and not administering the Statute [which] is what has to be done' (ibid. at p. 812).

Quite evidently from the terms of his judgment he treated the analogy drawn with s.18 of the Offences Against the Person Act as the crucial turning-point justifying his acceptance of the defendant's motion:

Mr. Abdela has called attention to the fact that section 18 of the Offences against the Person Act, 1861, an Act passed in the same year, uses the identical wording. . .Nobody has apparently heard. . .of anybody being prosecuted under that section for unlawfully and maliciously causing grievous bodily harm to himself. One only has to state the proposition to realise what a remarkable interpretation it would be. . . [O]n the whole I think that the reasonable construction of [s.2 of the Malicious Damage Act] is not the one which has been acted upon for many years. . .'[A]ny person being therein' must, upon a reasonable construction, refer to some person other than the setter on fire (Ibid. at p. 813)

Yet it is no less clear that the analogy used did not make the decision given obligatory. The existence of the analogy did not compel Howard J. to reach the conclusion he reached; rather it was in his view crucial in showing that a conclusion otherwise desirable was permissible in law. The analogy provided legal support for, not legal compulsion of, the decision given. The passages cited from the judgment make it crystal clear that Howard J. would not have deemed it justifiable to quash that count of the indictment but for the existence of a sufficient analogy between the two Acts. Again, it may be observed that the underlying justification of this approach lies in the presumed value of consistency as between related branches of law. Only given the presupposition both that a rational legislature ought to have a similar policy in mind in adopting similar phraseology in two codifying criminal statutes passed in the same year, and that the British Parliament is, or should be treated as, a rational legislature adhering to such coherent policies, can the observed use of the analogy in question be conceived as a relevant justification.

A not dissimilar, though perhaps weaker[28] case showing the same points is *Norwich Pharmacal Ltd.* v. *Commissioners of Customs and Excise* ([1972] Ch. 566) in which Graham J. ordered the Commissioners to disclose to the plaintiff company the names of importers who had to their knowledge imported into the country a chemical substance for which the plaintiff had the patent, in alleged infringement of the patent. The Commissioners contended that the statutes conferring on them power to require importers to disclose the nature of goods imported by them imposed also an implied duty of confidentiality such that it was unlawful for them to make discovery of the particulars sought by the plaintiff. The learned judge, rejecting this contention, found supporting justification in the practice whereby the police are authorized to give to parties involved in car accidents particulars as to the other parties involved,[29] even though such particulars were learned by them in the exercise of public powers and in pursuit of public duties. 'As a practical matter, both cases are

[28] [1972] Ch. 556 'Weaker' in so far as the analogy mentioned was in its context less all-important. Graham J.'s decision was reversed by the Court of Appeal, [1974] A.C. 133; but restored by the House of Lords on final appeal [1974] A.C. 133.

[29] 'Ultimately derived' as Graham J. pointed out, from such statutory rules as s.27 of the Vehicle and Driving Licences Act 1969. There were other supporting grounds: see ibid., pp. 582–4. And for the evaluative justification, see pp. 578–9.

in principle analogous, although the former [the police practice] may be ultimately derived from a statute, such as s.27 of the Vehicle and Driving Licences Act 1969. . .and if the interests of justice demand it in the one case, why should they not demand it in the other?' (ibid. at p. 584).

The power to order discovery of documents exercised in the case is a power conferred upon judges by the Supreme Court of Judicature Act 1925, and regulated by Rules of the Supreme Court made thereunder; prior to 1969 there was a common-law rule in virtue of which Ministers of the Crown had power to make conclusive claims of privilege from discovery in relation to documents belonging to classes of documents whose disclosure they deemed injurious to the public interest. That rule was, however, reversed by the House of Lords in the case of *Conway* v. *Rimmer* ([1968] A.C. 910), in which they laid down that the Courts had power to override such ministerial claims of privilege where they were of opinion that that public interest in ensuring the proper administration of justice outweighed the public interest in non-disclosure. That common-law rule—a rule of mandatory character *vis-à-vis* a puisne judge—in conjunction with the statutory rule, was applied by Graham J. in making the order he made. Be it observed that in this aspect, the justifying argument of the judge does not involve argument from analogy. If we are to use terms with any precision, we must distinguish the direct application of rules whose application is mandatory, from instances in which a statute or precedent laying down a clear rule for one set of operative facts is cited in justification for a decision establishing that a similar or the same normative consequence is to follow from a similar set of operative facts. The former case, the case of direct application involves expressly or impliedly the use of deductive argument as a sufficient and conclusive justification; the latter does not. In the *Norwich Pharmacal* case, the rule 'If a party to litigation seeks discovery of relevant documents, then the judge has power to order the party having custody of the documents to disclose them for inspection, and to override claims of Crown privilege on the following grounds. . .' yields by simple deduction the conclusion that the particular judge has power to grant an order for discovery at the instance of the particular plaintiff.

The difficulties in the case concerned whether or not the judge should exercise that discretionary power; against the argument that he should not because there was a duty on the Commissioners to maintain confidentiality, he advanced (*inter alia*) the police analogy mentioned above. A further and more central difficulty was that the normal use of the power to order discovery is only as between two parties to a dispute; but in the instant case the plaintiff's substantive claim for infringement of their patent lay against as yet unidentified third parties, whose names were known to the Commissioners in virtue of importers' customs declarations made to them. Thus it was contended for the Commissioners that the power to order discovery could not legitimately be exercised as against them. In Graham J.'s judgment, the decisive counter-argument 'the vital matter in this case' derived from the cases of *Orr* v. *Diaper*,[30] *Upmann* v. *Elkan*[31] and related authorities. He said:

The plaintiffs in [*Orr's* case] had had their rights invaded by third parties, exporters, whose names they did not know. The defendants were shippers of the exporters' goods which were counterfeits of the plaintiff's marks. The defendants refused when asked to give the names of the exporters and were sued for discovery. It was submitted that the defendants were mere witnesses, but Hall V-C said[32] [that their position, they being the actual shippers, was different from that of mere witnesses, and that a denial of justice to the plaintiffs would result if the shippers could refuse to disclose the consignor's name.] (Ibid. at p. 579)

I do not think that the fact that the confidential information had been obtained as a result of statutory powers rather than in some other way makes any difference to the circumstances under which it should be retained or disclosed as the case may be. This is supported by the recent decision of Forbes J. in *Alfred Crompton Amusement Machines Ltd.* v. *Commissioners of Customs and Excise*.[33] (Ibid. at p. 582)

It seems to me that in order that justice may be done and done as speedily and cheaply as possible thus avoiding the cost of extensive further enquiries by the plaintiffs it is highly desirable that the short cut should be taken and the commissioners made to disclose the names in question. (Ibid. at p. 584)

[30] (1876) 4 Ch. D. 92.
[31] (1871) L.R. 12 Eq. 140.
[32] See (1876) 4 Ch. D. at p. 96.
[33] Unreported (15 July 1971) see [1972] 2 Q.B. 106A–116G.

It is perfectly plain that a rational distinction could be drawn (as the Commissioners argued) between the *Orr* type of case, where a private party is in direct contractual relations with the potential (but unknown) defendant, and the instant case in which the relevant information had come into the Commissioners' hands in the exercise of a public power conferred by statute. Therefore it cannot be said that the ruling in *Orr* applied directly and of its own force to the circumstances of the *Norwich Pharmacal* case.

Apart from that potentially important dissimilarity, the points of similarity were (1) alleged infringement of a right having the nature of 'industrial property' (2) by improper use of goods (3) belonging to unidentified third parties (4) alleged to be guilty of the infringement (5) whose identity was known to the defendant (6) who had some degree of control over the goods whose use constituted the infringement (7) therefore being more than 'mere witnesses'. So the question remains *ought* the instant case to be decided in the same way as the precedent (by ordering discovery), given the significant difference of relationship between the defendant and the unidentified third party in the two cases? There are two levels to the answer: first what were the underlying reasons of principle by which the precedent decision was justified (or what such reasons can justifiably be imputed?) If these justifying policy considerations apply with similar force to the different circumstances of the instant case, then at least the argument from coherence is applicable. Then secondly, is the policy a good one to pursue (a) in itself and (b) in the circumstances of the case before the Court? This is, of course a matter for judicial evaluation along the lines earlier discussed, and that evaluation is the ultimately decisive factor. Looking at it in this abstract way, we may say that the first level is more or less cognitive, the second more or less evaluative, although as scrutiny of Graham J.'s opinion reveals—and the observation is essentially a general one—in the concrete, real-life argument the two levels are inextricably intermingled.

Again, of course, it has to be remarked, when we speak of relevant similarities in the context of analyzing analogies, that similarities are made not found. There is probably no marked visual similarity (for instance) between the Commissioners sitting in their London office receiving declarations about goods imported and the shipper, Diaper, shipping counterfeit trade-marked goods out of the country. What is crucial is that in an earlier case a Court in making and justifying its ruling in law subsumed the facts in issue within certain categories. The new case partially overlaps in the sense that its facts can be assigned to a partially similar set of categories, or a set of categories which, together with the earlier set, can be presented as species of some larger genus. The 'similarity' between the cases is similarity in respect of those categories. In so far as there were stated or can be suggested good consequentialist arguments which justify the prior ruling in law, these arguments can be advanced to justify a similar ruling for the present partially similar case, and indeed for any case belonging to this new category. But of course there may be counter-arguments based on adverse consequences arising from consideration of the differentiating material facts. Thus does 'argument by analogy' support without compelling innovative judicial decisions. This explanation further indicates why no clear line of distinction can be drawn between argument from legal principle and argument from analogy. Analogies only make sense if there are reasons of principle underlying them.

The difference really is only in the degree of explicitness with which a principle has hitherto been stated. The 'neighbour principle' once stated makes explicit a ground for treating as relevantly analogous cases similar in some respects to *Donoghue* v. *Stevenson* ([1932] A.C. 562; 1932 S.C. (H.L.) 31). On the other hand, the following of an analogy in a particular case may often provide the ground for making articulate some new, wider, statement of a principle, as the *Norwich Pharmacal*[34] case and *Steel's*[35] case show; but it need not, as *R.* v. *Arthur*[36] shows.

If such forms of argument are not compelling in the sense of a judge's having a duty to decide the new case similarly to

---

[34] [1972] Ch. 566; [1974] A.C. 133.   [35] 1944 S.C. 237.
[36] [1968] 1 Q.B. 810.

the analogous one, or to interpret the statute in question similarly to the authoritatively received interpretation of the analogous one, then two conclusions follow. First, there must be (or at least ought to be) some good evaluative argument for the decision given, minimally the value of coherence in the absence of any countervailing consideration, and preferably something more such as Graham J.'s[37] 'It seems to me that in order that justice may be done and done as speedily and cheaply as possible thus avoiding the cost of extensive further enquiries by the plaintiffs it is highly desirable that the short cut should be taken and the commissioners made to disclose the names in question.' Secondly, there must be some general reason why arguments by analogy or from legal principles should be conceived as providing 'legal support' for novel decisions, in the sense of being necessary conditions of their permissibility, rather than making them obligatory as do directly applicable mandatory rules. Such a general reason is not far to seek. Wide issues of legislative policy ought to be the concern of the political legislature, especially in democratic societies. Judges ought to abstain from taking side on issues of actual or potential partisan political controversy. Yet on the other hand the law as administered in the courts ought to exhibit coherence of principle, and should not be 'a wilderness of single instances', and so far as a society has, or is believed or perceived to have, certain values shared across party political differences and personal tastes, these 'common sense values' ought to be realized in its laws. These potentially conflicting principles can be kept in equilibrium by maintaining the principle that distinction and separation ought to be maintained between legislative and judicial functions and powers, not in the oversimplified terms of legislators making the laws and the judges only adjudicating upon those laws, but in terms that the necessary judicial law-making function required in the interests of consistency and the pursuit of 'commonsense' values ought to be subject to definable restrictions. The highly desirable recognition of a judicial power to make law must be restricted by recognition of a

[37] [1972] Ch. at p. 584.

duty to make it only 'interstitially'. Therefore there must be a criterion for distinguishing interstitial from architectural legislation. One possible criterion is that either a relevant analogy or an established principle is a necessary element of justification of an innovative decision. So if we seek a reason why arguments from analogy or from principle have the force they have in legal argument, the answer is the existence of a highly desirable conventional rule conferring power on judges to extend the law to cover circumstances not directly or unambiguously governed by established mandatory rules, but imposing limits on the extent of that power.

It seems true to say that the often hot but always arid controversy over whether or not judges do can or should 'make law' or 'legislate' is in essence a verbal or terminological question. In the last resort it is a matter of *fiat* whether we should use a different word to describe the process of enactment of statutes by Parliaments, after political debates in which it is irrelevant to the justification of the enactment that it conflicts with previous rules or principles of law (for that is often the purpose of such enactments) and the process of judicial rule-making justified by reference to analogies and principles in the existing law so far as these promote 'commonsense' values. Of course, there is a sense in which decisions and rulings so justified only make explicit what was implicit in the pre-existing law; and that is an important difference between the two processes. But equally it is true that the law is changed the moment after a great 'leading case' is decided from what it was the moment before; and that is an important similarity. What is important is to see both the difference and the similarity. The terminology is a good deal less important, though there is much to be said for reserving 'legislation' and 'legislate' to describe the former process, and to find some other term, for the latter—why not the much derided eighteenth-century usage of 'declaring' the law? At least such a distinction helps us to see the point of the doctrine of separation of powers, and to perceive the reality of the limits upon judicial powers of legal innovation.

To conclude the argument of this chapter, it is necessary finally to demonstrate that the force of arguments from analogy and from principle is *only* to show the permissibility of proposed decisions, not to make them obligatory. *Rondel* v. *Worsley*,[38] already cited and discussed sufficiently shows that even so well established a principle as 'the neighbour principle' is not of mandatory effect even in a case—that of a barrister's relationship to his client—to which it is in clear terms applicable. Countervailing reasons of policy justified the assertion that no liability for negligence exists between two such parties.

Phipps v. *Pears* ([1964] 2 All E.R. 35) neatly illustrates the same point. The owner of two houses on adjoining plots demolished one of them and built a new one with its flank wall flat up against that of the old one still standing. Some years later the two houses devolved into the separate ownership of the plaintiff and the defendant who on the orders of the local authority demolished his (the older house). Because of the way in which the adjoining wall of the newer house had been built slap up against the older, it had never been pointed, rendered, or plastered. So after the demolition rain got in and during the winter it froze, cracking the wall badly. The plaintiff sued for damages.

By pulling down No. 14, the defendants, he said had infringed his right of protection from the weather. This right, he said, was analogous to the right of support. It is settled law, of course, that a man who has his house next to another for many years, so that it is dependent on it for support, is entitled to have that support maintained. His neighbour is not entitled to pull down his house without providing substitute support in the form of buttresses or something of the kind, see *Dalton* v. *Angus*[39] . . .[In effect the plaintiff's case raises the question:] Is there an easement of protection. (*per* Lord Denning M.R., ibid. at p. 37)

The Court of Appeal declined to recognize any such easement of protection from weather. Their grounds were that the easement asserted was negative in nature, in that (if it existed) it would give the dominant owner the right to stop the other party doing something otherwise lawful on his own land. As such, it had to be 'looked at with caution, because the law has been very chary of creating any new negative easements'.[40] Instances illustrative of such caution were the denial of a right to a view in cases like *Bland* v.

---

[38] [1969] A.C. 191.   [39] (1881) 6 App. Cas. 740.
[40] [1964] 2 All E.R. at p. 37 (*per* Lord Denning).

Moseley,[41] or of a right to the free flow of wind for a wind-mill, as in *Webb* v. *Bird*[42]

The reason underlying these instances is that if such an easement were permitted, it would unduly restrict your neighbour in his enjoyment of his own land. It would hamper legitimate development, see *Dalton* v. *Angus* per Lord Blackburn. Likewise here, if we were to stop a man pulling down his house, we would put a brake on desirable improve-ment. Every man is entitled to pull down his house if he likes. If it exposes your house to the weather, that is your misfortune. It is no wrong on his part. . .(Ibid. at p. 38, *per* Lord Denning)

The argument may be open to criticism[43] ; it seems paradoxi-cal if the result is that the owner of the top flat of a block of separately owned flats should have a right to support from the proprietor below, but the latter no right to protection from weather (unless by express convenants) if the owner of the top flat sees fit to demolish his flat. Be that as it may, it is clear that although there was an obvious analogy between the right of protection claimed by the plaintiff and the legally recognized easement of support, the analogy was not of itself conclusive. The Court being persuaded of the policy reasons against recognizing any such novel easement—the undue restriction of development point—it was perfectly free to do so, the existence of the relevant analogy entailing no obligation to follow it. Of course, the counter-argument from policy was itself supported by the analogy of cases in which ease-ments of prospect or free flow of air had been denied. *Non sequitur* that in the absence of the competing analogy the judges would have been obligated to recognize as an ease-ment the right of protection.

That the similarity between a right of support and the postulated right of protection in cases such as the instant case where there is actual physical contiguity of buildings is so marked and obvious makes it worthwhile to observe also that 'closeness' of analogy is not decisive one way or the other way. We are speaking metaphorically, but even allowing for that it would be hard to say in any approximately quantitative way that there is any purely cognitive test whereby one could say that there is greater (or less) 'closeness'

---

[41] (1587) 9 Co. Rep. 58a.   [42] (1861) 13 C.B. (N.S.) 841.
[43] See R.E. Megarry, case note, (1965) 80 *L.Q.R.* 318–21.

of analogy as between rescuers and salvors than as between support for a contiguous building and protection from weather of a contiguous building. Yet in *Steel's* case the former analogy was held to justify an extension of liability, whereas in *Phipps's* case the latter was held insufficient to justify extension of the category of easements. The point is that in the former case the Court concluded that the better argument of principle and policy was in favour of treating the new class of case as falling under a wider principle capable of comprehending both cases, on the grounds that to draw a dividing line between rescuers and salvors such that the latter have no right to compensation would be to create an arbitrary and irrational distinction. In *Phipps's* case conversely the Court contended that there were good reasons of principle and policy for drawing a line between 'support' and 'protection', such that the distinction in rights was sound and rational despite the degree of similarity of the type-cases on either side of the line.

So unless we equivocate and use 'closeness' in an evaluative rather than a cognitive sense we cannot ascribe the persuasiveness of analogy to 'closeness' rather than to policy considerations. Nevertheless, there must be some limiting requirement as to what can count as even a prima facie sufficient analogy if we are correct in saying that the function of the judicial obligation not to innovate save with the justification of supporting analogies or statements of general legal principle is to set limits on the judicial power of making new law so that they do not trespass into the wider area of legislation reserved for the constitutionally defined legislator or legislature. To make the point obvious, any situation whatever in which one person can show that he has suffered some harm as a consequence of some other person's wrongful act or omission is *pro tanto* analogous to every instance of an existing delict or tort. But what if one tradesman secures an advantageous contract by driving from Oxford to London in excess of the speed limit all the way thus beating a trade rival who drove at the proper speed and who can demonstrate that he would have secured the contract had he not arrived in London later than his competitor? Such conduct does not fall within the ambit of any recognized delict or tort in Scots or English law, and few if any lawyers would suppose that the beaten competitor has even an arguable case for claiming compensation for loss of profit from the winner. Why should this be so?

The reason is the extreme degree of generality with which we have stated the ground of delictal liability as such. So soon as we descend even slightly in the scale of specificity, we find, for example, that harm may be divided into physical injury to person or property, with consequent economic loss, and pure independent economic loss. Since that is what is involved in our figured case we shall have to find our analogy if we can with torts involving pure economic loss. When we consider the 'wrongfulness' of the potential defendant's act, we find that it arises from breach of a criminal statute; so again, our analogies if any will have to be from the context of 'breach of statutory duty'; but there we ordinarily find that the plaintiff to succeed must belong to a class for whose special benefit the statute is supposed to have been enacted, and must base his claim on his role as a member of that class. Considerations such as these will probably lead us to the conclusion that, however much we sympathize with the losing tradesman, he simply hasn't a legal leg to stand on. Those observations point to the conclusion that sufficiency of analogy depends on the existence of similarity between the facts of the novel case and the operative facts of reasonably specifically stated rules or principles embedded in precedents or statutes. That is not an exact test, admittedly, but it is a real and important one. 'Closeness' of analogy in this sense is indeed a requirement of the law, though within the range of sufficiently close analogies degrees of closeness are not in themselves decisive either way but must be tested by consequentialist arguments for and against competing rulings in law.

Lastly, the opinion is frequently expressed that argument by analogy is especially a feature of case law rather than of statute law. There is certainly a degree of truth in this, in so far as bodies of case law are regularly built up by the steady accretion of decisions gradually extending the concrete application of a principle from case to analogous case. The modern development of the law of negligence in

Scots and English law is a clear illustration of this, as may be partially gathered from the numerous illustrations so far cited from that branch of the law. And there are many other areas of law of which the same might be said—such as the development of 'strict liability' (or 'presumed fault') from such cases as *Rylands* v. *Fletcher*[44] and *Kerr* v. *The Earl of Orkney*;[45] or the development in English law of the doctrine of 'promissory estoppel' from *Hughes* v. *The Metropolitan Railway*;[46] or the development of such parallel doctrines as *rei interventus* and homologation in Scots law and 'part performance' in English; or much of the (different) laws of trusts of both systems.

Nevertheless, as many of the illustrations chosen in this chapter show, argument from analogy is by no means uncommon or unimportant in the application and interpretation of statutes; we saw in the cases of *R.* v. *Arthur*[47] and *Norwich Pharmacal*[48] instances of analogies drawn from one statute used to solve a problem concerning the application of a statute in the one case, or the exercise of a statutory power involving a discretion partly worked out by case law in the other. *Beith's Trustees* v. *Beith*[49] cited in an earlier chapter involved the reversal of a common law doctrine partially justified by reference to the wide principle underlying a particular set of statutes in a relevantly similar area of the law, and so on. And conversely, statutes such as the Companies Acts have been worked out and concretized by elaboration in case law. The modern law of judicial review of administrative action consists in the application of wide common-law principles to specific statutes creating public authorities with public powers, often with a markedly restrictive effect on the statutory provisions; cases such as the *Anisiminic*[50] case (discussed in Chapter VI above) or *Malloch* v. *Aberdeen Corporation*[51] mark the current high-water mark

[44]   (1868) L.R. 3 H.L. 330.
[45]   (1857) 20 D. 298.
[46]   (1887) 2 App. Cas. 439.
[47]   [1968] 1 Q.B. 810.
[48]   [1972] Ch. 566; [1974] A.C. 133.
[49]   1950 S.C. 66.
[50]   [1969] 2 A.C. 197.
[51]   1971 S.C. (H.L.) 85 [1971] 2 All E.R. 1278.

of such judicial activity; the elaboration of the doctrine of *ultra vires* and natural justice has proceeded by the analogical application of precedents relating to one statute in cases involving other statutes in the public field. So it is false to suppose that there is any essential difference between statute and common law as to the force and function of arguments by analogy and from principle, even though we may assent to the proposition that perhaps the most characteristic use of such arguments is in the elaboration and concretization of doctrines from case to case—whether the *fons et origo* of the doctrine in question be a 'leading case' or an important statutory provision, or, for that matter, a principle stated by an institutional writer, or by foreign judges in persuasive foreign precedents.

For the Scottish and English legal systems, at least, there does appear to be abundant evidence in favour of the account of principles offered at the beginning of this Chapter, and in Chapter V. From their use, we can infer the importance ascribed to coherence of values within the working of a legal system. The same goes for the closely related use of arguments by analogy. Both together help us to form some understanding of the limits of what is regarded as legitimate in the way of judicial law-making. But it would be unhelpful and mis-leading to take too seriously metaphorical notions of the 'weight', far less relative weight, of principles singly or in competition *inter se*. It is the interaction of arguments from principle and consequentialist arguments which fully justifies decisions in hard cases—and even at that we have yet to consider the important matter of 'consistency' mentioned earlier. A ruling in law may be shown to be supported by principles and to be desirable in its consequences. But still it must be shown not to conflict with established and binding rules of law. That is for the next Chapter.

VIII

THE REQUIREMENT OF CONSISTENCY AND THE PROBLEM OF INTERPRETATION: CLEAR CASES AND HARD CASES

(a) *Clear cases and hard cases*

It is easy to put across in a few short words the point about arguments from consistency in law. There is a fundamental judicial commandment: Thou shalt not controvert established and binding rules of law. If there were not, the 'validity thesis' in any of its versions would fall flat on its face. But the commandment is indeed sufficiently observed to keep that thesis standing, occasionally a little unsteadily.

Take a case: in *Anisminic* v. *Foreign Compensation Commission* ([1969] 2 A.C. 147), it was not enough for the plaintiff company to show reasons of justice, common sense, and policy why the Commission's decision ought to be set aside. Of course, even to get to first base Anisminic had to persuade the court of that. There remained however, the formidable obstacle of s.4(4) of the Foreign Compensation Act, providing that a 'determination' by the Commission 'shall not be called in question in any court of law'.

As the Court of Appeal thought,[1] that provision can well be taken as meaning that even if the Commission gives a decision in a case which is unsatisfactory 'on the merits of the case', the Courts are precluded from setting it right—precluded by the plain words and evident intendment of Parliament. As one would expect, that argument was at all stages pressed by counsel for the Commission.

The only way in which counsel for Anisminic could argue round that was to find some ground for showing that the Commission in purporting to determine Anisminic's application (an application to share in funds recovered by the U.K. Government from the Egyptian Government in compensation for expropriation of British Nationals' property after the

---

[1] *Anisminic* v. *Foreign Compensation Commission* [1968] 2 Q.B. 862.

Suez Affair of 1956) had delivered itself not of a 'determination' but of a 'mere nullity'. That established, counsel could then press the point that what s.4(4) of the 1950 Act protected from judicial scrutiny was a 'determination'— understand a 'valid legal determination'—not a mere nullity. It is a tribute to the skill and ingenuity of counsel that they succeeded in making out such a case to the final satisfaction of the House of Lords.

What needs emphasis is this very point that no amount of persuasive consequentialist argument or argument from well-understood principles of public law would have sufficed to justify granting the declaration which *Anisminic* sought as against the Commission if it had not been possible to square that with the statutory provision. Thou shalt not controvert an Act of Parliament—but to find an interpretation of an Act which is consistent with the ruling one thinks right on other grounds is no breach of that commandment.

In all the cases we have considered from Chapter IV onwards this is a crucial element. Not merely must a decision be justified by good arguments from consequences and/or from principle or analogy. It must also be shown to be not inconsistent with established rules. But whether a given proposed ruling is or is not inconsistent with an established rule may plainly depend upon the interpretation which is put on the established rule.

To revert to our formulaic expressions: a proposed ruling is arguably or on the face of it in conflict with a rule *if p then q*. That precludes giving such a ruling unless it can be shown (a) that the rule in question is ambiguous as between *if p' then q* and *if p" then q*, and (b) that one of these versions of the rule squares satisfactorily with the proposed ruling.

Many disputes over the correct 'explanation' and possible 'distinguishability' of binding precedents arise in just such an argumentative context. Many disputes likewise arise, as in *Anisminic*, over the 'correct' interpretation of some statute or other article of written law. And the reason why such disputes do arise is precisely that judges recognize an obligation not to controvert established rules of law, not to institutionalize conflicting rules; but rather to give only such rulings as can be fitted without inconsistency into an already established body of rules. That these processes of explanation or interpretation involve modifying our understanding of the previously established rules is obvious—but not an objection to the present thesis. It would be a very radical version of 'rule scepticism' which suggested that statutes and case law are in all circumstances so indeterminate as to impose no limits whatever on possible ranges of 'interpretation' or 'explanation'. No one has ever advanced such a theory, though textbook writers have sometimes ascribed it to 'American Realists'.[2]

It is important to appreciate the above points, as a way of tying together our account of legal reasoning and correcting an oversimplification which has been tolerated until now. Hitherto, it has been assumed without much argument that there is a relatively simple disjunction as between clear cases and hard cases. In the former, justification of decisions can be achieved by simple deduction from clear established rules. In the latter, since we face problems of 'interpretation' of 'classification' or 'relevancy', we have to have recourse to 'second-order justification'. Deduction comes in only after the interesting part of the argument, settling a ruling in law, has been carried through.

But in truth there is no clear dividing line between clear cases and hard cases. Let us recall the argumentative context. A plaintiff/pursuer or prosecutor (P) has a complaint against someone (D). His best chance of obtaining legal redress is if he can prove some facts 'p' which will enable him to invoke some rule *if p then q*. But the defence may then raise a doubt as to the facts, or challenge the legal footing of the claim, the latter being the possibility which is of present interest. What that will involve in a case where P has a rule to invoke is D's raising an argument on the interpretation of the rule or the classification of the material facts in the specific terms of the rule. Sometimes this tactic will not get off the ground—recall how in the *Daniels* case Lewis J. rejected in summary terms (and quite rightly) the suggestion by counsel for the second

---

[2] See, e.g., G.W. Paton, *A Text-book of Jurisprudence* (1st edn. Oxford, 1951), pp. 18–19, 68–9; but compare 4th edn. (Oxford, 1972, by Paton and Denham), pp. 23–8, 87–8. Hart, *Concept of Law*, pp. 132–7, is not free of faults on this count.

defendant that sale of 'a bottle of R. White's lemonade' was not a 'sale by description' within the meaning of the Sale of Goods Acts 14(2). On the other hand, in *Maclennan* v. *Maclennan* (1958 S.C. 105) the defender succeeded in sustaining the argument that a wife's artifical insemination by a donor is not adultery within the meaning ascribed to that term by Scots Law.

It may be the other way round, of course, when in cases like *Donoghue* v. *Stevenson* ([1932] A.C. 562; 1932 S.C. (H.L.) 31) or *Anisminic* ([1969] 2 A.C. 197) it is P who sets out to found a claim on arguments of principle backed up by consequentialist argument, while D retires behind a rule of law which, he says, precludes a decision in favour of P. Then it is P who must seek out and exploit possible doubts and ambiguities so as to show that ostensibly adverse case law can be explained and/or statutes interpreted so as to clear the way for the ruling which he seeks, there being no conflict with the established law as 'properly' understood.

Thus, even if it is true that there are some, even many, cases like *Daniels* ([1938] 4 All E.R. 258) where the established facts leave no reason seriously to doubt or to contest the applicability of a clear rule, the line which separates such a case from a highly disputable one like *Donoghue* is not a sharp one. There is a spectrum which ranges from the obviously simple to the highly contestable, and across that spectrum it could never be judged more than vaguely at what point some doubt as to 'relevancy' or interpretation' or 'classification' could be raised so as to clear the way for exploiting consequentialist arguments and arguments of principle or analogy.

Among the reasons for vagueness on this point must figure differences of style, approach and even temperament as among different judges. A Viscount Simonds or a Lord Clyde takes a very different view of the desirability of a flexible approach to established law than a Lord Denning or a Lord Cooper or a Lord Reid. As Karl Llewellyn has observed there are also differences in the dominant style of different periods in the history of legal systems; in *The Common Law Tradition* he demonstrates the range of difference between an ideal typical 'Formal Style' and an ideal typical 'Grand

Style'.[3] In a very exact sociological study of the British House of Lords between the late 1950s and the early 1970s Dr. A.A. Paterson has traced the development of a change of judicial style in terms of a shift in the role perceptions of appellate judges, in which a key part was played by leading personalities among the Lords of Appeal.[4]

That such changes occur is perhaps neatly exemplified by reconsideration of the *Anisminic* case. Anyone familiar with the post-war development of British administrative law will readily appreciate that the decision given in that case, dependent on a very bold interpretation of the 1950 Act, would have been wholly unacceptable within the more formalistic approach which prevailed in the House of Lords in say 1956. The point can well be pressed home by animadversion to the contrast between the *Anisminic* case and such a case as, for example, *Smith* v. *East Elloe R.D.C.* ([1956] A.C. 736.). (In that case, when a challenge was made to a compulsory purchase order, Viscount Simonds strongly denounced the view that there was any ambiguity at all in the statutory provision that such an order 'shall not, either before or after it has been confirmed, made or given, be questioned in any legal proceedings whatsoever'. His Lordship's view was that the question even of the good faith of an order could not be judicially considered without depriving the quoted statutory words of 'their full meaning and content'.)

Even at a given point in time and before a particular court there can be no specification in exact terms of what is a seriously arguable point of law; though of course one of the things advocates and barristers are paid for is knowing what is worth trying on and what is not. The cases which do proceed to decision by simple deductive argument are those in which either (a) no doubt as to interpretation of the rule or classification of facts could conceivably have arisen; or (b) no one thought of raising and arguing a point which was in truth arguable; or (c) where such an argument has been tried but dismissed as artificial or far-fetched by the Court. Of these types (b) and (c) in principle belong in a penumbral area as

---

[3] Karl N. Llewellyn, *The Common Law Tradition* (Boston, 1960), pp. 35–45, 182–7.

[4] A.A. Paterson, op. cit. *supra*, Ch. I n. 13.

distinct from the sharp certainty of (a), but it is hard to figure examples of (a) which are not capable of some discussion on the issue whether they may not be truly cases of (b) or (c).

In terms of what is visible in the law reports, cases of the types (a) and (b) are very much the submerged part of the iceberg. A case which is simple, as was the *Daniels* case so far as concerned the Sale of Goods Act point, would not normally be reported, just because as a simple case it has no great significance as a 'leading case' of the kind which the law reports are in business to publish—the point only got reported on the coat-tails of the discussion of aspects of the *Donoghue* v. *Stevenson* rule which the case also involved. For a like reason, when a case goes to law and counsel fail to take a point of law which might have been pursued, treating the matter as simply one of 'fact', the case does not get reported.

Cases belonging to type (c) are more interesting; counsel for one party has put an argument which in some respect requires a relatively bold interpretation of a statutory provision or a point of case law. *Smith* v. *East Elloe R.D.C.* ([1956] A.C. 736), already cited, is such an example, where the House of Lords was not prepared to accept that the statutory provision precluding judicial review was in any way ambiguous so as to admit the exception for orders made in bad faith which counsel for the appellant had urged upon the House.

Another example is provided by *Temple* v. *Mitchell* (1956 S.C. 267), an oversimplified version of which runs as follows. The Mitchell family lived in a rented house belonging to the pursuer, the legal tenancy being in Mr. Mitchell's name. Under the provisions of the Rent Acts, the tenancy was a 'statutory tenancy', which entailed *inter alia* that 'so long as [the tenant] retains possession' of the house, his tenancy continues, and he cannot be evicted notwithstanding any provisions of his original contractual tenancy. (See Increase of Rent and Mortgage Interest (Restrictions) Act 1920, s.15.)

At a certain point in time, however, Mr. Mitchell deserted his wife and disappeared, leaving her and the children and all the furniture and household effects in the house. Mrs. Mitchell stayed on, and duly tendered payment of rent to the land-lord at the appropriate time, but he refused to acknowledge her as tenant by accepting the rent, and in due course raised an action of removing against her.

Had the tenant 'retained possession' or not? If he had not, the landlord had a right to be granted possession of the house as against the family; if he had, then under the Acts the land-lord had no such right. Precedents, both Scots and English, on the interpretation of the Acts established that a tenant who had left a house with no intention to return to live there himself could not be classed as 'retaining possession' even if he put friends or relations into occupation of the house on his behalf. On the other hand, people such as sailors who are away from home for long periods of time do not thereby lose possession; provided there are appropriate indiciae of con-tinuing occupation, such as furniture, or relatives occupying the house as the tenant's licensees, they 'retain possession' so long as during periods of absence they retain the intention to return to the house when on shore. (Those familiar with analytical jurisprudence will note the echo of the classical theory[5] that possession requires both physical control of the *corpus possessionis* and an appropriate mental element, *animus possidendi*; and to reinforce that echo, one might remark that the judges latinised the necessary intention to return to a house after periods of absence as *animus rever-tendi*.)

In the Second Division, Lord Mackintosh was for upholding the view that in the circumstances the tenant had retained possession:

There is...in my view, nothing in the common law of Scotland to stand in the way of it being held that a tenant's possession of a house may be retained by his leaving his wife and family in it although he himself goes away from it. If he allows his wife and family to remain on there when it was open to him—as it would be under our law—to have them ejected by legal process if necessary, the fair inference is that they are there at least with his tacit permission. That inference is strengthened when in addition the tenant husband leaves his furniture

---

[5] See, e.g., Paton's *Text-book of Jurisprudence* (4th edn.), pp. 553–89; D.R. Harris 'The Concept of Possession in English Law', in *Oxford Essays in Jurisprudence* (ed. A.G. Guest, Oxford, 1961) criticizes the inflexibility of the classical theory.

in the house, so that it is available for the use of his wife and family. In such circumstances I think that, for the purpose of construing the words 'retains possession' in section 15 of the Rent Restrictions Act of 1920, the wife's possession may properly be regarded as the husband's possession...The protection of the home being the whole policy and intention of the Rent Acts...the words 'retains possession' in section 15 of the 1920 Act ought, in my opinion, to be construed in a sense wide enough to cover possession vicariously exercised by the continued presence of the wife and family of the tenant in the house which had before the separation been the matrimonial home of the parties...(Ibid. at p. 281)

His argument to that effect was supported by reference to Scottish precedents, and to the leading Scots book on the topic, Rankine on *Leases*.[6] It was further buttressed by the fact that there were English precedents establishing that in cases of desertion, a deserted wife's occupation of controlled property constitutes her husband's retention of possession under the Act. Since the Act extended to the whole U.K., it should so far as possible be construed similarly throughout the U.K.

But Lord Mackintosh was in a minority. His three judicial brethren all took the opposite view. The English precedents were explained as turning on a special doctrine of the English law of husband and wife not received in Scotland. And as Lord Justice-Clerk Thomson put it:

I should very much like to decide the case on this obviously equitable and sympathetic line if I could. There is no doubt that these Acts, which started out as a moratorium on rents, have developed into something of the nature of a social housing code. But I cannot find in the Acts anything which puts a deserted wife in any privileged position. The argument which makes the deserted wife a vicarious tenant...is equally valid for any tenant who disappears leaving somebody like a housekeeper, a caretaker or a member of the family in the occupation of the house. (Ibid. at p. 272)

I am not satisifed that [English precedents] support the argument that there is an exception in favour of a deserted wife on the basis of the Acts alone. There is no express provision, and I cannot discover any clear implication. (Ibid. at p. 275)

The other Lords of the majority, Lord Patrick and Lord Blades, delivered themselves of concurring opinions substantially similar to that of the Lord Justice-Clerk.

---

[6] Sir John Rankine, *The Law of Leases in Scotland* (3rd edn., Edinburgh, 1913).

This case can thus be classed within my type '(c)', being one in which counsel tried but failed to persuade the Court that the statute in question was capable of bearing a meaning consistent with granting to his client the right she claimed. Despite such argument, the majority of the Court held that the interpretation of the Act was unproblematic and unambiguously excluded treating the deserted wife as possessing vicariously on behalf of the tenant, the husband in desertion.

(To recur to a point made earlier: it will be seen that the structure of the argument is unaffected by whether we choose to regard the point raised as one of 'interpretation' or of 'classification'. Whether we treat the question as being 'What meaning ought to be ascribed to the statutory phrase "retains possession"?' or as being 'Do the primary facts proven and admitted constitute "retaining possession" within the meaning of the Act?', the factors relevant to justifying the answer remain the same. Though the difference between the 'problem of interpretation' and 'the problem of classification' is of practical importance in some contexts, being treated as a difference between questions of 'law' and of 'fact' (or 'secondary fact'), there is no theoretical difference between them so far as concerns the theory of justificatory arguments in law.)

(b) *Problems of Interpretation and Classification: Statutory interpretation*

Temple v. *Mitchell*—like other examples cited in this and other chapters—can thus be taken as a useful illustration of aspects of the handling of problems of interpretation, or of classification, when they arise in law, with particular reference to the interpretation of statutes.[7] First, we may ask with reference to it, whether it is the case that one of the rival interpretations of the Act contended for by counsel in the case was more 'obvious' than the other. It seems that the

---

[7] The best current work on the subject of statutory interpretation is Rupert Cross, *Statutory Interpretation* (London, 1976); except that I prefer to speak of 'obvious' rather than 'ordinary' meaning (because 'obviousness' can be more or less, but not 'ordinariness') I am much in agreement with Cross; see also the Law Commissions, *The Interpretation of Statutes* (1969, Law Com. No. 21, Scottish Law Com. No. 11).

answer to that has to be affirmative. If we restrict ourselves to considering the words 'so long as he retains possession' in s.15(1) of the Increase of Rent and Mortgage Interest (Restrictions) Act 1920, the most obvious meaning is that a person who actually occupies a house with the intention to continue occupying it satisfies that condition, and somebody who has left a house with no intention ever to return does not.

Admittedly, there is a well-known conception of 'possession in law', whereby A is deemed to 'possess' property actually occupied by B, if B is A's tenant or licensee. But authoritative decisions on the interpretation of the Acts had before Temple's case ruled out the use of that sense of the words. 'The fundamental principle of the [1920 Act is] that it. . . is to protect a resident in a dwelling house, not to protect a person who is not a resident in a dwelling house, but is making money by sub-letting it' (*per* Scrutton L.J., in *Haskins* v. *Lewis*, ([1931] 2 K.B. 1 at p. 14). So the more obvious meaning of 'so long as he retains possession', taking account of the prior course of interpretation, is that it excludes the case of someone who has left a dwelling house of which he is tenant, having no intention of returning thereto.

The idea that there is, or could be, a 'literal rule' of statutory interpretation postulates or presupposes this possibility that statutory words normally have an obvious or plain meaning. In so far as that is true, there are no doubt good grounds why judges should approach the application of enactments with some presumption in favour of applying whatever is the more 'obvious' of the meanings appealed to by litigants before them. In a democratic constitution, it is the elected Parliament which must enact new laws; whether or not all the members of the legislature have the least idea of the contents of clauses of Bills, the least unsuccessful way of securing that the will of elected legislators will prevail will be to take the words enacted by them at their face value and so far as possible apply them in accordance with their plain meaning. In so far as Governments effectively control the business of Parliament, they are then at least put to the necessity of making exactly explicit the policies for which they solicit Parliamentary approval in legislation. And the ordinary citizen will be able to take statutes at their face value.

On the other hand, the 'obviousness' of an interpretation of enacted words may, perhaps must, depend on understanding of the principle or principles which are supposed to inform the enactment. The quotation above from Scrutton L.J. makes the point very neatly—indeed as he said earlier in his opinion, in relation to the Rent Acts the Courts had since 1920 'been trying to frame a consistent theory of what must happen' when the Acts fell to be applied ([1931] 2 K.B. at p. 9). What is obvious is, perhaps, obvious only given some such a theory of the aim and object of the Act. (That the judicial theory was in this instance confirmed by Parliament is nicely indicated by the terms of s.3(1) (a) of the Rent Act 1968 which now ascribes a statutory tenancy to a formerly protected tenant 'if and so long as he occupies the dwelling house as his residence', s.3(2) further providing in effect that the judicial interpretations of the previous terminology of 'retaining possession' are to stand in relation to the new and more exact terminology.)

Given that all that is so, what must be done by someone whose case depends on displacing the 'more obvious' interpretation in favour of a less obvious one? In *Temple's* case, the argument of counsel for Mrs. Mitchell briefly reported (1956 S.C. 267 at p. 270) shows them contending that 'The Rent Restrictions Acts should be interpreted in a broad and practical way so as to give effect to their principal object, the preservation of the family home.' It being desirable in itself that families should not be deprived of adequate housing, and it being the very principle or underlying 'theory' of the Rent Acts that family homes were to be protected as against the private landlord, the Act ought to be interpreted in the 'broad and practical way' required. The English precedents were cited as persuasive authorities on this point.

As we have seen, this argument prevailed with Lord Mackintosh, but was rejected by the majority because it was thought to involve reading into the express words of the Act an implied exception for deserted wives which simply was not to be found in it as enacted. (The 1968 consolidation of the Rent Acts does not contain any response to Lord Thomson's regretful conclusion that 'if the homes of deserted wives are to be protected in Scotland, Parliament alone can do it' (ibid. at p. 275); although the Matrimonial Homes Act 1967 clarified a confused area of case law, and gave explicit protections to deserted spouses in owner-occupied or rented houses, that Act is expressely excluded from application to Scotland.)

There are, in effect, two requirements to be met by lawyers who seek to persuade a court to adopt a less than obvious meaning for statutory words. First, they must persuade the Court that the sense in which they wish the court to read the words is a sense which can consistently with English usage be ascribed to them, even if not the most obvious. That was where counsel for Mrs. Mitchell failed in *Temple's* case, as we saw in the quotation from Lord Thomson, cited above. It is not sufficient that the party in question have a case which attracts sympathy or is well founded in general principles or on good consequentialist arguments; he can get nowhere unless he can show that the statutory words are capable of bearing a meaning consistent with the desired decision. It is not infrequent to find judges expressly stating that counsel has persuaded them of such a possibility despite the first-sight 'obviousness' of another meaning. For example, in *Barker* v. *Bell* ([1971] 2 All E.R. 867 at p. 869) we find Fenton Atkinson L.J. saying in relation to Mr. A.A.M. Irvine that

On reading these papers, until I heard counsel for the third party's argument, I had been unable to see how he could escape from the combination of the words 'was' and 'any' in s.29(3) of the Hire Purchase Act 1964. But having heard his argument, I am persuaded that he is right and that a man should be taken to be a purchaser without notice if he has no actual notice of any relevant hire-purchase agreement.

The second requirement, although not sufficient in itself, is indubitably a necessary one. Courts neither do nor ought to apply statutes in less rather than more obvious senses unless they have good reason to do so. The whole argument of this book has been that the reasons which constitute 'good' reasons for doing so are either consequentialist reasons, or reasons of legal principle, or (most powerfully) both sorts of reasons operating in combination. To persuade a judge that to apply a statute in the sense *if p' then q* will involve conflict with accepted principles, or will in the generic case conflict with justice or common sense or expediency, is to give him good reason for preferring some alternative reading *if p" then q* so long as he is also persuaded that that really is a possible reading of the original *if p then q*, not involving the importation of words or ideas wholly absent from the Act as written. The stronger the judge considers these reasons of consequence or of principle to be, the better justified will he consider himself in overriding the presumption that more obvious meanings are to be preferred, and the more willing he will be to 'bend' the enacted words, if not quite to breaking point.

When we talk of a difference between judicial styles— whether in terms of 'Grand' versus 'Formal' style, à la Llewellyn, or in other terms—what we are talking about is or includes the degree of readiness which a judge manifests to permit that presumption to be overriden.

It may be thought that these remarks are rather far removed from what is ordinarily discussed or described under the rubric of statutory interpretation. But in fact they provide a framework for understanding that very topic even in its most standard presentations. Take for example, the idea that there are 'rules' of statutory interpretation[8] —the 'literal rule', the 'golden rule', and the 'mischief rule' (alias the 'rule in *Heydon's* case'); and various canons of construction— *eiusdem generis, noscitur a sociis*, and all the rest of them. The trouble, as has often been pointed out about such 'rules' and 'canons' is that they tend to 'hunt in pairs'[9] ; for almost any one of them, another can be found which in an appropriate context will point to a different result from that which it itself indicates.

So far as concerns the 'rules of interpretation' the burden of this chapter so far has been to indicate that and why there is a presumption in favour of applying statutes in their more 'obvious' meaning; and at all events a fairly rigidly observed obligation only to give decisions which can be justified under some ruling which is compatible with *some* sense which is without excessive violence to understood linguistic usage

---

[8] See Cross, op.cit., ch. 3; Law Commissions, op.cit., ch. 4.

[9] See Llewellyn, 'Remarks on the Theory of Appellate Decision etc.' (1950) 3 *Vanderbilt L.R.* 395. As Rupert Cross points out, the 'hunting in pairs' can be exaggerated; op.cit., pp. 169–70.

ascribable to relevant statutory provisions. Within that limit, however, reasons of consequence and principle can justify resort to less obvious meanings. To advert to the 'golden rule' or to the 'mischief rule' in such contexts is simply to express in terms of standard justifying reasons the justification for departing from the more obvious meaning—namely, so as to avoid interpreting the Act in a way which will give rise to some 'absurdity' (the golden rule), or in a way which will defeat the actual objective of the legislator to remedy some prior 'mischief' or defect in the law. Especially the term 'absurdity' should be sufficient to indicate to us that we are in the realm of evaluative judgments of the kind which in law are inextricable elements in consequentialist reasoning and arguments of legal principle.

The trouble, it may be said, is that the notion of any 'obvious' or 'plain' or 'literal' or 'ordinary' meaning of expressions in an enactment is not itself a notion which is incontestable, nor free from any element of value judgments. That is not quite true, for sometimes statutory expressions are utterly unambiguous and plain in their meaning. Section 1(1) of the Murder (Abolition of Death Penalty) Act 1965, for example, provides that

No person shall suffer death for murder, and a person convicted of murder shall, subject to subsection 5 below [which makes special provisions for persons who 'appear to the court to have been under the age of eighteen years at the time the offence was committed'], be sentenced to imprisonment for life.

That section clearly and unambiguously obligates a judge after the return of a verdict of guilty in a murder trial to sentence the person convicted to life imprisonment, and it disables him from validly pronouncing sentence of death; that is clear beyond a shadow of doubt. Nobody in a legislature who advertently voted for or against enactment of these words could doubt what he was voting about, nor could any reader of the Act doubt what its meaning or intended effect was. The aim of abolishing the Death Penalty for murder having commended itself to a majority, the words chosen are an unambiguously appropriate means to achieving that end. Both from the words of the act, and from the surrounding circumstances of the Parliamentary and public debates, one can learn what was intended, and one can tell how to satisfy that intention: by sentencing convicted murderers (and everybody in the world either is or is not a convicted murderer) to life imprisonment, not to death by hanging or other means.

Such all-purpose clarity is no doubt relatively unusual. Nevertheless, what makes us able to make sense of statutes is our appreciation that they are forms of utterance which have legislative effect, and which pass through a procedure which has the function of establishing legal rules, and which those who participate in it understand as having that function. On that ground, it is justified to ascribe to the legislative body the intention that the clauses enacted shall take effect as valid legal rules; to understand their meaning as legal rules it is therefore proper to ask how a normal speaker of the language would intend his utterance of such a rule to be understood. (It is the qualification 'normal' which imports valuations.) In that sense, and in that way, we can without absurdity use the concepts of 'legislator's intention' and of a 'plain' or 'literal' meaning of the enacted words. What is more, we can by reading a whole Act construct a view of the policies and principles which it was (in the relevant sense) 'intended' to further which can in turn aid us in making reasonable inferences as to the effect particular sections might have been intended to procure. What I mean by my words, what I mean to achieve by using these words, and what my words mean, exhibit a similar interplay.[10] We are on safest ground when, as in case of the 1965 Act, all three 'meanings' exactly converge.

What is postulated is that independently of their use in some particular utterance words have meanings dependent on conventional semantic (and other) rules of 'normal' linguistic usage. To 'suffer death' for example, has a meaning independent of the use of the words in the Act, and it is that fact which makes them appropriate to the use to which they were put in the Act. But these conventions can themselves be vague and ambiguous, to which extent, for special purposes special conventions can be adopted. That is the

---

[10] Cf. G.C. MacCallum 'Legislative Intent', 75 *Yale Law Journal* 754, reprinted in *Essays in Legal Philosophy* (ed. R.S. Summers, Oxford, 1968) p. 237, esp. at 241.

role which 'canons of construction' play. The proposition
that general words ought to be construed as referring only to
the same class of things (*eiusdem generis*) as the particular
words to which they are appended is such a special convention. Since the convention is shared by the judges who apply
statutes and by the draftsmen who advise Parliament on the
drafting of legislation, there is justification for its use to
clarify or reduce the range of potential ambiguities, since
each party to the dialogue can reasonably impute to the
other knowledge of the convention and readiness to act on it.

All this goes to show, not that it is always possible to
ascribe a clear meaning to an enactment (of course it is not)
but to show that and why it is sometimes so possible. Even
so, there remains a permanent tension between following
the ostensibly obvious meaning, and seeking to establish in
particular cases generic rulings which satisfy other desirable
aspects of policy and principle. For just that reason, the
'literal rule' is defeasible in favour of the other 'rules';[11]
provided that the statutory words *can* bear a meaning other
than the more obvious one, judges, albeit to differential
degrees, regard it as proper to apply on grounds of policy
and/or principle less obvious meanings of statutory expressions.

There is a danger of treating 'literal' approaches to statutory
language as though they were synonymous with 'restrictive'
as against 'liberal' approaches. This is both confused and
confusing. Sometimes the 'literal' approach contrasts with
what counsel in *Temple's* case described as a 'broad and
practical' approach. But when we compare the *Anisminic* and
the *East Elloe* cases, we find that in the former the narrow
and restrictive interpretation of the provision precluding
judicial review is in contrast with the broader interpretation
achieved via the 'literal rule' in relation to the similar pre-
clusion in *East Elloe*. Again, in the *Ealing London Borough
Council* case ([1972] A.C. 342), the majority in the House
of Lords read the phrase about discrimination on the ground
of 'national origins' less broadly than Lord Kilbrandon, who
considered that 'national origins' should be interpreted as

---

[11] Cf. Cross, op.cit. *supra*, Ch. VIII n. 7, p. 43.

including legal nationality. Who was being 'literal,' who 'liberal', who 'restrictive'?

The confusion may be partly ascribable to judicial practice itself. British judges have (a) ascribed importance to giving statutes what I call their 'obvious' and other commentators their 'ordinary' meaning, as a measure of deference to the sovereignty of Parliament; but (b) they have also adopted in many cases a policy of upholding the common law (especially in relation to common law liberties) as against statutory incursions into it. Thus, in so far as the Race Relations Acts inhibit the former legal freedom to discriminate or not as one chooses, and especially since the phrase 'national origins' is used in the criminal provisions relating to incitement to racial hatred in the Race Relations Act 1965, the majority in the House of Lords was following a recognizable pattern in favouring the narrower of the possible interpretations of 'national origins', and in ruling that discrimination on ground of legal nationality fell outwith the statutory prohibition.

In such cases of genuine ambiguity judges themselves are apt to obfuscate the difference between construing Acts literally and construing them narrowly or restrictively, hence the aforementioned confusion. But it will be observed that such justification as there is for this general approach is justification in terms of common-law principles favouring a certain conception of the liberty of the individual citizen. Far from casting doubt upon the general thesis of this book, that confirms it. When problems of interpretation arise, they can be resolved only by recourse to consequentialist arguments and/or arguments of principle, both of which involve an appeal to values conceived as being basic to the law. These are matters which can be and are controversial, hence the fact that hard cases do not admit of easy answers.

It behoves me to adduce some evidence that the foregoing account is not wholly based on my own idiosyncratic conjectures. In the *Ealing* case itself, there is a nice instance of judicial exposition of the proper approach to statutory interpretation. Lord Simon of Glaisdale said this:

[T]he Courts have five principal avenues of approach to the ascertainment of the legislative intention:

1. examination of the social background. . .in order to identify the

social or juristic defect which is the likely subject of remedy;

2. A conspectus of the entire relevant body of the law for the same purpose;

3. particular regard to the long title of the statute to be interpreted (and, where available the preamble) in which the general legislative objectives will be stated.

4. scrutiny of the actual words to be interpreted in the light of established canons of interpretation

5. examination of the other provisions of the statute in question (or of other statutes in pari materia) for the light which they throw on the particular words which are the subject of interpretation. ([1972] A.C. at p. 361)

As will be seen, items (1) and (2) in that list import precisely the matters of policy and principle which I have described, whereas items (3) to (5) go to the business of establishing in context some interpretations as more 'obvious' than others. In the *Ealing* case, Lord Simon was of the opinion that pursuit of all five avenues of approach led to the same conclusion, in favour of treating 'national origins' as not including legal nationality.

With all due respect, I must say that I find Lord Kilbrandon's reasoning more persuasive. His 'consequentialist' argument cited in an earlier chapter shows what seem to me good reasons of policy and principle for treating 'national origins' as including nationality in this context; and as for 'avenue' number (4), 'established canons of interpretation' were mutually cancelling in this instance. As Lord Kilbrandon said:

I would not accept the view that there is some presumption here in favour of freedom from liability; the race relations code does, of course, contain some criminal sanctions, and it restricts liberty, but, on the other hand, it is conceived as a measure of social reform and relief of distress. Not much help is to be got from presumptions either for freedom or in favour of benevolent interpretation. (Ibid. at p. 369)

When a question is finely balanced, as the question here was and when either answer can be given consistently with the words used in the Act, a ruling must be made for one or the other; that ruling, to be justified, must show it to be the more acceptable given a consistent and principled 'theory' (to recall Scrutton L.J.'s word quoted earlier at p. 205) of the Act as regulating race relations in this society. Since no unequivocal intention can on this point be ascribed to Parliament without begging the very question at stake, our answer must depend upon the values we bring to bear on the question.

The answer is and must be an essentially contested or contestable one. My answer is the same as Lord Kilbrandon's. I share the theory by reference to which that is the right answer. But there is another theory by reference to which the other answer is right, and to have reasoned grounds for saying that one theory as against the other is right, we should require a third, higher-order, theory, which might in turn be challenged by a fourth—and so on. Short of an infinite regress we, must make, and live with, our own choices—but I am here anticipating a point for argument in the next chapter.

So far as concerns problems of statutory interpretation I have shown to my best ability how problems of interpretation can arise and must be settled within a legal system in which (in accordance with the validity thesis) there is a requirement that cases must not be decided on the basis of rulings inconsistent with the body of valid legal rules. There is a justified presumption in favour of applying statutes in accordance with their more obvious meanings, but provided there are other *possible* meanings the presumption can be displaced by good arguments from consequences and/or from legal principles.

(c) *Problems of interpretation in case law*

But what of the interpretation of precedents? It is often stated or assumed that the process of reasoning from or with precedents is radically different from that of reasoning from or with statutes. But in fact the differences are at most differences of degree not of kind.

For a start, as we saw in relation to *Temple's* case some time ago, the interpretation of a statute is quite standardly a matter of interpreting it in the light of glosses already imposed by precedent. Section 15 of the 1920 Rent Act did not present itself in virginal purity to the Court of Session in 1956, but came already pregnant with judicially ascribed meanings. What had to be decided in the particular problem situation was how to apply the Act consistently with its own terms and with prior authoritative rulings on aspects of its meaning—in particular the ruling that 'so long as he retains possession' refers to a tenant's actual occupation of the dwelling house as his home, not his 'possession in law' for example by subletting to a subtenant. In trying to make sense of, and act consistently with, established law in order to make and justify its decision for the instant case, the Court cannot be supposed to be directing its mind to radically different problems according as it is the *ipsissima verba* of Parliament or the more rambling discourse of a judge which furnishes the material for excogitation.

The point that differences in law between the use of precedents and the use of statutes is a difference of degree, not of kind, is, in the context of the present chapter, an important point. Hitherto I have tried, as it were, to explain the cash value of the requirement of consistency so far as it concerns statute law. If, as I claim, the same requirement has reference to case law as well, it must be similarly explicable. The commandment that thou shalt not controvert established and binding rules of law is to be understood as applying to rules derived from case law also.

But how can rules be derived from case law? The point has already been touched on in Chapter IV, but may be restated. Cases which pose problems pose them precisely because parties, or their lawyers, take different lines on the matters we have described as concerning 'relevancy', 'interpretation', or 'classification'. The parties move the Court for a decision in their favour supported by a particular 'version' or 'reading' of the law, in turn backed up by reference to consequentialist arguments and arguments of principle. The Court must decide the case by granting or refusing the remedy sought, and to justify its decision it must give its ruling on the disputed question of law, and must in turn justify that ruling. If it has ruled on one question which sufficiently disposes of the case in that it covers the actual decision, it may, but it need not, make rulings on further points which have been argued; or it may indicate its opinion on such matters subject to an express proviso that such a statement of opinion being unnecessary to the decision is not to be taken as conclusive.[12] (This is a more or less explicit way of saying: 'The following remarks are to be regarded technically as *obiter dicta, not ratio*'.)

In Chapter IV it was shown at some length that this practice of expressly or implicity making a ruling on the point of law at issue, in a 'universalized' form, is both required and justified by respect for the principle of formal justice. It has also been noted that failure to make a ruling when necessary, and to show its derivation from or compatibility with relevant legal principles, is treated by the judiciary as being worthy of criticism, which reinforces the theoretically justified opinion that the practice has normative force from the judicial point of view.

Professor Rupert Cross, the leading English authority on judicial precedent in English law has put forward the following as a 'tolerably accurate description of what lawyers mean by *"ratio decidendi"* ':[13] 'The *ratio decidendi* of a case is any rule of law expressly or impliedly treated by a judge as a necessary step in reaching his conclusion, having regard to the line of reasoning adopted by him.'

By taking full account of the justificatory function and the general structure of the type of legal reasoning involved in judicial opinions, we can perhaps improve on that.

The *ratio decidendi* is the ruling expressly or impliedly given by a judge which is sufficient to settle a point of law put in issue by the parties' arguments in a case, being a point on which a ruling was necessary to his justification (or one of his alternative justifications) of the decision in the case. (The caveat must be repeated here that, on this view, by no means all cases—even 'leading' cases—have *a* single *ratio decidendi*.)

Having given that elucidation of the thesis that rules are derivable from case law, because the ruling given by a precedent court can be taken as supplying a rule for present relevant cases (and because within a doctrine of binding

---

[12] A randomly chosen example is Salmon L.J.'s words in *Gallie* v. *Lee* [1969] 1 All E.R. 1062 at pp. 1081–2: 'On the view I take of this case, no question of estoppel arises. Perhaps I ought, however, briefly to express my conclusions on this question out of respect for the able arguments addressed to us by counsel. . . [but] the defence of non est factum never gets off the ground and, therefore, it is unnecessary to consider whether the plaintiff is precluded from relying on it.'

[13] Rupert Cross, *Precedent in English Law* (2nd edn., Oxford, 1968), p. 77.

precedent it either must be so taken, or prima facie ought to
be so taken, subject to the hierarchical arrangement of the
court system), we may turn to considering how reflection on
the requirement of consistency in law bears upon it and confirms it subject to minor qualifications. I shall treat of the
matter by considering first the application of case-law rules
in a relatively uncontroversial way, secondly the topic of
distinguishing precedents, especially where this involves
'explaining' them in a restrictive way; thirdly, the topic of
extending and developing case-law rules—which of course
shades off into the type of argument from analogy or general
principle discussed in Chapter VI.

(i) *Applying a precedent*

In the *Daniels* case ([1938] 4 All E.R. 258), so far as
concerned the action against R. White and Sons Ltd., the
lemonade manufacturers, we have already seen that what was
involved was the application in a straightforward way of the
Donoghue ruling ([1932] A.C. 562, 1932 S.C. (H.L.) 31)
on the duty of care owed by manufacturers to consumers.
Even if a doubt could have been raised whether that ruling
covered all manufacturers of consumer goods as *per* Lord
Atkin, or only manufacturers of articles of food and drink as
per Lord Macmillan, it would have been immaterial to the
instant case which concerned lemonade. As we saw, the rule
that a manufacturer, at least of such a product, owes a duty
to the ultimate consumer to take reasonable care was applied
by Lewis J. In this case, its application favoured the manufacturer, because the plaintiff failed to prove that the manufacturer had in fact broken his duty by failing to take reasonable care.

Such a case is directly comparable with, e.g., *M'Glone* v.
British Railways Board (1966 S.C. (H.L.) 1), where likewise
one issue at stake was whether the Railways Board had taken
reasonable care for the safety of the pursuer, who had been
electrocuted while climbing a power-line pylon on an elect-
trified railway line; that the rule in this latter case was
established by legislation, viz. the Occupiers' Liability (Scotland) Act 1960, is a point which in no way differentiates the
style of reasoning involved. There is a rule requiring somebody

to take reasonable care for somebody else; what the court has to do is to decide whether reasonable care was taken, and that regardless of the source of the rule. In *M'Glone* and in *Daniels* as it happened, the judges decided that reasonable care had been taken.

The application of a rule may of course necessitate making a ruling as to its proper interpretation for a given species of facts. We have just been discussing that in relation to the Rent Acts and the Race Relations Acts. In the same way, questions can arise about the proper interpretation (and thus application) of case-law rules. We have already seen how, in *B.T.C.* v. *Gourley* ([1956] A.C. 185) the House of Lords gave a ruling which Lord Goddard expressed in the following terms:

In this opinion I am dealing solely with damages in personal injury and wrongful dismissal cases. In the present case all we are concerned with is whether in calculating the damage the incidence of tax should be taken into account and whether it is an element to be considered in assessing general damage. In my opinion, it is, and I would therefore allow the appeal. . .(Ibid. at p. 210)

That is straightforward and clear as far as it goes; but it does not by any means anticipate all possible doubts and problems. Take the case which, putting it in simple terms, arose in *Lyndale Fashion Manufacturers Ltd.* v. *Rich* ([1973] 1 All E.R. 33). The company wrongfully dismissed Mr. Rich, who in due course succeeded in mitigating his loss by obtaining alternative employment. During the relevant tax year before and after his dismissal, he earned £x gross; had he remained employed with the company, his gross earnings would have been $(x + y)$. So in terms of gross earnings, his wrongful dismissal had cost him £y.

Given a progressive system of income tax, the marginal tax rate bites upon earnings above a certain level. The effective rate of taxation of Mr. Rich's £x was quite low after taking account of all his allowances against tax. But if he had in fact earned £y on top of that, a substantial proportion of it would have gone in tax, say £z. The Company's case was that it ought only to pay £$(y - z)$ by way of damages; but Mr. Rich argued that that was unfair, and that there should be set against his damages not tax charged at the marginal rate for the top 'slice' of his income, but only the average

rate of tax payable on the whole income of a person earning
£$(x + y)$ in all. As against the company's offer of £$(y - z)$
he demanded the considerably larger sum represented by
£$(y - \frac{z}{n})$.

The Court of Appeal ruled that the Company's was the
better view; thus it gave an authoritative ruling on the interpretation of the *B.T.C.* v. *Gourley* rule in relation to this
type of case. As we would expect, it justified that ruling by
reference to the basic justifying principle of the *Gourley*
case; if damages are for compensation only, and if the interpretation favoured by Mr. Rich would make him better off in
terms of net earnings than he would have been had he stayed
in the Company's employment, then that is a good reason
for rejecting his argument. It would have, and so the court
rejected it.

This case illustrates the characteristic process whereby an
initial ruling, in principle simple, on an important point of
law, is in turn concretized and elaborated in details by a
succeeding series of satellite rulings.[14] Nowadays, to understand the law on the question of the offsetting of tax liability
against lost earnings in actions for damages for personal
injuries or wrongful dismissal, one has to refer not only to
the initial basic ruling in *Gourley*; one has to refer also to the
series of precedents which have elaborated the doctrine in
its application to a series of generic contexts. The same is,
of course, true of Acts of Parliament—a glance at Commentaries on the Rent Acts, the Race Relations Acts, the Sale
of Goods Act, or whatever, is sufficient to show how each of
the sections has been glossed and concretized through the
process of judicial interpretation.

In France, where in theory precedent has no binding force,
the standard editions of the codes in like manner list in
footnotes to each section of each article the leading decisions
which have ruled on points of interpretation of the relevant
law. Reading the codes in themselves tells one something of
the general spirit and principles of French law. But one
could be greatly misled as to the detailed practical effect

---

[14] A similar point is made via the different metaphor of plotting points on a
graph in Paton's *Text-book of Jurisprudence*, 4th edn., pp. 219–21.

of the law, if one did not study also the precedents revealing how it has been judicially interpreted. In this matter, the difference between statute law and precedent, and indeed between codified and non-codified systems, certainly ought not to be exaggerated.

(ii) *Distinguishing and explaining precedents*

Just as judges, on the basis of consequentialist arguments and arguments of principle which seem to them good, sometimes apply a very narrowly restricted interpretation of a statutory provision (e.g. s.4(4) of the Foreign Compensation Act 1950, in *Anisminic* ([1969] 2 A.C. 197), so do they on occasion, and for the like justifying reasons, interpret precedents very restrictively in order to 'distinguish' them from the point in issue in a given case.

Sometimes, of course, the distinguishing of a precedent involves giving full effect, but no more than full effect, to the original ruling. When in *Phipps* v. *Pears* ([1964] 2 All E.R. 35) the Court of Appeal was invited to rule that the owner of one house could have, and did in the instant case have, a right against the neighbouring proprietor by way of an easement of protection from the weather (see above, p. 189), the court in rejecting that invitation drew a distinction between the situation in hand and the situation covered by precedents establishing the easement of support. *Dalton* v. *Angus* ((1881) 6 App. Cas. 740) was, as Lord Denning noted, such an authority. But the ruling that one person may not knock down his house so as to remove the physical support of his neighbour's is in no sense incompatible with the ruling that he is not obliged to preserve its protection from damage by adverse weather. The one case is plainly distinct and therefore distinguishable from the other. As was said before, the former could be extended by analogy to cover the latter; but in the absence of sufficient reasons of policy or principle, it need not be; and given that the law is properly 'very chary of creating any new negative easements' ([1964] 2 All E.R. 37, *per* Lord Denning M.R., *cit.sup.*, p. 189), it ought not to be.

Distinguishing in this way is simply the obverse side of applying case law rules; to the extent that a rule can be or has been formulated in clear terms authorized by binding precedent, it is to be applied according to its terms when its operative facts are satisfied; when they are not, it cannot be directly applied, though it may given other sufficiently good grounds be used as an analogy justifying extension of the law. In the absence of such grounds it can simply be taken at its face value and distinguished—for despite the analogical similarity between it and the instant case, the opposite ruling in the instant case does not controvert the precedent ruling.

What is more interesting is the conscious restatement of the point made in a precedent, the 'explanation' of it, which clears the way for treating it as distinguishable from the instant case. We have seen how in *Steel* v. *Glasgow Iron and Steel Co.* (1944 S.C. 237) the Court of Session used the analogy with 'rescue' cases to justify recognizing the right of a salvor who saves property endangered by negligence to damages against him whose negligence endangered it. But their Lordships had an obstacle (not hitherto mentioned) to surmount in so doing.

In *Macdonald* v. *David MacBrayne Ltd.* (1915 S.C. 716), a salvor's right was denied in the following circumstances: MacBraynes, the shipping company, being under contract to deliver two drums of paraffin to Mr. Macdonald's store in Fort William, in fact delivered two drums of paraffin and one of naphtha. Taking it for a drum of paraffin, he kicked it to see if it was full, and it exploded setting fire to the store building. Mr. Macdonald escaped from the conflagration, but was severely injured while trying to extinguish the blaze. On appeal from the sheriff, the Second Division held that MacBraynes were liable for the damage to the store directly arising from their careless misdelivery in breach of contract. But they held that the pursuer's acts in trying to extinguish the blaze constituted a *novus actus interveniens*, breaking the chain of causation, and that accordingly he had no right to reparation for his own injuries.

In *Steel's* case, counsel for the pursuer put the following argument:

Macdonald v. *David MacBrayne Ltd.* [was] an example of voluntary self-exposure to an unreasonable danger, and so was distinguishable from the present case in which no such unreasonable actings had taken place. It was important to keep in mind the responsible position held by Steel in relation to his train. . .(1944 S.C. at p. 243)

In effect he offered to the Court an explanation of the *Macdonald* decision which would be consistent with a ruling in the pursuer's favour in the instant case: that it ruled that unreasonable self-exposure to risk excluded a salvor's right, not that a salvor never had a right to damages against the party negligently endangering property.

Among the majority in *Steel's* case, Lord Cooper went even further than that and declared roundly that '*Macdonald* v. *David MacBrayne Ltd.* appears to me to be no more than a decision on its own facts' (ibid. at p. 247). In short, he denied that the precedent contained any considered ruling on the question of salvor's rights; it assumed rather than stated any proposition of law, and, as counsel had argued, must be presumed to be based on a factual appreciation of the pursuer's conduct as unreasonable. Lord Mackay, on the other hand, who dissented in *Steel's* case, urged that the 'rescue' cases were distinguishable (which they certainly were), and that they ought to be distinguished, because *Macdonald* ought to be followed as much by authority of its reason as by reason of its authority: 'I see no other just result, and that is the effect of *Macdonald*' (ibid. at p. 261).

It is an important point that it is the proposition of law, not the particular words in which the precedent court has expressed it, which if anything constitutes binding *ratio* under the doctrine of precedent. This does indeed distinguish practice in relation to precedents from practice in relation to statute law. Statutes lay down rules 'in fixed verbal form' as Twining and Miers put it;[15] precedents do not. Any interpretative gloss on a statutory provision must be consistent with the *ipsissima verba* of Parliament in some sense which can reasonably be applied to them. That restriction does not apply to judicial interpretation even of authoritative rulings on points of law to be found in the precedents. For that reason the latitude available in 'explaining and distinguishing' precedents in unquestionably greater than that

[15] Loc.cit. *supra*, Ch. III n. 7.

available in the restrictive interpretation of statutes. Provided that the ruling in a precedent can be restated in a way which is consistent with the decision of the case, and in line with the ulterior arguments of principle to which appeal was made in the case, judges will accept and use 'explanations' of the precedents which clear the ground for what are deemed to be desirable rulings on the points at stake in a given case.

But the presumption is against far-fetched explanations, just as in statutory interpretation the presumption is in favour of the most 'obvious' meaning of the relevant terms of the Act. What is crucial is the perceived strength of the consequentialist arguments and arguments of principle in favour of the case which is prima facie obstructed by adverse binding precedents (or, for that matter, adverse statutory provisions). Judges treat it as permissible to explain restrictively and to distinguish binding precedents when there are strong reasons for doing so, but the onus of argument is very much on the party who needs to make the distinction in order to set up his own case.

It is commonly said that it is only the ratio of a precedent which is binding, not the ulterior justificatory reasons which are only *obiter dicta*. This is, technically, true enough; but it should also be realized that the respect which is in practice accorded to judicial rulings on the law is to some extent conditional on the strength and persuasiveness of the supporting arguments adduced therefor. In *Steel's* case, Lord Cooper was no doubt the more ready to treat lightly the *Macdonald* decision, because the issue in that case was dealt with fairly summarily and without careful argument of principle, whereas in Lord Cooper's opinion the argument from legal principle favoured the pursuer in *Steel*. In *White & Carter (Councils) Ltd.* v. *Macgregor* ([1962] A.C. 413, 1962 S.C. (H.L.) 1) the boot was on the other foot, in that Lord Reid justified overruling the adverse precedent of *Langford* v. *Dutch* (1952 S.C. 15) on the ground *inter alia* that in that case Lord President Cooper in holding that an advertiser was not entitled to claim the full contract price for a cancelled advertising contract had failed to explicate any reason of principle for that ruling. (The current legal consensus appears to be that Lord Reid, however, was wrong, and Lord Cooper right,[16] but that's another story.)

Here again, there is a difference with respect to statutory interpretation, in the sense that statutes stand as law in their own right, without the support of express arguments of principle. Nevertheless, it is statutes which appear to Courts to lack underlying principles which are the likeliest candidates for restrictive interpretation, especially when they trench upon common law principles (not that one always agrees with the judicial view about what constitute good principles in such contexts). We saw in relation to *Temple* v. *Mitchell* (1956 S.C. 267) how a difference in background principles of matrimonial law as between Scotland and England was treated by the Second Division as fatal to construing the Rent Act provisions concerning a tenant's security of tenure in favour of the deserted wife. And cases like *Ridge* v. *Baldwin* ([1964] A.C. 40) or *Malloch* v. *Aberdeen Corporation* ((1971) S.L.T. 245) indicate how ready courts are to treat statutory powers of dismissal of public servants as importing the requirement to observe the principles of natural justice.

At the very least one can say that the process of and the grounds for restrictively explaining and distinguishing precedents are markedly similar to those of and for restrictively interpreting statutes; the difference is only in the degree of freedom which judges ascribe to themselves in effectively rewriting precedents which they deem to be unsound in principle or unacceptable in their consequences. It is sometimes no more than decorum which leads a judge to argue that the apprehended adverse consequences which would flow from adopting a certain interpretation of a statute cannot have been intended by Parliament—what price *Anisminic*?

One last point which ought to be obvious: the dominant values and principles of the law change over time. When in *Derry* v. *Peek* (1889) 14 App. Cas. 337) the House of Lords held that A had no right to damages for losses arising from A's reliance on B's false statement negligently but not wilfully

---

[16] See, e.g., D.M. Walker, *Principles of Scottish Private Law* (2nd edn., Oxford, 1975), i. 642n.

or recklessly made, it was no doubt acting in accordance with the then dominant principle that parties must secure their own protection by contracts. By the 1960s the law in relation to negligence in general had developed (or in Scotland returned) to a very different point.

It was therefore not surprising that in *Hedley Byrne & Co.* v. *Heller & Partners* ([1964] A.C. 465), *Derry* was distinguished on the ground that it ruled only that proof of actual intention to deceive or of wilful recklessness as to the truth was essential to an action for damages for the tort of deceit. But since *Hedley Byrne*, in ruling that A has a right to damages against B when A has reasonably acted in reliance on B's statement which turns out false, B having had grounds to foresee that he would so rely but having failed to take reasonable care to be accurate, set up a right to damages for economic loss independent of physical harm, it was in turn controversial. Despite the dissent of Lords Reid and Morris of Borth-y-Gest, the Privy Council in *Mutual Life etc. Co.* v. *Evatt* ([1971] A.C. 793) restrictively explained and distinguished the *Hedley Byrne* ruling, towards which the pendulum has in turn swung in later decisions in which *Evatt* has not been followed.[17]

Whether a precedent is distinguished or not is not conditioned simply by the question whether it is in some way distinguishable; it is also, and crucially, conditioned by whether or not there appear to the court good reasons to distinguish it. Such reasons are in the nature of the case controversial and the values which they necessarily incorporate change over time.

(iii) *Extending and Developing Case-Law Rules*

The very point just made is the key to considering how case law in the process of interpretation is extended and developed. Nobody is ever under an obligation to distinguish a given precedent just because it *can* be distinguished. On the basis of the majority speeches taken together it was at one time *possible* to have argued that *Donoghue* v. *Stevenson* did

---

[17] See, e.g., *Esso Petroleum Co. Ltd.* v. *Mardon* [1975] Q.B. 819, [1976] Q.B. 801 (C.A.).

no more than establish that manufacturers of articles of food and drink owe a duty of reasonable care towards those who consume the food and drink they make. That point was open to argument in *Grant* v. *Australian Knitting Mills* ([1936] A.C. 85), where sulphite-impregnated underpants gave the wearer dermatitis. But nothing was made of it and the Privy Council further held that under *Donoghue* the point was not whether it was *possible* for the harm-inducing defect to be discovered or removed by intermediate inspection or by the consumer's own act, but whether it was reasonably foreseeable that it *would in fact be* so discovered or removed. The purchaser of the underpants *could* have washed them before wearing them, but it was reasonably foreseeable that many buyers of such articles would do no such thing. So, too, as we noted earlier, in *Haseldine* v. *Daw* ([1941] 1 K.B. 688) it could have been held that *Donoghue* did not cover, but was indeed distinguishable from, cases involving the repair of lifts and the like. But it was not so held, the Court of Appeal indicating that it saw no good ground of policy or of principle for drawing any such a line. And so on.

To go into this at any great length would be otiose, since it would merely repeat the points made in Chapter VII about the understood legitimacy—and legitimating force—of analogical extrapolation from established law. A case can be supporting authority for a great deal more than that for which it is binding at the level of minimal indistinguishability. Case law is open ended, in that essentially a judge or Court seeks to give a ruling in law which *sufficiently* justifies its decision.[17a] There is a great difference between saying '*At least* if *p* holds good, then the consequence is *q*' and saying '*only if p, then q*'—and the former is much more characteristic of case law rulings in novel areas than the latter.

The controversy[18] as to what was the ratio of *Barwick* v. *British Joint Stock Bank* ((1886) L.R. 2 Ex. 259) turns on failure to observe this. A bank manager acting in the course of his employment fraudulently induced the plaintiff to

---

[17a] Cf. A.W.B. Simpson 'The *Ratio Decidendi* of a Case etc.' in *Oxford Essays in Jurisprudence*, ed. A.G. Guest (Oxford, 1961), ch. 6.

[18] See Cross, *Precedent in English Law*, 2nd edn., pp. 72–4, and Goodhart, op.cit. *supra*, Ch. IV n.7.

accept a worthless guarantee, whereby his employer the Bank obtained a benefit; it was held that the Bank was vicariously liable for its servant's fraud. Plainly, the decision could legitimately have been distinguished later in cases involving fraudulent employees whose frauds in the course of their employment did not benefit their masters.

But in *Lloyd* v. *Grace Smith & Co.* ([1912] A.C. 716) the House of Lords, reversing the Court of Appeal, held that the element of benefit to the master is not necessary to the master's vicarious liability for an employee's fraud committed in the course of his employment. The House of Lords *said* that in *Barwick's* case Willes J.'s reference to the master's benefit was merely an allusion to particular facts of the given case. But it could have *said* the opposite had it been minded, as was the Court of Appeal, to deny liability in such cases. What was involved here was a quite proper extension of the ambit of vicarious liability for fraud, by removal of the earlier cautious qualification—expressible as 'at least if the master benefits'. To attempt, as Dr. Goodhart appears to have attempted,[19] a doctrine of *ratio* which includes both the least a case must be followed for and the greatest point to which it can be extended is to essay the impossible.

Of course what starts out as an open ended development in law can be closed off. 'At least if. . .' can be turned into 'only if. . .'. The doctrine of *Rylands* v. *Fletcher* ((1868) L.R. 3 H.L. 330) was in just that way closed off in *Read* v. *Lyons* ([1947] A.C. 156), as was discussed earlier. The *Rylands* doctrine *could* have been extended to cover escape of dangerous substances from control by the defendant, regardless of escape over the perimeter of his property, and could have been extended to cover personal injuries to the plaintiff, not just harm to a neighbouring proprietor. *Read's* case, on grounds of principle already reviewed, set up an 'only if' barrier establishing escape out of the defendant's land and damage to neighbouring proprietor as necessary, not merely sufficient, conditions of strict liability.

Although, as we have seen, statutes can be and are on occasion appealed to as establishing principles and con-

---

[19]   Goodhart, op.cit.

statute law within our legal systems than is the use of stituting analogies justifying developments outside of their specific sphere, that is a less marked feature of the use of case law doctrines and principles to that effect. If on any point, it is on the point of 'open endedness' that case law differs most from statute law at least in our tradition as distinct from that of e.g. France. But that does not affect what has been here said about the demand of consistency in relation to statute law and case law alike. 'Thou shalt not controvert established and binding rules of law' is a command-ment which applies to both, and which imposes genuine and important limits to judicial freedom of action even after we have made all appropriate qualifications to allow for the possibility of restrictive interpretation and explaining and distinguishing.

Open-endedness has another aspect too, in that case law rules are in a sense only relatively binding. In a hierarchical system of Courts, only confusion and expense is caused by lower courts declining to follow precedents set by higher courts; so, standardly, the latter's decisions are binding on the former. But not vice versa, of course, and at any given level, it is not necessarily the case (and is actually so only for the English Court of Appeal and Divisional Court) that an appellate court must treat as absolutely binding its own prior decisions and those of co-ordinate tribunals. Such decisions are at the material level only presumptively binding, and precedents from below are only persuasive, so that observance of precedent rulings lacks the cast-iron obligatory quality presented by valid statutes. Overruling or not follow-ing is always a possibility. Again, it is the reason of justice, of not departing from like decisions in like cases without very good reason, and the reasons of policy and principle supporting the precedents, coupled with the public-con-venience argument for certainty in law, which account for the standing of precedent as a 'source of law' in the system, and which enable us to grasp its essentially open-ended quality.

The relevance of that is more to the ideal of coherence than to the requirement of consistency. But taking the two together, we can see why it is that there is not a clear line dividing 'clear cases' and 'hard cases'. What makes a case clear in law is that facts can (it is believed) be proved which are unequivocal instances of an established rule; but the established rules are susceptible of variant interpretations depending on the pressure of consequentialist arguments and arguments of principle. To be confident in advance that one has a clear case, one must be sure both that it is 'covered' by a rule, and indeed by that interpretation of the rule which is best justified by consequentialist arguments and arguments of principle—whose application will not offend judicial conceptions of the justice and common sense of the law. At once we are in the area of the essentially contestable. Of course there are open-and-shut cases, and we all know then when we see them. But in the spectrum from the pellucidly clear to the long-shot try-on, no one can with confidence (unless he is a fool) claim to discern the point at which the clear cases stop and the hard ones start.

IX

LEGAL REASONING AND LEGAL THEORY

(a) *Principles and Positivism*

A theory of legal reasoning requires and is required by a theory of law. As was seen in Chapter III, any account of legal reasoning, not least the account here given, makes presuppositions about the nature of law; equally, theories about the nature of law can be tested out in terms of their implications in relation to legal reasoning. This is a point which has been strongly pressed by Ronald Dworkin.[1]

Dworkin indeed argues that legal positivism, at least that form of positivist theory ascribed by him to H.L.A. Hart, can be shown to be fundamentally flawed when we consider the implications it has in relation to legal reasoning. The gist of his argument can be grasped, albeit compressedly, in the following way.

A legal system, on the Hartian model,[2] comprises a set of mutually interrelated primary rules, which regulate the duties of persons in a society, and secondary rules which empower individuals in private or public capacities to vary the incidence of, or alter, or apply others among, the whole set of rules. What unifies the whole set into a system is the existence of a secondary rule which sets criteria for identifying all those rules which belong to it, and which thus settles the duty of officials to observe and give effect to all the other rules. The existence of that 'rule of recognition' is constituted by its common acceptance 'from the internal point of view' by at least the superior functionaries of the system, as a shared social standard for them at least; its existence as the rule of recognition of an actually operative legal system requires that the rules which it identifies be effectively in force among the population of the society in question.

---

[1] Dworkin's case is made out in a series of well-known articles, now reprinted in *Taking Rights Seriously* (London, 1977), of which see especially cc. 1–4, 12, 13 (hereinafter cited as *TRS*).

[2] As expounded in *Concept of Law* (Oxford, 1961).

According to Dworkin, that thesis is untenable because it necessarily misrepresents the process of adjudication. First of all, it leaves no room for the operation of principles within the judicial process.[3] Secondly, it wrongly characterizes the nature and extent of judicial discretion:[4] rules according to Hart's thesis have a core of certainty and a penumbra of vagueness and open texture, so in cases outside the core of certainty, in which the rules supply no unequivocal guidance, judges must have discretion in the 'strong sense', in the sense that they can only in a quasi-legislative way choose the decision which seems to them best on whatever grounds they think appropriate to such choices. The truth, says Dworkin, is that they have only a weak form of discretion, in that they must exercise their own best judgment (whose else could they use?) as to the proper application of relevant principles and other legal standards. Thirdly, these principles, although genuinely legal, are not identifiable by 'pedigree' via a rule of recognition.[5] Fourthly, the theory of social rules on which the account of the rule of recognition is based is in any event untenable.[6]

So much for the destructive arguments. Constructively, Dworkin argues that the basic feature of legal principles, as a subclass of political principles generally, is that they identify rights of citizens as individuals, and so are distinct from policies which identify 'collective goals'. In hard cases as truly as in clear cases, it is rights of citizens which are being enforced—and not least of one's rights is the right to a judgment vindicating the other rights one has. Of course it is contestable which of the parties in litigation has the better substantive right and thus the right to judgment in his favour. But rights must be 'taken seriously'—not trivialized as positivism trivializes them by implying that the winner in a hard case is simply the beneficiary of a 'strong' discretion exercised in his favour by way of retroactive law-making.[7]

What shall I say about all that? It must be obvious that the

---

[3] *TRS*, pp. 22–8, 71–82, 90–100.
[4] *TRS*, pp. 31–9, 68–71.
[5] *TRS*, pp. 21, 36, 39–45, 64–8.
[6] *TRS*, pp. 46–80.
[7] *TRS*, pp. 81–6, 279–90.

approach which I have taken in this book is vastly influenced by, though not simply derivative from, Hart's. Is the book then a mere rehash of a version of positivism which has already been bypassed or rather steam-rollered into oblivion by the Herculean power of the 'Rights Thesis'?

Unsurprisingly, I am inclined to think that there is more to be said for it than that. What is more, though it contains many excellent insights, the 'Rights Thesis' itself is fundamentally flawed as a theory of law, and the general theory of this book in fact gives a better account of those very aspects of the legal process which Dworkin takes to be inexplicable by positivists. Let us consider first the four points of the destructive argument, excepting the second, on discretion, which will be considered later.

Dworkin, like Pound[8] (to whom he acknowledges his debt) and many others before him is indubitably correct in asserting that arguments from legal principle play a profoundly important part in legal reasoning—and it is a defect in Hart's *Concept of Law* that this is touched upon only in passing.[9] Chapter VII of this book—also following many precursors— shows indeed that arguments from principles and from analogies play a vital part in the decision of hard cases in our laws, and to that extent though not unqualifiedly confirms Dworkin's point. Most recently, Chapter VIII has shown also that the interpretation of rules is much affected by considerations of principle. The decision whether to interpret a statute restrictively or extensively, or the decision whether to explain and distinguish or follow by extending a case-law rule is, as a matter of observation, in part at least based on arguments from legal principles, so that we can't tell whether the case we are faced with is easy or hard until we have reflected on the principles as well as on the prima facie applicable rule or rules.

The last point however is as much a point against as for Dworkin. One of the distinctions he draws between principles and rules depends on the view that rules have 'all or nothing' quality,[10] so that if valid they either determine a decision or

---

[8] R. Pound, *An Introduction to the Philosophy of Law* (rev. edn., London, 1954), p. 56; see *TRS*, p. 38.

[9] See the opening sentence of ch. 7 of *Concept of Law*: at p. 121.

[10] *TRS*, pp. 24–6.

contribute nothing to it, while on the other hand principles having the dimension of weight (a metaphor on which doubt has already been cast) may compete without either of the competitors being invalidated by loss in the competition.

One of the defects in that view, that it leaves the use of rules in argument by analogy unexplained, was sufficiently pressed home in Chapter VII. In the light of Chapter VIII we may now add the converse point, that in problems of interpretation rules in effect compete with principles, and are not invalidated by loss in the competition. That reasons of principle (coupled with consequentialist arguments) justified the decision in *Anisminic* ((1969) 2 A.C. 197) to construe narrowly s.4(4) of the Foreign Compensation Act 1950 does not imply that the section was invalid. (In terms of the weight metaphor, the Court of Appeal could be said to have ascribed greater weight to s. 4(4) than did the House of Lords). What the House of Lords did was to determine the ambit of the rule in a given context, not its validity or invalidity. *Per contra*, in *Temple* v. *Mitchell* (1956 S.C. 267) the majority considered that the clear words of section 15 of the 1920 Rent Act overrode the principle of protecting the family home; in the relevant context, they fixed the ambit of that principle—just as much as when in *Read* v. *Lyons* ([1947] A.C. 156) the principle of no liability without fault collided with the principle of strict liability for damage caused by escapes of dangerous substances, and the ambit of the latter was fixed.

rules and principles (and it is a necessity both for the present thesis and for the 'rights thesis'), we shall have to look elsewhere than in the rights thesis. (The idea that principles identify rights wouldn't do either—so do many rules, as I have recently argued[11] at some length.)

The better view was stated in Chapter VII as being that principles are relatively general norms which are conceived of as 'rationalizing' rules or sets of rules. That postulates, of course, that we know what rules to rationalize. But we do. We know the rules of law because we have 'criteria of

---

[11] N. MacCormick 'Rights in Legislation' in *Law, Morality, and Society*, ed. P.M.S. Hacker and J. Raz (Oxford, 1977).

recognition' or something like that. (To avoid repeating at length an argument I have made elsewhere, let me say that I would rather make the point through the notion of 'institutive rules' which set criteria of validity for other rules of law;[12] I have here, for simplicity, used the more familiar Hartian formulation.) If we could not and did not know rules of law, law examinations would be even more pointless than those who sit and those who mark them are in their gloomiest moments inclined to think them.

That is what knocks down the third point ascribed to Dworkin above. There is a relationship between the 'rule of recognition' and principles of law, but it is an indirect one. The rules which are rules *of law* are so in virtue of their pedigree; the principles which are principles *of law* are so because of their function in relation to those rules, that is, the function which those who use them as rationalizations of the rules thus ascribe to them.

This, it may be said, suggests antipositivistically that law is not after all value—free. Not so much does it suggest it, it thunderously proclaims it—but there is nothing antipositivistic about saying that law is not value free.[13] Nobody in his right mind—and there are at least some positivists who are in their right mind—has ever suggested or would ever suggest that law itself is value free. If human beings did not value order in social life, they wouldn't have laws at all, and every legal system embodies not merely a form of social order, but that form of order which is specifically valued by those who have control of the legislative executive or adjudicative process—or at least, it is a patchwork of the rival values favoured by the various groups taking part in such processes.

The point of being a positivist is not to deny obvious truths of that sort. The point is rather in the assertion that one does not have in any sense to share in or endorse these values wholly or in part in order to know that the law exists, or what law exists. One does not have to believe that Soviet law or French law or Scots law is good law or the repository of an objectively good form of social order in order to believe

---

[12] N. MacCormick, *Law as Institutional Fact, cit. sup.*, Ch. III n. 6.
[13] Cf. Ch. Perelman, *Logique juridique* (*cit.sup.*, Ch.I n. 14), s. 37.

that it is law, or to describe or expound or explain it for what it is.

Nor does one have to regard 'the law' as being objective or neutral or impartial as between competing interests or classes or religious groups or other groups or sexes or whatever.[14] Historically and for all present systems that would be an absurd belief. What is more even though a good legal system (in my view) would not favour one class or race or sex or religion over others, it would be absurd to suppose that it would not favour some interests over others. The interests of those who pursue their own ends by fraud ought not be favoured against the interests of those they defraud in any circumstances. Law not merely is never, it ought never to be, neutral as between such interests.

But I am in danger of digressing. Law certainly embodies values and these values are characteristically expressed in statements of the principles of a given legal system. But when we say that law 'embodies' values we are talking metaphorically. What does it mean? Values are only 'embodied' in law in the sense that and to the extent that human beings approve of the laws they have because of the states of affairs they are supposed to secure, being states of affairs which are on some ground deemed just or otherwise good. This need not be articulated at all—it is difficult indeed to be articulate about it, and it would even be mistaken to suppose that many people devote to it the kind of attention necessary to such articulation. The formulation, haltingly and hesitatingly and subject to improvement, of statements of principle in law is one way of making such values relatively more explicit. But observe, this is not necessarily nor even usually a matter of making explicit what is already known clearly; it is a matter of *making sense* of law, as much as of finding the sense which is already there. The point was argued at length in Chapter VII.

Just because that is so, it would be false to argue that the principles are themselves determined by the 'rule of recognition': there may be more than one set of normative

---

[14] Cf. Perelman, loc.cit.; Z. Bankowski and G. Mungham, *Images of Law* (London, 1976), pp. 10–11.

generalizations which can be advanced in rationalization of the rules which 'belong' to the system concerning a certain subject matter—recall the differences between majority and minority in *Donoghue* v. *Stevenson* ([1932] A.C. 562; 1931 S.C. (H.L.) 31) about the proper principles of law to apply in relation to negligence. Nevertheless, over time there develop more or less widely received views as to governing principles, as indeed occurred in relation to the 'neighbour principle' by the time we reached the 1970's in the U.K.

This may seem to involve putting the cart before the horse. Surely, it will be argued, we have the rules because we hold to the principles, not vice versa. Because at least a majority in Parliament was convinced that it would be wrong in principle to let landlords exploit as against tenants the market shortage of houses for private letting after World War I, the Rent Restrictions Acts were enacted. Because a majority in Parliament in the 1960s held it to be wrong in principle to tolerate racially discriminatory practices in areas of public activity, the Race Relations Acts were enacted. Does not the argument that principles belong to the legal system because of their relationship to valid rules get this reality backside foremost?

No, it does not. Recall the dictum of Lord Morris of Borth-y-Gest quoted earlier: 'by enacting the Race Relations Acts 1965 and 1968 Parliament introduced into the law of England a new guiding principle of fundamental and far-reaching importance' ([1973] A.C. at p. 889). That public discrimination between people on racial grounds ought not to be tolerated is a political principle to which some people (myself included) subscribe, while others do not. One can argue out a case why it is a good principle to have, and why it ought to be enacted into law; though the former position does not necessitate the latter, for it is possible to be genuinely opposed to racial discrimination yet to think it unwise or undesirable to institute legal controls in relation thereto, as scrutiny of the Hansard debates over the Race Relations Bills discloses.

Even so, a political principle which commends itself as such even to a majority of people, or to a majority of the thoughtful and unprejudiced people whose views on such matters Dworkin is prepared to admit as relevant,[15] is not *eo ipso* a principle of law. Dworkin himself allows this to be true, in terms of his distinction between principles establishing 'background rights' and those establishing 'institutional right'.[16] What then can transform such a principle into a legal principle?

One part of the answer is Lord Morris's: it can be adopted into law by the enactment of appropriate legislation, by the making of a set of rules which give the principle, as it were, concrete legal form and force by prohibiting or otherwise regulating discriminatory conduct. *Mutatis mutandis* the same could be said of the Rent Acts, in relation to which we saw how, as Scrutton L.J. put it, the Courts subsequently had to work out a 'theory' of how the basic principle was to be put into effect in the application of the enacted rules of law.

But of course that is only part of the answer. The law is indeed not hermetically sealed from morals and politics, and we must heartily welcome Dworkin's energetic assertion of that truth, without necessarily conceding that 'positivism' would lead us to suppose otherwise. The Courts are not immune, nor should they be, from developments in political opinion (which is not to say that there are not extremely good reasons why they ought studiously to avoid taking sides in areas of party political controversy).

I have already suggested that in evaluating the apprehended consequences of possible rulings on points of law the Courts take as one relevant test the bearing of 'common sense', and I have suggested that that refers in part to 'the sort of rough community consensus on social values to which judges conceive of themselves as giving effect' (Ch. VI, p. 149 above). In just that way contemporary opinion on matters of moral and political right comes to be filtered into the law, no doubt subject to the distorting lens of the judges' conceptions of 'contemporary opinion', a phrase whose nebulousness has been consciously chosen to reflect the rather nebulous quality of the reality it describes.

In this way, albeit slowly and incrementally rather than by the 'big bang' of legislation, new principles are adopted into

[15] *TRS*, pp. 246–55.
[16] *TRS*, pp. 93–4.

the law through judicial decision making. Thus, to continue with the race-relations example, in *Scala Ballroom (Wolverhampton) Ltd.* v. *Ratcliffe* ([1958] 3 All E.R. 220), the Court of Appeal held that the Musicians' Union had not acted unlawfully in boycotting a ballroom which operated a colour bar, for, as a union which had black as well as white members it had a legitimate interest in resisting colour bars. That the matter was argued on the footing of actual interests of members of the union, rather than straightforwardly on the wrongness of colour bars, was due to the need to relate the point at issue to existing legal principles concerning civil conspiracy. Why such a need exists in addition to the necessary appeal via consequentialist argument to 'commonsense' moral and political values was fully explained in Chapters V to VII above. (The necessity for common law to develop in this way, not by a 'big bang' is ignored or dismissed in Lester and Bindman's recent *Race and the Law*[17].)

Similarly, *Nagle* v. *Fielden* ([1966] 2 Q.B, 633), in the related field of sexual discrimination, struck down as being in breach of 'public policy' a rule of the Jockey Club whereby women, including the plaintiff who was an experienced horse trainer, were excluded from being granted Jockey Club trainers' licences. Here, support was drawn by the Court of Appeal from general doctrines of unlawful restraint of trade, and from the analogically relevant but in no way directly applicable Sex Disqualification (Removal) Act 1919—yet another example of 'statutory analogy' and a further nail in the coffin of the view that statutes cannot have in themselves Dworkinian 'gravitational force'.

Lester and Bindman describe *Nagle* as a 'rare example of the creative development of the Common Law by the Courts in response to changing social values'.[18] But they are simply wrong in that; for reasons which ought by now to be obvious the Common Law can only be developed incrementally. New values come in only where old principles and analogies can give them a toe-hold. But once they are in they are in, and they can become the focus over time for new and increasingly

---

[17] A. Lester and G. Bindman, *Race and the Law* (Harmondsworth, 1972), p. 53.
[18] Op.cit., p. 52.

bold statements of legal principle. The process is beautifully described in E.H. Levi's *Introduction to Legal Reasoning*.[19] It is not, as the present book also shows, rare for the common law to develop in response to changing social values as understood by the judges. But this can only happen relatively slowly. The enactment of statutes like the Race Relations Acts or the Sex Discrimination Act can change things overnight.

In short, when we ask what gives a principle *legal* quality we must give the answer in terms of its actual or potential explanatory and justificatory function in relation to law as already established, that is, in relation to established rules of law as identified by reference to criteria of recognition. That is thoroughly compatible with the equally true proposition that in the law-making process it is people's adherence to political and moral principles which gives them reason to enact or judicially enunciate statutes or legal rulings. In that way of course a well-framed theory of law meshes with a well-framed theory of legislation, but there is no reason to collapse the one into the other.

Does this involve drawing a sharp disjunction between principles of law and moral and political principles? Yes and no. It involves asserting that there really is a difference between principles which are and those which are not legal, subject to an intermediate *terra incognita* of principles struggling for legal recognition, like the 'neighbour principle' before 1932 and perhaps for some time after. It does not involve the assertion that a principle which is a legal principle thereby stops being a moral or political principle, on which again we are indebted to Dworkin for vigorous statement of the neglected truth.

But again we must be cautious about meanings. Principles which are legal principles are also political, in the sense that they are concerned with the good governance of the polity; they are not political in the specific and narrow sense of that which is a focus of party controversy—as in the 'political question' doctrine. They are 'moral principles' only in the descriptive sense: South African Nationalists adhere to the

---

[19] E.H. Levi, *An Introduction to Legal Reasoning* (Chicago, 1948).

principle of apartheid as a part of *their* conception of political morality. From *my* point of view, if I call that a 'moral principle' I imply only that it is a principle of their morality, not that it is (normatively) a principle which it is moral to hold or act on. If I want to try and grasp contemporary South African law, rules, principles, and all, I must be able to expound what its principles according to my understanding are, without thereby committing myself to any moral endorsement of them. Am I to say that it has no principles, or that it has principles, but bad ones?

The latter seems to me far the better view, and it is in that sense that the positivist programme of keeping distinct the description and the evaluative appraisal of legal system seems to me an essential requirement of clear thought about and discussion of law. Again, I repeat, that is not to say that any law could be grasped at all or its principles and its rules understood if it were not appreciated that *for those who willingly subscribe to* a legal system it is oriented towards values, oriented towards ordering society in what they consider a good and just way. Here let us recognize that Dworkin's critique of positivists for having concentrated to excess on one type of legal standards, legal rules, makes a very palpable hit.

But the positivist must respond not by surrendering the duel, but by extending the ambit of his inquiry. I cannot have a full grasp of a particular legal system in terms of its principles as well as its rules unless I 'get myself inside it' to the extent of grasping the conception or conceptions of justice and the good by which it is animated. I am not incapacitated thereby from rejecting the governing conceptions of justice and the good as corruptions of rather than manifestations of justice and the good life among human beings—which involves normative judgment by reference to my conception of justice and the good.

Thus, although I would argue as strongly as Dworkin that we must take full account of principles and other standards in law as well as of legal rules, if we are to have an adequate theory of law or of legal reasoning, that does not require abandonment of legal positivism characterized minimally as insisting on the genuine distinction between description of a legal system as it is and normative evaluation of the law which is thus described. (Among the most pointless questions which could be asked is whether that is the essence of positivism; there is no such thing as an essence of positivism. The term positivism serves only to characterize an approach to or a programme for legal theory held by some theorist or theorists. There is a range of possible uses of the term from which all one can do is stipulatively select that which characterizes the approach one wishes to defend—or attack.)

Nor does acknowledgement of the place of principles force us to abandon the thesis that rules which count as rules of law do so because they belong to legal systems, and that rules belong to legal systems because they satisfy operative criteria of recognition. So far from making the *legal* quality of certain moral or political principles inexplicable, that thesis ('the validity thesis') is essential to explaining just that point —in terms of the indirect relationship of principles of law to the 'rule of recognition' as argued above.

Dworkin's specific criticism of Hart's way of describing or explaining the existence of a rule of recognition (an explanation which is located within his general theory of social rules) is, however, a criticism in which with considerable difference at least of emphasis I would join. In Chapters III and VI I considered the topic of 'underpinning reasons' for accepting particular criteria of recognition, and pointed out in agreeement with Sartorius[20] how these necessarily come to the surface in hard cases of constitutional import, and require the articulation of constitutional principles and values.

As I said (Ch. VI, p. 139), 'what must be essential to the "internal aspect" of the rule of recognition is some conscious commitment to pursuing the political values which are perceived as underpinning it, and to sustaining in concrete form the political principles deemed inherent in the constituted order of the society in question.' Some such attitude seems to be necessarily engaged in genuine acceptance of an obligation to apply validly enacted statutes, or authoritative precedents, or whatever other rules are derivable from sources

---

[20] R. Sartorius, op.cit. *supra*, Ch. VI n. 2.

of law specified by criteria of recognition. At least one must extrapolate beyond Hart's own discussion of the 'internal aspect' to take fully into account the 'volitional' as well as 'cognitive' components of it, as is argued in the Appendix of this book.

But even in the terms in which the point is put in *Concept of Law*, Hart's suggestion that the 'existence' of a rule of recognition is a matter of 'social fact' is a suggestion only about the *observer's* view of it.[21] There is a point here which must be given full weight, namely that however different might be their several sets of 'underpinning reasons', the judges must at least agree to a very high degree on what does count as a rule of law, and on what are the *immediate* conditions of validity of law, or else there would not be a legal system at all, only chaos. And other officials of Government must at least be willing to work along with these closely convergent judicially operated criteria of validity of law. What is more, it would not be enough that judges just happen to converge in applying criteria of validity which each regards as a purely personal matter settled by each for himself. From the point of view of each judge what is accepted as a criterion of validity must be by him conceived as a social, not a purely personal standard; conceived, that is, as settling what it is right for *any citizen*, himself and other judges included, to act on as valid law.

Since only a madman would frame and adopt such a standard without conscious animadversion to the standards he sees and understands others in a like position of responsibility to be using, there are strong reasons to expect a high degree of agreement and conformity among the judiciary in this matter—so that it is indeed not uncommon for the observer to be able to specify with reasonable accuracy the rule of recognition as it 'exists' at a given time. (What is more, conformity tends to reproduce itself because of the pressure which it generates upon potential 'mavericks', or indeed, to be cynical about it, because of the strong prudential reasons which those who run a system have for keeping it running on an agreed basis. Even so, there is room for, and

---

[21] Hart, *Concept of Law*, pp. 106–7.

there are, strong-minded mavericks to be found like Lord Denning M.R.—if one may so describe him without discourtesy.)

Hart's account as he left it is, then, insufficient, though it is doubtful whether the present account is inconsistent with anything he said, or does more than extrapolate from it. The important point is not, however, the genealogy of the account, but its correctness. Although this account shares or adopts much of what is in Dworkin, one must not throw the baby out with the bathwater. If the question is, 'Can we do without a rule of recognition?', the answer is 'No.' So we must have it as well articulated as possible.

Some, perhaps far too much, vagueness has been tolerated, indeed exploited, in this book so far in the talk about rules or criteria of recognition, criteria of validity, the validity thesis, and all the rest of it. The time has come to lay it on the line with some exactitude. What is all this rather vague talk about?

What distinguishes a judge from, for example, an arbiter is his institutionalized position and duty. A person appointed to be a judge takes up a position within a fairly well-defined institution, 'a court', and as a consequence of his appointment he incurs a duty to resolve disputes coming before him in accordance with law—not just to arbitrate according to the equity of an individual case (whatever that might be supposed to mean) nor to conciliate or procure compromises. He is to do right to all manner of men, and he is clothed with the necessary powers to run proceedings and bring them to a definitive conclusion by issuing binding orders or decrees. The duty to judge according to law would be vacuous unless law were identifiable.

We postulate therefore that in fulfilling his duty he applies some test or tests to distinguish among norms cited before him 'laws' and 'non-laws' or merely 'purported laws'. A fictitious example might be:

(1) The Constitution adopted by the people in 1900 is supreme law, as amended in accordance with its own provisions as to amendment; every rule ('norm') expressed in that constitution is a rule of law.

(2) The Constitution empowers the Legislative Assembly to enact

statutes by a simple majority procedure in each of three stages within each house; every rule ('norm') expressed in any statute enacted by that procedure, in so far as it does not controvert any rule expressed in the constitution as amended from time to time, is a rule of law.

(3)   If a valid rule of law enacted by the Legislative Assembly confers power on another person or body having qualifications q and acting by procedure p in circumstances c to make valid rules on subject matter s, every rule so made in relation to s, in so far as it does not controvert any rule expressed in the Constitution or in an unrepealed valid statute, is rule of law.

(4)   If on any subject matter s, the Supreme Court or the Court of Appeal has given a ruling on a disputed point of law in a case decided by it within its constitutional competence such a ruling, in so far as it does not controvert any rule of law instituted under (1), (2) or (3) above, is a valid rule of law, save that: (a) the Supreme Court may reverse rulings previously made by itself or the Court of Appeal; and (b) the Court of Appeal may reverse rulings previously made by itself.

We postulate further that before his own appointment he considered that all the judges ought to apply as valid rules the rules which were thus identifiable, and that he believed that each of the judges both held that he and his brethren ought so to act, and did normally so act subject to occasional lapses which did not pass without critical comment. We postulate that since his appointment he continues firm in both beliefs, and that he makes no secret of his normative opinion that everyone ought to accept relevant rules as laws, and no secret of the fact that he considers this a generally held and the correct belief. When challenged, he can explain reasons of principle for thinking that such rules so identified ought to be applied as laws; so can other judges, and constitutional writers, and politicians and journalists and various writers of letters to the editors of the newspapers circulating in the country. There is much less agreement about the principles and values which underpin the four rules mentioned than about the content of the rules themselves. There is considerable agreement about that, though quite a few who think that (4) is meaningless because of the difficulty of specifying what is meant by a 'ruling', and in private interviews two of the judges have conceded that they think it enables them to pick and choose pretty well at random from

among statements in judicial opinions in the precedents and
call them 'law', so as to facilitate giving the decisions which
they think intuitively right. At least one Professor of Law
has advanced the thesis that since the constitution does not
empower the Legislative Assembly to delegate legislative
power, the widely held belief in rule (3) is a mistake.

Maximum clarity would perhaps be achieved if we agreed
to call these four rules the 'institutive rules' for valid law
of the imaginary state. Be that as it may, how does the more
familiar 'rule of recognition' terminology fit the postulates?
The answer is that the four taken together compendiously
are the rule of recognition of that state (one legal system,
one rule of recognition, *per* Hart[22]). The rule of recognition
includes four criteria of recognition ranked in descending
order of priority: (i) the Constitution, (ii) Legislative Assembly
acts not inconsistent with (i); (iii) delegated legislation
not inconsistent with (i) and (ii); (iv) judicial precedent of
appellate courts not inconsistent with (i), (ii), and (iii),
subject to the hierarchy of the Courts, and subject to a power
of reversal within that hierarchy. 'Criteria of recognition' and
'criteria of validity' are equivalent phrases.

The 'validity thesis' is the thesis that our imaginary state
is not really imaginary at all, but is, with appropriate sub-
stitutions for (1), (2), (3), and (4), an exact model of every
state having an institutionalized legal system. The concept of
'a legal rule' is defined via that thesis, as being any rule which
is either a rule of recognition or a valid rule of a given legal
system operative within a state (in my preferred terminology:
either an institutive rule or a validly instituted rule).

But the concepts of 'law' and of 'legal system' are, as has
been elaborately asserted and reasserted herein, not exhausted
by reference to the whole set of legal rules. Principles also
belong within the genus 'law', legal systems comprise principles
and all the rest of it as well as laws. And in all the ways
discussed in this book the principles interact with the rules,
underpin them, hedge them in, qualify them, justify the
enunciation of new rulings as tested out by consequentialist
arguments, and so on.

---

[22] Ibid., pp. 97–100.

As with all rules, the rule of recognition or institutive rules can be verbally stated with the kind of relative clarity with which my imaginary ones were stated above. But no reader of this book will doubt that relative clarity of expression does not guarantee clarity or uniformity in application. As I have put it elsewhere, they are perhaps best seen as stipulating 'ordinarily necessary and presumptively sufficient' conditions of validity.[23]

Is it a paradox then to claim that there are principles of law which are *legal* only given their indirect relationship to the institutive rules ('rule of recognition'), but that these very rules and the other rules validly instituted are in turn qualified in the light of and fully understandable only by reference to the aforesaid principles?. There is apparently a logical circle here, but is it a vicious one?

I think not. When we view the law in action what we see is a constant dialectic between what has been and is taken as settled, and the continuing dynamic process of trying to settle new problems satisfactorily and old problems in what now seems a more satisfactory way. Kelsen's conviction that the law has to be represented both in a static form and in a dynamic form[24] in order that its full nature may be captured both testifies to this continuing dialectic and represents a brilliant attempt to grasp and explain it. Or we might instead borrow from Rawls[25] and say that fully to understand law we have first to take a crude statement of all the rules in the statute book and all the precedents in the case books; then inquire into the motivating principles and values of those whose rules they are; then in the light of that modify our initial crude grasp of the verbally replicated rules; then consider again the principles and values, and so on until we reach a stage of 'reflective equilibrium'. But by the time we have got there the law will have moved on—new legislation, new precedents, new textbooks, new review

---

[23] *Law as Institutional Fact* (*cit.sup.*, Ch. III n. 6), part 3.
[24] See Hans Kelsen, *General Theory of Law and State* (tr. A. Wedberg, New York, 1961), pp. 100–13.
[25] J. Rawls, *A Theory of Justice* (Cambridge, Mass., and Oxford, 1972), pp. 319 f., 456 f. For Dworkin's observations on the idea of 'reflective equilibrium', see *TRS*, pp. 159–68.

articles; so we have to start again, this time not quite at the beginning, and work towards reflective equilibrium again. But by the time we have got there. . .(If nothing else, that would certainly well capture the way of thought intrinsic to real legal scholarship.)

It is as though the law were to be compared to the tracks of a 'caterpillar' tractor; an endless belt which is continuously moving through time. Endless, but not gapless, the gaps being filled in by extrapolation from what is already there. If the phenomenon we describe is circular, a circular explanation of it is not vicious, but required by veracity.

(b) *Discretion, Rights, and Right Answers*

Having thus dealt with three of the main points of Dworkin's 'destructive' argument, we are left with the 'discretion' argument still to be considered, together with closely related matters in the constructive argument for the rights thesis. To restate the Dworkinian themes briefly in order to indicate the interlocking quality of the arguments: judges have no 'strong' discretion in hard cases, for even in such cases they are obligated to seek out and give effect to existent legal rights, not to invent them retroactively for one lucky citizen as against his unlucky opponent. This does require the exercise of 'weak' discretion, the 'discretion that involves judgement' over the proper weight to be ascribed to the various legal standards bearing upon the decision. It is highly controversial, and reasonable people inveterately disagree over what is the right answer. But the very fact that they genuinely disagree shows us that there is in principle a right answer, even though in practice we can never be certain what it is or who has it.

An analogy may reveal the force of the last point: I can only disagree over the distance in miles between Edinburgh and Glasgow with someone who uses the same standard of mile measurement as I do. I say it is 44 and he says it is 50. We *seem* to disagree. But it afterwards turns out that his criterion for saying it is 50 miles is that the last time he went from Edinburgh to Glasgow he sneezed fifty times in the train, whereas mine is the more usual one: then we can only compare notes and etymologies—we don't after all disagree, but only seem to. Real disagreement on such a matter postulates common standards which can in principle be applied so as to achieve a correct result, however difficult it is to carry out the measuring process accurately.

As that example shows, the argument from genuineness of disagreement is a forceful one. It has been recognized as such at least since Thomas Reid used it[26] against David Hume. If of two people, judges or not, one states that d is the right decision of a case, and the other says that c is the right decision of that case, it seems evident that they do genuinely disagree. So there must be a right answer in principle, even if it is not in practice possible for anyone to be certain which of them is right.

Powerful though it seems, the argument is false because of a concealed ambiguity in the idea of disagreement. 'Disagreement' includes both conflict of opinion on speculative questions and conflict over projects for practical action. The example of the people who really disagree about the distance in miles from Edinburgh to Glasgow is a case of speculative disagreement.

For an example of practical disagreement, let us consider the following: Mr. and Mrs. X have set aside £25 in their joint account for buying a picture. They go to an exhibition of watercolour paintings and find that there are four pictures within their price range which they both like at first sight, pictures A, B, C, and D. Mr. and Mrs. X each have fairly articulate aesthetic standards which, from long discussion, they both know quite well, and they partially overlap but partially differ—say, they both prefer representational to abstract pictures, but Mr. X has a penchant for impressionist, Mrs. X for pre-Raphaelite styles.

Initially Mr. X's order of preferences is A, B, C, D; Mrs. X's is C, D, B, A; but they talk it over and Mr. X comes to realize that by his standards B is indeed better than A. Both

---

[26] Thomas Reid, op.cit. *supra*, Ch. I n. 5, Essay V, Ch. 7 (1819 edn., vol. iii pp. 571–2). In 'No Right Answer' (*Law, Morality, and Society*, Oxford, 1977, ed. P.M.S. Hacker and J. Raz, pp. 58–84) Dworkin, of course, accuses positivists of using the 'argument from controversy' in a different way. But his own opinion depends effectively on the view that when people disagree on the answer to hard cases, the fact that they really disagree indicates that there is something to disagree about—to wit, the right answer to the case. See esp. pp. 78–9.

of them after discussion agree that by Mrs. X's standards, the right order is C, D, B, A. There is no longer any speculative disagreement. But there remains a practical problem: which to buy. All things considered, Mrs. X regards C as the best buy and Mr. X regards B as the best buy. Neither thinks the other has made a mistake, but they really disagree about what to do, and the disagreement matters to them because they will both have to live with the painting they buy. There is a real practical disagreement, but is there a right answer?

There are indeed real disagreements in law, but the most basic ones are in my submission practical disagreements over what it is best, all things considered, to do. They are not speculative disagreements whose existence forces us to recognize that there is a uniquely correct answer to a given problem. In law moreover, one of the ways open to Mr. and Mrs. X is not open to the judiciary; Mr. and Mrs. X can decide to avoid rather than resolve their disagreement by not buying a picture but going for a slap up meal. Judges who disagree still have to decide. Hence, characteristically, in appellate courts there is commonly though not invariably an uneven number of judges, so that disagreements can be resolved by votes. But the resolubility of the disagreement does not mean that it does not matter to anyone which way the decision goes. The parties and the judges have to live with the result, just as Mr. and Mrs. X have to live with one painting or the other, or with none.

Let me stress that the force of my picture-buying analogy is not dependent on any particularly strong asserted similarity between aesthetic standards and legal standards. Its use is only to establish the reality of the difference between disagreeing over what to do and disagreeing over what is the case. Genuine practical disagreement, about which the parties really care, arises not because of irrationality, not because there is a truly right answer which someone has failed to see but because—or when—the decision one way or the other cannot be avoided and must be taken by people who cannot 'each go his own way' but who must decide together one way or the other and live with the decision.

It does not seem possible to dispute that disagreements over legal decisions in hard cases involve practical disagreement of just that kind. 'Non liquet' is not an available judgment; the Court must rule on the law and decide for one party or the other, and all concerned must live with the result.

It therefore follows that one possible knock-down argument against those who deny that there is a single uniquely correct answer to every possible dispute in law fails as a knock-down argument. The important truth that there are genuine disagreements about the proper solutions of legal problems is explicable otherwise than by reference to the 'one right answer' theory.

Non sequitur that there is not *also* speculative disagreement. A Dworkinian could accept the foregoing point but contend that practical disagreements are only *part* of legal disagreements, for, after all, practical disagreements are often the outcome of speculative disagreements (e.g. economist A and economist B disagree about the cause of inflation, A being a monetarist and B an antimonetarist. They have a real disagreement about a theoretical point to which there is in principle a true answer. They are also likely, as a direct consequence, to have heated practical disagreement over what economic policy the Government should adopt). Having knocked down that knock-down argument, we still face the problem of disputing Dworkin's claim, which can be translated into the proposition that disagreements in hard cases are not only practical but also speculative.

That proposition is intimately associated with the discretion argument. If judges do have 'strong' discretion, then the only possible disagreements in hard cases are practical disagreements, whereas to say that they have only 'weak' discretion is to imply that disagreements in such cases are always in the first instance speculative disagreements, of which practical disagreements are the consequence.

For my part, I certainly agree with Dworkin that judges do not have 'strong' discretion, if that is characterized as I characterized it at the opening of this chapter: to say that in hard cases judges have strong discretion would be to say that 'they can only in a quasi-legislative way choose the decision which seems to them best on whatever grounds they think appropriate to such choices'. But we must not falsely apply the law of excluded middle. Let us not suppose that the only possible alternative to that is to say that judges only have discretion in Dworkin's 'weak' sense[27] with all that it implies.

In summary, the theory presented in this book has been that the judicial duty to do justice according to law is a highly complex one. It is a duty to give only such decisions as can be justified by a good justificatory argument. In the simplest situation, where a clear rule is agreed by all parties to be clearly applicable, the only problem is over proof of facts, and once a conclusion on that is reached, the decision is justified by a simple deductive argument. But the alleged clarity of a rule is intrinsically disputable, and problems of interpretation or classification may be raised; and moreover claims may be put forward in circumstances in which no pre-established rule at all seems to govern the issue—the 'problem of relevancy'. The justification of decisions when such problems are raised must look beyond 'rules' as defined by the validity thesis to principles of the law. Principles of law certainly authorize decisions: if there is no relevant principle or analogy to support a decision, that decision lacks legal justification; and if there is a relevant principle or analogy the decision supported thereby is a justifiable decision—but the adduction of the principle or analogy although necessary to is not sufficient for a complete justification of the decision. The ruling which directly governs the case must be tested by consequentialist argument as well as by the argument from 'coherence' involved in the appeal to principle and analogy. And just as the absence of any supporting principle or analogy renders a decision impermissible, so the test for consistency must be applied: it must be shown that the ruling in question does not controvert any established rule of law, given a 'proper' interpretation or explanation of such a rule in the light of principle and policy.

All that, and especially the role of consequentialist argument, presupposes an adherence to the principle of formal justice. There is much evidence that judges do adhere to that principle in both its forward looking and its backward looking implication; and in my own right I argue that they ought to.

[27] See *TRS*, pp. 31–32, 68–71.

I argue that the interrelated elements of consequentialist argument, argument from coherence, and argument from consistency are everywhere visible in the Law Reports, providing strong evidence that they really are requirements of justification implicitly observed and accepted by judges; and in my own right I argue that these are good canons of argumentation to adopt because they secure what I regard as a well-founded conception of the 'Rule of Law'.

So my theory is presented as a true description of the legal process, and the norms which I describe are also norms which I commend. In either aspect, what does it say about judicial discretion?

It says that judges in our system are, and in every good system of law would be, cribbed, cabined, and confined in the exercise of the great powers which they wield. It does not say that they cannot or that they do not on occasion, perhaps even often, act against the norms of justification stated above. Such evidence as there is suggests that if they do so act, they at least cover their tracks by clothing decisions which are otherwise motivated in contrived justifications of the proper form. But whether such things were done blatantly or covertly, the theory gives us reason to condemn the misconduct (a) as infringing the existing requirements of the system the judges purport to serve; and (b) infringing requirements which it is good to have and observe.

The discretion is then indeed a limited discretion: it is a discretion to give the decision which is best justified within those requirements, and that is the only discretion there is whether or not it is or can be often abused or transgressed. (*Quis custodiet ipsos custodes?*) But although it is only such a limited discretion, it is not what Dworkin means by discretion in the 'weak' sense, with all that is implied in that. The requirements and the sustaining theory tell us by what modes of argument to justify a decision, they do not settle what decision is in the end *completely* justified. Within them there may arise many issues of speculative disagreement which can in principle be resolved, but there is an inexhaustibly residual area of pure practical disagreement.

To say what that means via an example: in *Donoghue* v. *Stevenson* ([1932] A.C. 562; 1932 S.C. (H.L.) 31) Lord

Buckmaster, as we saw, made a factual prediction about manufacturers having to meet hosts of unmeritorious claims which they could not possibly investigate or answer. Lord Atkin implicitly disagreed. In 1932, it was a matter for the future to settle which of them was correct; both honestly held his view and nobody could be certain which of them was correct. But subsequent events have confirmed Lord Atkin's and disconfirmed Lord Buckmaster's view. Again, Lord Atkin asserted and Lord Buckmaster vehemently rejected 'the neighbour principle' as a statement of the 'general conception' of the duties of care variously instantiated in negligence cases in various contexts. Whether that could or could not be—even in 1932—asserted as a reasonable general explanation of the decided cases is (on a generous view) a question admitting of an objective answer. For my part, I agree with Lord Atkin that it was, and disagree with Lord Buckmaster's view that it was not, a reasonable statement of a principle already implicit in the law. We could go through the whole report in this way and line up all the points of speculative disagreement, and if we were so minded we could send for Hercules[28] (Dworkin's demigod *ex machina*) to resolve them correctly.

But at the end of the day there would remain an inexhaustible residue of pure practical disagreement. That would remain locked in the interstices of the consequentialist argument which, as I have stated and restated to the point of boredom, was in *Donoghue* and must be in any hard case the clinching point of the justification, that which moves us from the eminently justifiable to the fully justified decision.

Consequentialist argument involves framing the universalized ruling necessary to the instant decision, examining its practical meaning by considering the types of decision which it will require in the range of possible cases it covers and *evaluating* these as consequences of the ruling. This evaluation does not use a single scale of measurable values (the Bethamistic fallacy is the belief that practical choices can be reduced to testing by such a single scale of measurable values). It involves multiple criteria, which must include at

[28] These labours of 'Hercules' are described in *TRS* at pp. 105–30.

least 'justice', 'common sense', 'public policy', and 'legal expediency'.

Is there, then, the possibility of some theoretically correct answer to the question whether a ruling ought to be given that (e.g.) manufacturers ought to be liable in damages to consumers of their products when in consuming the products they have been caused harm which could have been prevented by the taking of reasonable care in the manufacturing and packaging processes? According to the conceptions of justice, common sense, and public policy held by Lords Atkin, Macmillan, and Thankerton, the answer was 'Yes', and for my part I agree with them.

But if we purge Lord Buckmaster's and Lord Tomlin's views of all speculative errors, can we not suggest that the opposing conceptions of justice, common sense, and public policy also disclose a tenable view? There is a general public interest in cheapness of consumer goods, but there is always a risk of defects in consumer goods. By their own free contracts people in a commercial society can stipulate for such protections as they want against defects, fixing their own valuations of the balance between cheapness and safety. Manufacturers who know with whom they deal directly and on what terms can insure themselves with full foreknowledge of their possible contractual liabilities, and in free competition can reduce their prices to a minimum having made clear allowance for the cost of insurance. Consumers can insure themselves against general risks of injury whether arising by non-actionable negligence or by sheer accident. On these assumptions, to hold manufacturers responsible to persons with whom they are not in contractual relations is (a) unjust, (b) inimical to the public interest in cheapness of consumer goods, and (c) contrary to common sense.

Somebody who holds that view does not have to deny 'the neighbour principle' as a satisfactory generalization about legal duties of care, nor does he have to deny that there is in such a case as *Donoghue* (as Lord Macmillan put it) a real contention between the principles of privity of contract and liability for negligence apart from contract. For what he has done is to have expressed a powerful consequentialist argument favouring adoption of the ruling supported by the contract principle and rejection of that supported by the negligence principle; he has given reasons for according supremacy in this context to the contract principle—for *ascribing* to it, rather than finding in it, the greater 'weight'.

And so we see that once we purge the opposed arguments in such a case of genuine speculative errors, we find ourselves faced with a disagreement which it is in principle impossible to send to any theoretical 'Hercules' for objective resolution by delivery of the right answer. We have reached that point of pure practical disagreement at which we have to reach out beyond that which is already settled among us and decide how we are to live, how our society is to be organized. Between two possible rational extrapolations from our legal and political tradition a choice has to be made, and not merely are the parties stuck with the specific decision, but the judges and all of us in the society have to live (*pro tem.* at any rate) with the ruling and its manifold practical effects on social and commercial life.

Here we find ourselves beyond that which can be reasoned out, although we got there *for reasons*. We got there because to the persons with whom the decision resided the state of affairs represented by a society in which the manufacturers' liability ruling holds seemed in the light of their conception of justice public policy and common sense preferable to the alternative.

Is there any way in which their choice in that matter can be stigmatized as wrong in theory, as distinct from being reversed by repealing legislation? First of all, they could be corrected by reference to their own conception of justice, as perhaps the Lords of the majority in *White & Carter (Councils) Ltd.* v. *MacGregor* ([1962] A.C. 413, 1962 S.C. (H.L.) 1) could be corrected for ignoring the principle of damages-as-compensation-only and its associated principle of mitigation of damages which played such a part in *B.T.C.* v. *Gourley* ((1956) A.C. 185). That would be correction internal to the given conception of justice, which is a possibility but not a relevant one when we are considering the choice which of rival conceptions of justice etc. to put into effect. Secondly, they could over time correct themselves.

In living with the consequences of the ruling they could find them after all unacceptable, and so change their conception of justice etc. (Compare what happened in *Conway* v. *Rimmer* ([1968] A.C. 910).) But that involves a discovery about one's own attitudes and true long-run preferences—not the demonstration of a theoretical error.

There is only one remaining possibility of correction. As between the two rival theories of the disagreeing judges, a third theory could be constructed as the Archimedean point for discriminating between them. But it might in turn be challenged, and a fourth theory constructed to resolve the challenge; but the fourth theory would in turn be challenged—and so on. 'Correction' presupposes criteria of correctness, but (as Dworkin and I both hold), such criteria have to be framed in the context of some relevant theory. So every time I 'correct' a theory as a whole, I am pre-supposing some further theory. Dworkin postulates a Hercules who can construct a best-possible theory of a given legal system. But Hercules can construct that only at the far end of an infinite regress of theories. Dworkin has landed his Hercules in Augean stables in which the dung cannot run out, because it is in infinite supply.

(c) *Rights and Right Answers*

I should be sorry if it were inferred from the foregoing that I do not take rights seriously. That is the last challenge which must be faced.

Dworkin contends that decisions are about rights, and that positivism trivializes these rights in effectively asserting that in hard cases rights are arbitrarily allocated to one side or the other after the event. We must go some way along the road to agreement with him, but not the whole way, since his theory is untenable for the reasons just demonstrated.

To have a legal right presupposes the existence of a relevant legal norm. Under the rules of the Succession (Scotland) Act 1964 and other such laws, various people have in various circumstances rights of intestate succession. Let us call such rights 'rule-based rights', to contrast them with 'principle-based rights'—rights whose justification is asserted on the basis of some principle. Most moral rights and political rights are principle-based; but some legal rights are rule-based, some principle-based. Under the neighbour principle, everyone has a right that others in 'proximate' relations show reasonable care for their safety; under the privity of contract principle (which does not hold, of course in Scots law) everyone has a right to be held liable on contracts only towards those who are also parties to the contract; under the principles of natural justice, everyone has a right to a fair hearing and an impartial judge; and so on. (Dworkin has done a great service in effectively drawing to legal attention the importance of principle-based rights, and I for one am glad of the lesson.[29])

For all the reasons which this book has explored, I cannot but conclude that litigation even in hard cases does concern rights. Since justified decisions in hard cases require the support of principles, and since each side has some principles or rules to appeal to (otherwise the litigation would not be hard), the decision in the end is the confirmation of somebody's principle-based or rule-based right.

But we must not be deluded by a conjuring trick into supposing that that disconfirms the previous argument. The reason why it does not, is that *both* parties in (say) *Donoghue* v. *Stevenson* have rights: they have competing principle-based rights: such that under the negligence principle the pursuer has the right to a favourable decision, and under the contract principle the defender has the right to a favourable decision.

In short, all that we have done is rephrase the truth about the contention of principles as a no less true statement about a contention of rights: a contention of principle-based rights, each based on one of the contending principles. Accordingly, in this phraseology, the point of practical disagreement is: whose right ought to be preferred? or, which is all things considered the better right?'

This may sound paradoxical, and may lead some to think that we should avoid talking about principle based rights.

[29] I omitted to include these in my discussion of legal rights in 'Rights in Legislation', *cit.infra*, Ch. IX n. 11; but they were at least considered in my 'Children's Rights', 1976 A.R.S.P. LXII 305–17.

But that would be dodging, not solving, the problem.

Those, like Dworkin or myself, who say that principles are a genuine part of the law, and that there are many principles of law which can on occasion come into conflict, the whole not being reducible to one great principle such as that of utility, find ourselves occupying a camp in legal theory next neighbours to the so-called 'deontological' or 'intuitionist' school of moral philosophy. For example Sir David Ross (the most distinguished twentieth-century British member of that school) held that[30] there were a variety of moral principles determinant of moral obligations or duties, and that these principles were not reducible to one single principle, as utilitarians argue. In easy cases, we know our duty simply by reference to the applicable principle. But sometimes principles conflict—we can be faced with a situation in which we must tell a lie or break a promise for example. We then have to direct our moral intuition to deciding between the competing principle-based duties, that is, to deciding what is the right thing to do, all things considered.

Ross, however, found it unsatisfactory to use the term 'duty' *both* to refer to the act which is the right thing to do all things considered *and* to refer to the act prescribed by a single principle considered in isolation. He therefore coined appropriate terminology to avoid the appearance of paradox or contradiction. Principles, he said, determine prima-facie duties; but in any choice situation, we must consider the bearing of all our moral principles in order to consider what among our prima-facie duties it is actually our duty to do (our duty 'all things considered').[31]

Exactly the same terminology resolves, in a very recognizable way, the apparent legal paradox. Principles of law determine prima-facie rights, as do rival interpretations of ambiguous rules determine prima-facie (rule-based) rights. Hard cases involve conflicts of prima-facie rights—that is just

---

[30] See Sir W. David Ross, *Foundations of Ethics* (London, 1939), ch. IV, esp. pp. 79–86, ch. VIII. *The Right and the Good* (London, 1931), ch. 2.

[31] *Foundations of Ethics*, pp. 84–5; *The Right and the Good*, p. 19; in the former (historically later) work, Ross admitted to dissatisfaction over the locution '*prima facie* obligation', though he continued to use this idea—see pp. 84–5, and ch. VIII, esp. pp. 190–1.

one way of saying that they are hard—and their decision involves settling whose is to be preferred as the (best) right, all things considered.

In *that* sense, it is true that adjudication always upholds pre-existing rights. But as it is now easy to see, that cannot lead us to suppose that there is no real choice to be made, nor that disagreement which prima-facie right to prefer is anything other than, in the last resort, a case of pure practical disagreement. A real choice has to be made between competing prima-facie rights.

A satisfactory theory of legal reasoning indeed requires and is required by a satisfactory theory of law. The theory of legal reasoning here presented gives full weight to the operation of principles and other standards in the legal process, and it shows that judges never have more than a limited discretion in hard—or any other—cases. But so far from being inconsistent with a 'positivist' legal theory, the present theory depends on and justifies what is, in one sense of the term, a positivist theory of law. Institutionalized legal systems do indeed revolve round what Hart has called a 'rule of recognition' though some departure from or extrapolation beyond his account of social rules is called for.

The reproach that all this involves failing to take rights seriously is readily rebuttable. Just as we must be alive to the distinction between prima-facie duties and duties all things considered, so we must distinguish with no less lively an awareness prima-facie rights and rights all things considered. For it is a mistake to suppose that all disagreements in law are speculative disagreements; there are also pure practical disagreements which remain after all possible speculative disagreements are resolved. There are limits to practical reason, and we ignore them at our peril.

Principles and Policies

It was mentioned in the text of Chapter IX that legal rights can be either rule based or principle-based. From this it may be thought that the present theory follows Dworkin's in assuming that principles are of necessity concerned with rights rather than with 'collective goals', or anything else. Consider, for example Dworkin's statement[1] that:

Arguments of principle are arguments intended to establish an individual right; arguments of policy are arguments intended to establish a collective goal. Principles are propositions that describe rights; policies are propositions that describe goals.

But the present theory in fact makes no such assumption.

It is of course perfectly legitimate to make stipulative definitions in any kind of theoretical work, laying down how particular terms shall be used and shall be understood in the context of the theory. But stipulations which ascribe special meanings to words in common and general usage are apt to mislead readers, if not indeed also the writer.

Dworkin's stipulation that principles shall be always and only considered as right-conferring is pregnant with such danger. The 'principle of utility' as propounded by an act-utilitarian (prescribing that in choice situations that act should always be chosen which maximizes total—or, in some versions, average—happiness) cannot in Dworkinian theory be called a 'principle' after all. The 'principle' of common law that contracts are void if they restrain trade in a manner adverse to the public interest is likewise not a principle after all, in Dworkinian terms. The 'principle of economy of effort' (that one ought always to choose the simpler among alternative possible means to a given desired end) is not after all a principle, in Dworkinian terms.

Likewise, but conversely, if we use the term 'policy' to describe the settled policy of Scots and English Courts to secure that in the absence of contrary enactments a fair hearing is given to everyone whose interests are directly affected by a public decision-making process, we find that

[1] *TRS*, p. 90.

Dworkinism convicts us of infelicity in usage.

The boot, as it seems to me, is on the other foot. It would be singularly eccentric to commit oneself to Dworkin's prescriptions for the usage of the terms 'principle' and 'policy', since to do so consistently would be to make unsayable all manner of things which are perfectly sayable within the ordinary usages of lawyers, philosophers and indeed laymen.

A principle, as I would ordinarily use the term, following what I believe to be a pretty common usage, is (as was said in Chapter VII) a relatively general norm which from the point of view of the person who holds it as a principle, is regarded as a desirable general norm to adhere to, and which thus has explanatory and justificatory force in relation to particular decisions, or to particular rules for decision. (If I believe in the principle that one ought to be temperate in drinking alcohol, and if I am well aware of my fleshly weaknesses, I may be wise to adopt the rule of not touching the stuff till after 5 p.m.)

Principles may therefore be as various in their modalities as any other legal or moral norms. The following is a list of norms which could perfectly well be considered as principles from certain points of view, the modality being different in each case:

(a) An owner of property is free to do what he will with his own, subject to any specific legal restrictions.
     (This principle, so characteristic of high capitalist law, delineates an area of Hohfeldian 'privilege' or 'liberty'.)

(b) Every human being has a right to be presumed innocent of crime until proved guilty according to law.
     (This principle, characteristic of liberal criminal law, asserts a 'claim-right', and is therefore a ground for asserting duties of police, prosecutors, trial judges etc.)

(c) The Queen's Courts have jurisdiction over all legal questions, unless expressly excluded by unambiguous statutory provision.
     (This charactertistic principle of English Common Law, whose establishment was confirmed by the Revolution Settlement, concerns what Hohfeld and others call 'powers'.)

(d) No person may be reduced to a servile status even by his own consent.
     (This principle, no less basic to common law, states a general 'immunity', protected by a self-referring 'disability'.)

(e)   Every citizen must assist the appointed officers of the law in
      quelling riot and civil disturbance.

      (Not merely is this principle of English law in the duty-stating
      mode; the duty it stated is a good example of an Austinian
      'absolute duty', and even the most enthusiastic adherent of
      theories of omnipresent 'jural correlativity' would find it hard
      to find a convincing correlative right. But see (f) below.)

(f)   Human beings have a duty to pursue spiritural perfection by
      mortifying the flesh.

      (This principle of moral asceticism is included finally to
      confute those who adhere to the eccentric opinion that 'duty'
      always implies 'right'.)

(g)   (i) There are no moral authorities.

      (ii) The Queen cannot impose taxes without consent of
      Parliament.

      (These two principles concern Hohfeldian disabilities; the
      former is a moral principle beloved of advocates of autonomy,
      the latter a principle of British constitutional law. The category
      'disability' is thus as apposite to morality as to law, and a
      possible modality of principles of either type.)

(h)   The security of the state ought to be protected in preference
      to private rights.

      (This widely held political principle does not belong to any of
      the Hohfeldian modalities: it is an 'ought-principle' rather
      than a 'duty-principle', though it may be used to justify duty-
      principles—such as that a citizen's duty is to forego private
      rights when the security of the state is at risk. But, observe: in
      Dworkinese 'salus populi suprema lex' *cannot* in logic count
      as a 'principle' at all.)

All the norms listed in (a)–(h) above are, I suggest, tenable
as principles, given certain well-understood points of view as
indicated in each case. But observe that none of (e) to (h)
counts as a principle at all on Dworkin's definition, and that
the status of (c) is at least doubtful.

Let me at once concede that (e) to (h) are not principles
of his, that he does not wish to admit them as principles of
his substantive moral/political/legal philosophy; that is
perhaps all that he really wants to say. But we should beware
of the risk of even seeming to define out of existence
positions with which we wish to engage in substantive philosophical disagreement. That *P* is not a principle of mine does
not mean that it cannot be a principle at all, not even if I
have good arguments which suggest that it is a very bad
principle to adhere to.

The last on my above list, the principle that the security
of the state ought to be protected in preference to private
rights, is perhaps of all of them the one which Dworkin
would most firmly and definitely reject as a principle, for it
belongs to what *he* calls the category of 'policies'. It concerns a 'collective goal' which is plainly non-distributional
in character. The security of the state is not even in principle
capable of allocation in equal (or unequal) shares among the
citizenry, though it may be hoped that it is something in
which everyone has an equal stake. So here we have a classic
case of a Dworkinian 'policy'.

Again, I must contest the reasonableness of Dworkin's
stipulative definition of 'policy'. In the more common
understanding of the term (as attested for example by the
Shorter Oxford English Dictionary), 'policy' refers to a
'course of action adopted as advantageous or expedient',
being especially apposite to courses of action adopted by
governmental agencies. What is important is the idea of a
'course of action', or perhaps we should say 'course of
interrelated actions'. If I as an individual make a policy of
reducing my personal and domestic expenditures over a
period of time—months or years—in order to eliminate my
overdraft, then each of my particular acts of parsimony is
an act within that policy, and justifiable by reference to the
policy-goal, provided of course that the determined course
of actions is in fact well adapted to achieving the policy-goal.
A government's 'incomes policy' denotes a course of actions
extended over time, all aimed at influencing rates of pay
increases as negotiated by trades unions and employers, rates
of company dividends, etc., the whole course of so acting in
this sphere being directed at the goal of reducing the rate of
inflation. In this case, of course, it is highly contestable
whether any such course of actions *is* or *can be* effective in
reducing the rate of inflation, and it is on a different plane
contestable whether such intervention in the free-bargaining
process is desirable even if it can be effective towards that
goal and even if it is agreed that the goal is in itself desirable
of achievement.

Argument over issues of policy can be conducted at three
levels: means-effectiveness arguments—will doing x in this

context actually achieve *y*?, means-desirability arguments—regardless of efficacity is it on other grounds undesirable to do *x*, or undesirable to use *x* as a means to *y*?, and goal-desirability arguments—is it desirable to procure *y* by any means?

But somebody who has a policy in relation to something has set himself to pursuing some relatively determinate course of actions over a period of time aimed at securing some state of affairs, achievement of which *he* must be presumed to think desirable. He must also be presumed to think his course of action likely to be effective in achieving the policy-goal, and not undesirable in itself or in context. The policy is the complex course of actions as articulated towards the postulated goal (which we may call the 'policy goal'); but the goal is not, as *per* Dworkin, the policy. For example, we cannot identify the government's incomes policy as 'reducing the rate of inflation'; rather, it is the Government's having decided to pursue a course of actions *c* with a view to reducing inflation which is its incomes policy.

And so with the law. 'Policy' has become a hideously inexact word in legal discourse, but if we wish to use it with any exactitude at all, we had better use it as denoting those courses of action adopted by Courts as securing or tending to secure states of affairs conceived to be desirable. A 'policy argument' for a given decision is an argument which shows that to decide the case in *this* way will tend to secure a desirable state of affairs. But, in law, the 'constraint of formal justice' so operates as to necessitate that such arguments may be used only by way of evaluating the *universal* or *generic* ruling in terms of its effects in producing desirable or undesirable states of affairs. Decisions in law are not justifiable *ad hoc* or *ad hominem*.

What is more, when in law or in any other sphere we raise the question whether a given policy goal is desirable or not, we are raising a question of principle. For any goal *g*, to say that it is a goal which *ought* to be secured is to enunciate a principle or a judgment dependent on some unstated but presupposed principle. For this reason, the spheres of principle and of policy are not distinct and mutually opposed, but irretrievably interlocking, as I argued in Chapter VII. To articulate the desirability of some general policy-goal is to state a principle. To state a principle is to frame a possible policy-goal. Hence it makes perfect sense (and is true) to say both that the British Courts have a standing policy of securing fairness in judicial and quasi judicial determinations of all sorts, and that the principles of natural justice are important principles of Scots and English law.

Thus I disagree very firmly with Dworkin's characterization of the terms 'principle' and 'policy'. I do so perhaps all the more firmly, because I am inclined also to subscribe to the substantive moral and political theory that the most fundamental principles are those which determine rights (in the sense of 'claim rights'). The reasons which, for me, point in this direction, have been partly expounded elsewhere.[2] We ought, in my opinion, to embark upon the question what are such basic goods for individuals that it would be in all normal circumstances wrong to deny or withhold these from any human being. On that footing we can establish basic principles of human rights. These principles would then, for me, settle the basic groundwork of a theory of justice, and the rights so identified would be treated as indefeasible in the face of other claims of principle or policy.

That does not, however, require me to *define* principles as *only* concerning rights—many less fundamental principles do not. Nor would it require me to define 'policy' so as to set up an artificial opposition between policy and principle. Nor would it require me to say that holders of opposed theories are *wrong by definition*. That is no way to cut off worthwhile arguments.

[2] In 'Children's Rights' and 'Rights in Legislation', *cit.sup.*, Ch. IX n. 29.

X

LAW, MORALITY, AND THE LIMITS
OF PRACTICAL REASON

This chapter confronts a vast topic, but it need not be a long chapter, for it will use rather than restate the arguments of the whole book in order to vindicate the position sketched out in the first section of the first chapter. It must by now have become clear that just as theories of legal reasoning and of law require and are required by each other, both in turn have to be based in some general theory of practical reason and its limits.

If it is a fair reading of Dworkin to take him as asserting that all legal disagreements are at bottom speculative disagreements (and his assertion that 'there is one right answer in [any] hard case'[1] must surely necessitate such a reading), his position has to be rejected as an untenable form of ultra rationalism. Reason *alone* cannot wholly determine what we ought to do.

But it is essential not to be swept to the opposite extreme, to the total irrationalism asserted by such as Alf Ross. The idea that talk of justice is no more than an expression of emotions, equivalent to banging on the table,[2] is at least as aberrant as the ultra-rationalism against which it is a reaction.

This book taken as a whole sets a course between these two extreme positions. As I said at the outset, 'any mode of evaluative argument must involve, depend on, or presuppose, some ultimate premises which are not themselves provable, demonstrable or confirmable in terms of further or ulterior reasons', yet on the other hand, 'that our adherence to ultimate principles in the evaluative and normative spheres is not derived by reasoning...does not show that our adherence to such principles is other than a manifestation of our rational nature'.[3]

---

[1] *TRS*, p. 290.
[2] Alf Ross, *On Law and Justice* (London, 1958), p. 274.
[3] *Supra*, Ch. I, p. 6.

Three particular elements in legal reasoning exhibit the role which reason plays in practical affairs. The analysis of deductive justification shows how we can deduce conclusions about the particular decision which ought to be made from normative premises taken together with premises of proven fact. (Albeit briefly, we saw also how 'proof' of facts involves a reasoned search for coherent patterns of events which allows us to reach conclusions far beyond the present evidence available to direct perception.) The analysis of arguments from coherence and consistency is even more revealing. The argument from consistency requires us not to tolerate the presence in a legal system of two rules which controvert each other. 'The determination of the Commission shall not be called in question in any Court of law' and 'The House of Lords is entitled to grant a declaration of nullity in case of a "determination" by the Commission' seem on the face of it to controvert each other, to be mutually inconsistent. Therefore, either they must be rendered reconcilable by interpretation, or one or other must be rejected.

The argument from coherence goes beyond even that, seeking not merely to avoid flat contradictions or inconsistencies, but indeed to find a way of making sense of the system as a whole, by making sense of branches of it at a time. This is more a matter of ideal than of actual achievement, of course; partly this is because the system changes through time, and there is always some messy old lumber lying around. But in arguing from coherence, we are arguing for ways of making the legal system as nearly as possible a rationally structured whole which does not oblige us to pursue mutually inconsistent general objectives. That is no doubt a bit vague; Chapter VII gave an account which injects some substance into the vaguely expressed idea.

Taking account of consistency and coherence takes us well beyond the minimal contribution of reason involved in deductivity. Many hard-headed irrationalists will concede that given normative premises we can of course make deductions from them while at once going on to point out that reason as such doesn't give us any norms to start with.[4]

[4] Cf. Alf Ross, *Towards a Realistic Jurisprudence* (Copenhagen, 1946), pp. 95–6.

These, they say, are sheer products of will begotten by blind emotion. Attending to arguments of consistency and coherence enables us to resist that irrationalist assertion. What is it other than reason which enables us to judge, after all the permutations of interpretation have been marshalled, whether two rules are or are not inconsistent? What is it other than reason which enables us to assess the coherence of a novel ruling with the body of pre-established law? What, indeed could be more obviously analogous with the process of attempting to construct a whole scientific theory, as distinct from lighting upon a particular scientific truth?

Hume has indeed too passive a view of reason. On at least this point Reid and Kant are right. Reason imposes an order and structure on the phenomenal world of our experience—whether there is in it a real order answering to that which our reasoning makes for us in the phenomenal world is in the nature of the case a question of faith, not knowledge. But equally it is possible for us to order the world of our activity: to shape it in accordance with rules and principles of action and to secure that the rules and principles of our action are mutually consistent and form a coherent set. We reason out questions of consistency and coherence in law, just as much as we reason out the lengthy chains of deduction involved in deciding even so simple a case as the *Daniels* case ([1938] 4 All E.R. 258). To the extent that we have in a nation an ordered legal system, and indeed to the extent that any of us has as an individual an ordered system of morality, we owe it to our capacity of reasoning, our gift for imposing an order of universals on a world of particulars.

The irrationalist is blind to this. The irrationalist has failed to see that not merely does reasoning enable us to deduce consequences from norms to which we adhere, it enables us also to check that the norms from which we reason belong to a consistent and coherent order. Reason may not determine but it does strictly limit the sets of norms we can have all together—whether by that we mean the set we can have all together, all of us together in a state; or the set each of us can have all together as the moral position of an individual, which may differ from the equally rational moral position of some other individual.

The irrationalist may reply that he is an irrationalist not merely in theory but in practice; that he sets no store by having a consistent and coherent morality or legal system or political creed. So be it. Let us ask him whether and why he sets store by having a consistent and coherent set of beliefs about the natural universe, about the world of science. Either he does set store by that or he does not.

If he does not, we are entitled to ignore his irrationalist legal or ethical theory for it will be a matter of sheer chance whether it makes sense. If he does, we can press the question why. One way or the other his answer must come down to the proposition that he values reason, or that he has some kind of irresistible propensity to set his thoughts in order and try to make sense of the world.

But here we touch on the truth which Hume was probably the first philosopher fully to grasp, the truth which ethical and legal irrationalism as theories distort. My belief that I ought to strive to be rational is not a belief which I can justify by reasoning. Of course, it can be explained why somebody with the kind of social and familial background which I have, brought up in a 'professional' family in twentieth-century Scotland, is likely to hold such a belief. Of course it can be conjectured that all human beings have a biological nature of which the propensity to favour rationality is an essential part however occluded by misfortune or adverse circumstance.[5] But these are explanations, not justifications.

If challenged as to why I think I ought to strive to be rational, or indeed why I think that every human being ought to strive to be rational—to avoid inconsistency and incoherence in thought—I really could only repeat Socrates' remark that, to me, an unexamined life is not worth living. I can, really, only express my revulsion from the prospect of a life without reasoned discourse.

Nor can I do other than express my revulsion from the

[5] Cf. Franz Neumann, *The Democratic and the Authoritarian State* (New York and London, The Free Press, 1957), pp. 3–4: 'Man. . .is an organism endowed with reason, although frequently not capable of, or prevented from, acting rationally.'

prospect of a life of arbitrary moment by moment decisions, whether decisions of mine or of others affecting me and my fellow creatures. I shall certainly endeavour to prevent the imposition of any such mode of government. Consistency and coherence, the treating of like cases alike and different cases differently, are *possibilities* for us in our practical acting, reasoning, and deciding, just as consistency and coherence of thought, and the seeking of similar explanations for similar phenomena and different explanations for different phenomena are *possibilities* for us in our attempts to understand explain and describe the natural universe. 'Shall we pursue rationality? Shall we strive for consistency and coherence?'—these are open questions for us in matters both of practice and of speculation.

For my part I cannot see why I should give different answers in relation to action and to reflection. If I were told that the idea of being rational in action as distinct from in speculation is meaningless, I would reply that this book demonstrates the falsity of that assertion. We have a choice, to be rational or not, and it is an ever-present choice in relation to all aspects of our life, whether as theorists or scientists working on explanations of the nature of things, or as practical agents going about the business of life interacting with other animate beings within some set of legal, moral, and social relationships.

The irrationalist fallacy lies in the assumption that moral and legal relations cannot be shaped into a rational order. The ultra-rationalist fallacy lies in the assumption that there is some way of establishing by reasoning and reflection an objectively valid moral or legal order. But any attempt to establish and justify such a theoretical order would simply lead one into an infinite regress of justifications, which is not just like, but the self same as, the road of infinite regress of theories to which Dworkin's Hercules is all unrealizingly consigned.

For although Hume is wrong about the passivity of reason, he is not wrong in contending that our affectively valuing anything belongs to the realm of our attitudes and predispositions; even in the case of reason, it is not *reason* which is expressed if we set value on rationality. If we set value on it, we shall follow it in trying to secure consistency and coherence at a given time and over time in our general attitudes to our own and others' conduct. But it is because we have affective attitudes (including, maybe, a favouring of reason and rationality) that we *care* about what happens to ourselves and other people, or that we care about anyone's acting reasonably or rationally. It is grossly overstating that to say that 'reason is and ought to be the slave of the passions'. But the arresting overstatement has its place even in philosophy.

So although reason is our guide in securing the consistency or coherence of a system of norms, it is an affective commitment to rationality in action which makes us follow that guide, if we do, or so far as we do. And, what is more, we would have no call for norms about conduct at all if we did not *care* about how to live with other people, or about how other people live with us. Shaping these attitudes of 'caring' into norms—rules and principles of action—involves the exercise of reason in framing the 'universal' formulation of a guide to action. But *testing* it to see whether we can live with it; engaging in consequentialist argument—here, as I said in Chapter IX, what is at stake is how we are to live, how we are to satisfy our long-run propensities (what Hume called 'calm passions').

This also shows why the study of 'processes of justification' can also be relevant to the explanation of actual actions. It is of course possible that judges always or sometimes have subjective reasons motivating them to decide cases as they do which are quite other than the justifying reasons they give. But this book shows that it is also possible that judges could commit themselves to trying always to give the best justified decision (as they see it) *because it is* the best justified decision. In that sense, it is *possible* that we can, and that judges do, consciously model our actions upon rules, principles, and other relevant standards. It is a vitally interesting sociological question to what extent, for particular judges, in particular legal systems, at particular times and in particular circumstances, this possibility is actualized. This book demonstrates that that is a real question, though it does not answer it.

Thus an examination of the modes of legal reasoning both confirms and reveals the meaning of saying that reason can play, and in law appears to play, an indispensable role in the governance of practical affairs, but that there are limits to practical reason. Arguments from consistency and coherence reveal the former, the evaluative element of consequentialist arguments, the latter.

Thus it is that we can have rationally structured but not rationally determined legal systems, and indeed 'systems' or 'theories' of morality (as distinct from theories *about* morality). That we can have such enables me to answer a possible objection to the thesis presented in Chapter II, that deductive argument in law is possible. In that Chapter, I committed what some would regard as the obvious error of postulating that there can be 'true' statements of legal norms which figure as major premisses in such deductions. It is with some people an article of faith that there can be no such thing as 'true' statements of norms.[6] (Many such people hold law chairs, and I hope that they never have the hypocrisy to deduct marks from candidates in law exams who make false statements of the law.)

If what they are objecting to is the implication that there are 'absolutely' true normative statements their objection is well enough founded. But given the possibility of a coherent and consistent set of rules and principles identified directly or indirectly by reference to a 'rule of recognition' we have no problem about ascribing *relative* truth to propositions of law. Such propositions can be indeed true or false, relatively to a given legal system at a given time. In consequence, of course, any conclusions we deduce from such relative truths will in turn be only relatively true themselves. But that is all that is needed to sustain the possibility of deductive justifications in law. If it is true, as a proposition of current Scots law, that any person who drives a car on a motorway at a speed in excess of 70 m.p.h. is guilty of an offence, then if it can be proved that I drove my car yesterday in the proscribed way, it is also true (in the context of and for the purposes of Scots law) that I was guilty of an offence.

The same goes for moral propositions. From the point of view of utilitarian morality, it is true that, if keeping promises

---

[6] See, e.g., Alf Ross, *Directives and Norms* (London, 1968), p. 102.

always maximizes happiness, then promises ought always to be kept. Grant the utilitarian premises and that is one true conclusion you can derive. Relatively to somebody who adheres to a utilitarian morality, that and many other true statements can be made. But to call utilitarianism a 'true' moral theory would require some meta-theory for adjudicating among rival moral theories—and so, equally, to call it 'false'. John Rawls's hypothetical contract theory[7] purports to be just such an engine for testing between rival theories as theories of justice. For my part, I cannot, however, truly believe in it as a substitute for the testing of moral theories to which we subject them in trying to live by them as creatures having whatever fundamental attitudes we turn out to have (not that trying to live consistently with a coherent moral philosophy is not an experience which enables us to change and develop our basic attitudes. Although initially given, these are not immutable—otherwise coming to a coherent and reflective set of moral attitudes would be impossible. There is a dialectical engagement between 'reason' and 'passion').

Finally, may it not be objected that it is the grossest form of 'legalism'[8] simply to assume, as this chapter has effectively assumed, that there is an analogy between legal reasoning and moral reasoning. Is this just another case of legal imperialism?

The reverse is really the case. It is not that moral reasoning is a poor relation of legal reasoning. It is rather, if anything, that legal reasoning is a special, highly institutionalized and formalized, type of moral reasoning. Of course the very features of institutionalization and formality create important disanalogies between legal reasoning and moral reasoning in the deliberations of individuals, or the discourses and discussions of friends and colleagues, or whatever.

But the compensation for these built in disanalogies is the publicity and publication which legal reasoning attracts.

---

[7] Op.cit. *supra*, Ch. IX n. 25; and see N. MacCormick, 'Justice According to Rawls' (1973) 89 L.Q.R. 393, and 'Justice—An Un-Original Position' (1976) 3 *Dalhousie L.J.* 367, for fuller support of my assertions about the limits of the contract hypothesis.

[8] See Judith N. Shklar, *Legalism* (Cambridge, Mass., 1964).

We have in the Law Reports a superb resource in the count-less instances they contain of people stating public justifi-cations for difficult decisions they have made affecting other people. Although W.D. Lamont in *The Principles of Moral Judgment*[9] showed moral philosophers how valuable a resource such reports are, it was long enough before anyone followed in his footsteps.

Anyway, I suggest that the disanalogies are greatly exaggerated, and they have been exaggerated because of a false emphasis on moral autonomy—every person his or her own legislature, judge, jury, and sheriff officer. None of us starts off other than totally heteronomous. We are as children (unless we are very unlucky) brought into a family which has a moral code or codes laid down by the governing authorities—parents, grandparents, uncles, and aunts, in due course primary-school teachers.

If autonomy is supposed to involve the experience of inventing a moral universe from scratch it is non-existent, just as much as if scientific originality were to be ascribed only to those who develop a whole branch of science where previously nothing was known.

If on the other hand it means that we become full moral agents only at the point at which we fully engage ourselves in applying moral norms as standards 'from the internal point of view', and that only at that stage does it become *our* morality, as distinct from the morality to which we are subject, autonomy is a reality and indeed an essential element of moral agency.

But then the development of autonomy means the gradual taking of responsibility for a 'moral code' which one already has and uses in a sub-moral heteronomous way. But then the judging and deciding one does as an autonomous moral agent presumably involves testing and modifying and extrapolating from an already established moral position. Revolution is no doubt possible, as in cases of religious or ideological con-version. But even then one does not invent a whole new moral position—one buys a ready to build kit, pre-packaged. And then as an autonomous moral agent one tests and

[9]   Oxford, 1946.

modifies and extrapolates from this new moral position. Even the great moral reformers like Jesus and Socrates appear to have argued their position by testing out the consistency and coherence and the acceptability all in all of elements of the currently received morality, and by extrapolating from it. They came not to destroy the law but to fulfil it.

In other ways, too, one's room for moral originality is restricted. Whatever one's own beliefs, one lives among human beings in a community or various communities. One's fellows have, and one knows they have, moral attitudes towards and moral expectations of oneself, which reflect their moral principles and, perhaps, rules—their 'moral code'. It would take exceptional and not necessarily commendable tough-mindedness to ignore or show indifference to these attitudes and expectations. Psychopaths, I suspect, are the only true existentialists—and vice versa.

As I said in an earlier chapter, 'the truth is that our moral, like our legal, life has a necessary social setting, which provides us with the basis of rules and principles of action in new or difficult circumstances. Autonomy is real, but only against a back-cloth of heteronomy.'[10]

The great difference in levels of formality as between legal and moral reasoning should indeed put us on our guard against assuming that there are no other differences. But I venture to suggest that all in all there are also real similarities and that we do in practical moral discourse regularly have recourse to consequentialist arguments as well as to arguments of consistency and coherence. There must be a unity in practical reason as well as a diversity in its particular operation in special contexts. A study of legal reasoning is by no means unhelpful towards the understanding of moral reasoning.

But for both we must be aware of the limits of practical reason. Between ultra-rationalism and sheer irrationalism there is a course to be steered. This book has attempted to steer such a course, and thereby to give a better understanding of practical reason, of legal reasoning, and of law itself.

[10] *Supra*, Ch. V, p. 124.

APPENDIX

ON THE 'INTERNAL ASPECT' OF NORMS

Readers of Swift's *Gulliver's Travels* will recall how, sometime after Gulliver had been washed ashore on the coast of Lilliput after his shipwreck, and had been captured by the tiny inhabitants, people no larger than his thumb, the King of Lilliput determined that his person should be searched. To that end he sent two commissioners, Clefren Frelock and Marsi Frelock, to make an inventory of all his personal belongings. In a document full of interest, one passage perhaps stands out more than others:

Out of the right Fob hung a great Silver Chain with a wonderful kind of engine at the Bottom. We directed him to draw out whatever was at the End of the Chain; which appeared to be a Globe, half Silver and half of some transparent Metal; for on the transparent Side we saw certain strange Figures drawn and thought we could touch them, until we found our Fingers stopped with that lucid Substance. He put this Engine to our Ears which made an incessant Noise like that of a Water Mill. And we conjecture that it is either some unknown Animal, or the God that he worships; But we are more inclined to the Latter Opinion, because he assured us (if we understood him right, for he expressed himself very imperfectly) that he seldom did anything without consulting it. He called it his Oracle, and said it pointed out the time for every Action of his life.

To the old riddle, 'What is it that God never sees, the King rarely sees, and ordinary people see every day?' The authorized version of the answer was 'An Equal', but the wit's answer was 'A joke'. The academic vice is not so much of not seeing, but rather of being under a compulsion to say what is involved in seeing, a joke; at any rate for present purposes, I must ask what is involved in seeing the joke in the passage quoted from *Gulliver's Travels*.

The joke turns on the point that in relation to the 'wonderful kind of engine' described, the Lilliputian commissioners have given so accurate an external description of the thing in terms of its visual appearance and auditory manifestations that *we* can know what it is; yet *they* have done so without themselves knowing what it is. Up to a point, but only up to a point, 'for he expressed himself very imperfectly', they know how the Man Mountain used this wonderful kind of engine—indeed Swift uses their limited understanding to turn the joke back on western man by putting in their mouths the conjecture about its being the 'God that he worships'; but that part of the joke I shall for the moment pass over.

Appearance is not the whole of human reality. Not the most meticulous physical description of every cog and spoke and their interconnections together, not even with super-added the most meticulous description of every act and utterance of the possessor of the 'wonderful engine' in relation to it, would amount to an understanding on the describer's part of the crucial fact which we to whom it is described know, and know even on the footing of a relatively imprecise external description: that the engine in question is a watch; that Gulliver 'consults' it in order to tell the time of day.

We know what the commissioners don't know, so for us the passage is a joke; we know it because we know a watch when we see one (or hear it described), and know how to use it, and know what to use it for. To use terms of H.L.A. Hart's which I find highly illuminating, we look upon these wonderful engines 'from the internal point of view', from the point of view of those who understand and work with that complex set of normative conventions in terms of which we can use these artefacts to measure the passage of time and thus to synchronize and co-ordinate activities with each other to a remarkably high degree of accuracy.

By contrast, the Lilliputians are outsiders. They are unaware of those conventional norms which for us make sense of our use of watches. Accordingly they can (for the moment at any rate) only appreciate Gulliver's watch and his use of it at the level of observable, or, rather, sensible phenomena. They can only describe it in such terms, together with vague conjectures as to the possible meaning of the object to Gulliver. Theirs is, by contrast with ours, an 'external point of view'. It is 'external' in respect of the set of conventional norms in question.

This contrast between 'internal' and 'external' points of

view is brought out particularly vividly by the example taken from Swift's *Gulliver*. Swift makes us realize what it would be like to see a watch and not know it as a watch; and thus makes us able to contrast the position of somebody like that with our own actual position. But it is the contrast itself which is of present importance. To have drawn such a contrast and explained its importance for an understanding of the law is in my opinion a major element in Hart's contribution to the philosophy of law. The purpose of this essay is to consider Hart's distinction further, and to make some suggestions in the way of constructive criticism aimed at improvement on Hart's version of the doctrine.

To recall the context and content of the doctrine: in *Concept of Law*[1] Hart develops his exposition of the notion of 'rule', which is central to his theory of law, by contrasting it with the concept of 'habit', which he interprets in a purely behavioural sense; in his terms it is a necessary and sufficient condition of the existence of a habit that a particular pattern of behaviour of an agent or group of agents be regularly repeated over a period of time. (Whether this is plausible as an account of the notion of 'habit', or fair as an account of Austin, who is criticized for his use of the notion of 'habit of obedience' in accounting for sovereignty and therefore law, is not of present concern.)

The explanation of 'social rules' is developed by expounding 'three salient differences' between them and that behavioural conception of habit. First, where a group has a rule about doing something or another, deviation from the normal pattern is treated as a fault or lapse open to criticism, whereas in the case of a mere habit, deviation from the normal pattern 'need not be a matter for any form of criticism'. Secondly, such criticism is regarded as justified or legitimate in the sense that someone's deviating from the normal pattern is regarded as a 'good reason' in itself for criticizing the lapse or fault involved.

[1] H.L.A. Hart, *The Concept of Law* (Oxford, 1961). The passage with which I am primarily concerned here, and from which I quote extensively in the present and succeeding two paragraphs, is to be found at pp. 54–6; the themes first developed there recur frequently throughout the book, notably at pp. 86–8, 96, 99–100, 101, 105, 112–14, 197.

Thirdly, there is the point about the 'internal aspect of rules', with which we are presently concerned. To constitute a habit, it is not necessary that anybody think about the habitual behaviour or be conscious of its generality in a group; 'still less need they strive to teach nor intend to maintain it'. But 'by contrast, if a social rule is to exist, some at least must look on the behaviour in question as a general standard to be followed by the group as a whole. A social rule has an 'internal' aspect in addition to the external aspect which it shares with a social habit and which consists in the regular uniform behaviour which an observer could record.' An example which Hart proceeds to give of this is drawn from the game of chess. It may be an observable fact that chess players move the Queen always in characteristically similar ways, but there is more to it than that, says Hart. They have a 'critical reflective attitude to their behaviour; they regard it as a standard for all who play the game'. That attitude is manifested in the way in which they criticize lapses, demand conformity with standard patterns, and acknowledge that some such demands and criticisms are justified.

The internal aspect of rules is often misrepresented as a mere matter of 'feelings' in contrast to externally observable physical behaviour. . . [But] such feelings are neither necessary nor sufficient for the existence of 'binding' rules. There is no contradiction in saying that people accept certain rules but experience no feelings of compulsion. What is necessary is that there should be a critical reflective attitude to certain patterns of behaviour as a common standard, and that this should display itself in criticism (including self criticism), demands for conformity, and in acknowledgments that such criticism and demands are justified, all of which find their characteristic expression in the normative terminology of 'ought', 'must', and 'should', 'right' and 'wrong'.

Surely it must be beyond doubt that Hart is correct in saying that an understanding of rules is possible only given attention to and analysis of the 'internal aspect' to which in this passage he draws attention (whether or not in all respects his account here and elsewhere is entirely satisfactory). Indeed, such a view would nowadays be almost a commonplace theory, and Hart himself in advancing his account with special reference to the law was following and developing accounts previously given by, among others,

Winch[2] , Wittgenstein[3] , and Weber[4] (by all of whom, especially the first mentioned, he was obviously much influenced).[5] The force of such an example as that with which this section commenced—Gulliver and his watch—is that it dramatizes the difference between seeing activities only as they manifest themselves externally to the senses, and seeing them with understanding, understanding in terms of the categories used by the agents themselves—for example, what is the difference between marking a cross on a paper, and voting in an election, and how would we explain the differences?[6]

I trust that it is obvious that the use of clocks and watches is comprehensible only in terms of the existence of shared social conventions of a kind, indeed, which could without any strain be called 'rules'. Why, for example, is a watch to be considered defective if its hands do not move in such a way that the larger one completes twenty-four revolutions, and the smaller two revolutions between one mid-day (as determined by the perceived position of the sun, or whatever) and the next? Why is it wrong to say 'It is 11 o'clock' when the longer and the shorter hands of a clock are both aligned with the numeral '12'? Why is it right to mark out the face of a clock with sixty equidistant points around its perimeter, every fifth of them marked out with one of the cardinal numbers from 1 to 12, in order?

The only possible answer to such questions is to explain that we have conventions for reckoning the passage of time in terms of which we envisage the passage of time from one 'mid-day' to the next as being divided into twenty-four

---

[2] See Peter Winch, *The Idea of a Social Science and its Relation to Philosophy* (London, 1958), esp. ch. 2, *passim*.

[3] See Ludwig Wittgenstein, *Philosophical Investigations*, ed. G.E.M. Anscombe and R. Rhees, 2nd edn. (Oxford, 1958), e.g. at 1.197−241.

[4] See, e.g., M. Rheinstein (ed.), *Max Weber on Law in Economy and Society* (Cambridge, Mass., 1954), pp. 11−12; also the passage and arguments from Weber cited in Winch, op.cit., pp. 45−51.

[5] See *Concept of Law*, p. 242, note to p. 54, citing Winch, op.cit., with reference to passages in which Winch's main argument involves close discussion of themes from Wittgenstein and Weber.

[6] For a discussion of this example, see, e.g., M. Lessnoff, *The Structure of Social Science* (London, 1974), p. 30; Lessnoff's book, esp. in chapter II contains a review of themes similar to those mentioned in this paragraph. Cf. also B. Wilson (ed.), *Rationality* (Oxford, 1973).

equal 'hours' and each of these into sixty equal 'minutes' and so on. Clocks and watches are artefacts which people make in order to reckon the passage of time in accordance with these units of measurement. The use of these artefacts in accordance with the measuring conventions further enables us to fix on names for different 'times of the day', and that in turn enables us to co-ordinate and synchronize our activities quite accurately, even when complex interrelations of many people's activities are involved, as for example in running a train service or a factory. But it is all a matter of convention. The units of measurement fixed on could have been quite different (indeed, those used in Republican Rome were quite different) the design of the artefacts could have been quite different and is indeed to some extent subject to changes of technology and of fashion over the years—I saw a television interview the other day involving a person who manufactured, *inter alia*, digital watches.

Certainly, to take one of Hart's points of distinction as between 'habits' and 'social rules', there is no doubt that the patterns of behaviour involved in telling the time is one which most contemporary parents in our society 'strive to teach' to their children, and 'intend to maintain'. Telling the time is an important skill for western man—the Lilliputians came nearer to the mark than perhaps they knew in supposing that Gulliver's watch might have been 'the God that he worships'. And it is a skill which must be learned, and learning it involves acquiring the capacity to distinguish correct from incorrect statements of the time for any given configuration of the hands on the face of the clock, how to correct the setting of the hands on any particular clock so as to make it conform to some standard time, e.g. Greenwich Mean Time, how to keep a watch properly wound up and so forth. The very fact that we are able to describe the skill, indeed only able to describe it, by reference to correct and incorrect performances in given contexts, draws attention to that particular feature of rule governed conduct which Hart places at the centre of his picture thereof: the manifestation of critical attitudes, the appraisal of actual performance against a conceived standard performance, which is manifested by the use of terms such as 'correct' and 'incorrect'.

This learning of correct and incorrect performance is, in a distinctive sense, the learning of a (conventional) skill, and this is a fact from which interesting consequences follow. To say 'it is 10 o'clock' when both hands of a watch are aligned with the 12 is to make a mistake, to tell the time incorrectly, to be wrong in what one says; but it is not a case of 'wrongdoing', not a case of acting badly, or being bad. There is a difference in the criticism proper to deviations from or lapses of skill, from that which is proper to breaches of duty. The explanation of the difference is interesting: a conventional skill such as telling the time is constituted by mastery of a complex set of interrelated norms none of which makes complete sense apart from the whole set. To know and understand the norms is to have the skill, in the sense of being able to use it whenever one has reason to. What is more, it is only when an agent has reason to, and does decide to, 'tell the time' that the norms are relevantly applicable. The only actions to which the norms of the skill are relevant are those which the agent (for some reason) intends as instances of it. Somebody who said 'It is 11 o'clock' may either mean his utterance as a statement of what the time is, or (for example) as a statement in the children's game 'What's the time Mr. Wolf?' and it is his intention which is decisive of the question which one of these (or what else) it is. A statement can only be correct or incorrect as a statement of the time of day, if that is the kind of statement which it is intended to be, or to be understood as being. If it is a move in a children's game, or something else, some other canons of criticism would be relevant, but not the time telling norms. Hence, since what makes the norms of the skill or practice applicable is the agent's own intentions in the matter, we can see why the particular mode of criticism applicable to breaches is criticism in terms of 'mistake' or 'incorrectness' or 'inaccuracy' rather than 'wrongdoing'. To get it wrong is to miss one's own intentions, by misapplying norms the applicability of which has been determined by one's own will. In terms of a distinction which I have drawn elsewhere the norms involved are 'procedural' rather than 'substantive'.[7] Of course, it does not follow, and has not been said, that the existence of the norms is dependent upon one's will. The social practice exists, and is available for one's use whenever one has reason to choose to involve oneself in it.

To that extent, the norms of this skill parallel those norms of a legal system which regulate procedures whose invocation is at the option of the individual. Conveyancing, for example, is a difficult and complex skill to the learning of which much effort has to be devoted. The law specifies what steps must be taken in order that ownership of Blackacre shall pass from A to B. But it is up to individuals to decide whether to convey or not to convey their own property, and if they do, to ensure that they (or their lawyers) conform to the required patterns. That the norms of conveyancing (considered as a practice) or of time telling (seen likewise) leave it entirely at one's option whether to invoke them on any given occasion or not in no sense implies that it cannot be on other grounds obligatory to invoke either set of norms. For example A may by contract bind himself to transfer Blackacre to B on 1st July, thus obligating himself on that date to execute a valid conveyance of Blackacre, in accordance with the relevant institutive rules. And so too, whoever accepts a job in a factory which works under a shift system accepts an obligation to tell the time at any rate to the extent required for keeping time properly. Indeed for us all time keeping is so very important a skill, just because the whole round of our business and social obligations, attending meetings, keeping appointments, going to the theatre, or whatever, is dependent at every point upon the clock; that is, on our accurate use of properly set and maintained clocks.

In criticizing an act as wrongdoing or breach of obligation, we are not concerned at all with the question whether the agent under criticism acted, or failed to act, with reference to the norms whose breach is at stake. Whether or not 'the

---

[7] See D.N. MacCormick, 'Legal Obligation and the Imperative Fallacy', in *Oxford Essays in Jurisprudence Second Series*, ed. A.W.B. Simpson (Oxford, 1973), esp. at pp. 116–29 for my attempt to elaborate and justify that distinction. The same essay contained a discussion of the idea of 'internal intention' (pp. 104f.) reference to which would be necessary fully to justify my assertion made above about intentions in relation to 'telling the time'.

subjective meaning' of his act was as a fulfilment or breach of the norm is irrelevant to the question whether it was such, and whether it can be relevantly criticized as such. (That is not to say that the agent's intentions are irrelevant—the criminal law in relation to murder or assault is certainly concerned with the question whether the accused intended to injure or kill his victim. What is not necessary at all to the application of the rule against assault or the rule against murder is that the act under consideration should have been performed with the intention of its being recgnized as an instance of 'assault' or 'murder'. This is a sharp contrast to what is necessary for an act to constitute a conveyance, or for that matter an act of telling the time.) So there is at least this characteristic difference between the norms of a skill and the norms of obligation: the former are only relevant to those acts which are, or are presumed to be, performed with reference to the norms themselves; but the applicability of, the latter is not conditional on an agent's subjectively intending to invoke them. These are distinctions which it is only possible to make from the perspective of an 'internal point of view'.

What has been said so far has shown how an activity which anyone who reads this essay is presumed to take for granted, the activity of using clocks and watches and telling the time by them, despite its superficially simple and taken-for-granted quality, is one which can in truth be understood only by reference to a set of conventional norms which is really very complex (so much so that most of us would find it difficult if not impossible to give any very clear or coherent explicit account of the whole set which we implicitly use with such ease and assurance). They are essentially social norms, both in the sense that all of us learned them from other people rather than inventing them for ourselves, and in the sense that their whole point is dependent on their being shared norms constitutive of a practice of telling the time which we can all understand in more or less the same way as each other. That it is the norms which make sense of the activity can be demonstrated by showing what one would make of the activity if one didn't understand the norms; a demonstration which Swift's literary skill makes it the easier to give.

By seeing that there really could be an external point of view, we make ourselves aware of the internal point of view and of its importance.

It is important to investigate further what is involved in this awareness. There is and must be here an appeal to an awareness of the content of our conscious thoughts and processes of thinking. A behaviouristic account of the use of clocks and watches would necessarily, however elaborately it were constructed, rest at the level of the Lilliputian commissioners' description, restricted to the perceptible phenomena, without reference to the categories which are essential to the conscious use of clocks and watches as instruments for measuring the passage of time. I do not say that there could not be interesting behaviourist accounts, e.g. of how children are taught to and learn to tell the time. But the product of the teaching, the skill learnt, could not itself be explained in such terms.

And so to generalize that: any account of rules and norms and standards of conduct must be in terms of this 'internal point of view'. That is to say, it must take account of the consciousness of those who use and operate with whatever standards of conduct may be in question. To anyone who would object that this is an unscientific approach, one could only retort by reiterating the wise saying that it cannot be wrong to be anthropomorphic about people. Let whoever doubts that, contemplate how he would seek to explain to the Lilliputians the true nature and uses of the wonderful kind of engine discovered in Gulliver's right fob.

It is not clear to me how far Hart himself would go in accepting this wholeheartedly mentalistic view of the nature of what he identifies as 'the internal point of view'. Let us recall that he treats as the necessary element of the internal point of view the existence of 'a critical reflective attitude to certain patterns of behaviour as a common standard', of which he at once goes on to say that 'this should display itself in criticism . . . demands for conformity, and in acknowledgements that such criticism and demands are justified, all of which find their characteristic expression in the normative terminology of "ought", "must", and "should", "right" and "wrong"'.[8]

---

[8] Op.cit., p. 56.

It isn't entirely clear whether such expressions of demands and criticisms are envisaged as being constitutive of, or merely evidentiary of, the critical reflective attitude envisaged. The use of the terms 'characteristic expression' has an empiricist flavour about it which may increase doubt. In fact, it is not so much that criticism is characteristically expressed in normative terminology, as that it is *appropriately* so expressed; and as that more candid phrasing indicates it is the conventional norms of the language which determine how we should express the criticisms, demands, and such like which we may wish to make. But to say that the attitude in question is *appropriately* expressed by such terminology is frankly to concede that it could be otherwise expressed, and indeed (most important of all) that its existence is logically independent of how it is expressed. What is more, it would not seem very satisfactory to offer in explanation of the nature of norms an account of the appropriate use of normative language. For among other things, what is at stake is to understand how we can have standards of appropriateness of this kind.

On the other hand, if we strip off these problems about how the necessary attitude displays itself, we are left with the unadorned idea of 'a critical reflective attitude to certain patterns of behaviour as a common standard', which is illuminating, but only incompletely so, since it seems almost to be circular. What, after all, is 'a standard'? Do we not have to account for it in much the same way as 'a rule', or in exactly the same way? The road to a further explanation in terms of the characteristic expression in which this is displayed being cut off, for reasons already given, there is a problem about the way in which to advance towards an improved explanation.

Let us consider what must essentially be involved in our having a critical attitude to, or making a critical appraisal of, the actual conduct of oneself or other people. In this there must be some element of appraising the actual against some other possible configuration of action in the given circumstances which confront us. We must indeed have in view some 'pattern of behaviour'; that we use such a conceived 'pattern of behaviour' as that against which to appraise actual behaviour is indeed what *constitutes* that pattern as a standard for us. But only given a certain sense of the term 'appraise'. When we speak here of appraising we mean more than merely indulging in some quite neutral comparison as between the actual and the conceived state of affairs, followed by a recording of any divergence between the two. The conceived pattern must be a pattern of preferred or approved as against disapproved conduct. What makes 'not wilfully attacking other people' or 'saying "It is 12 o'clock" only when both hands of the clock are aligned with the 12' standards of conduct? Not just that these are possible patterns against which we could conceivably appraise actual conduct, but that these are patterns of conduct actually willed, desired, preferred, approved as patterns *for* conduct and its appraisal in our own society just now. The relevant appraisal is appraisal for conformity or not with some pattern which is envisaged as a pattern of preferred conduct.

For a person to be *sincerely* critical of any given action of himself or another, there must be some alternative mode of acting in the circumstances in question which he would in some degree prefer over that actually undertaken. Common social standards must depend on shared preferences for certain modes of possible action over others. It can only be a will for conformity of actual actions to conceived patterns of action which is constitutive of standards of conduct. To make sense of the idea of 'critical appraisal' of actual conduct against some conceived pattern it is necessary that we consider the 'conceived pattern' as being willed by somebody. Such will, preference or approval need not be envisaged as arbitrary; for example, there may be eminently good reasons for preferring that people refrain from assaulting each other, or that they follow certain practices of measuring and telling the time. Such reasons for preference may themselves be further norms of a higher order, though outside of theological ethics, they cannot all be.

There is at least one obvious line of objection to the view here advanced. It is surely not the case that every judgment of action by reference to a given standard, every appraisal of any state of affairs by reference to some norm is necessarily an expression of the will or preference of the person who passes judgment or appraisal. Equally, and conversely, not every expression of will or of preference is an expression of a social (or any other kind of) norm, nor presupposes any such. How then could it be possible to assert any necessary connection between wills or preferences and standards of conduct? Is it not indeed a common and persistent source of error to set up a simple correlation of norm with will, as in all variants of 'the command theory' of law?[9]

The points made, though true in themselves, are not decisive as objections to the view here put. Plainly, for any given social grouping, a social norm can exist in relation to some behaviour even if not everybody wills conformity to the envisaged pattern. Some members may be indifferent, some even in some degree actively unwilling to conform to the pattern, or hostile to its being maintained. It would, one may suppose be highly unusual in any group of any size to find exactly similar attitudes among all members of the group, though perhaps there are easy cases like those of assault and murder.

What is more, one can understand, and work with, social norms, even in the case of being indifferent or hostile to them. Two years ago, there were many Scots lawyers who would greatly have liked to see the divorce law radically reformed, but who could nevertheless understand and work along with the law as it stood. But always the position of those who, while understanding a norm, and able to frame judgments in terms of it, remain indifferent or hostile to it, is a position which is parasitic on that of those who do for whatever reason will the pattern of behaviour in question as a standard for all in their group. This detached view of social rules makes sense only if those who hold it suppose (and it may be a false supposition) that there are some who do care about maintenance of the pattern of conduct in question. That there can be common patterns of criticism of conduct or states of affairs depends upon our conceiving that some patterns are willed as common patterns for all people in given circumstances. We can conceive of that independently of our own will in the matter, but not independently of our beliefs

---

[9] Cf. MacCormick, op.cit. *supra*, p. 282 n. 7, esp. at pp. 100–16.

about the will of other members of our social group—
or, if we are anthropologists or tourists, of the groups
we are studying or passing through and seeking not to
offend.

Why should anybody ever conform to a pattern of conduct
which he does not himself regard as a desirable or preferable
standard of social conduct? The answer is obvious: other
people's willing it as a standard entails their disapproving of
deviant conduct, and few people are very keen to attract
the avoidable disapproval of their fellows. What is more,
part of what is expected of us may be ostensible commitment
to the supposedly shared rules of our society, so that one
may seek to avoid disapproval by oneself expressing criticism
of deviant conduct, against one's own private sympathy.
Hypocrisy, as the saying goes, is what makes the world
go round; it certainly seems to be an essential ingredient
in the cement of an ordered society.

In his own account of the 'internal aspect' Hart, as
we saw, is anxious to reject the view that it is a matter
of 'feelings' about conduct. Specifically, he argues that
feelings of restriction or compulsion—'feeling bound'—
are not essential to the existence of rules though some
individuals may in fact experience such feelings 'where
rules are generally accepted by a social group and generally
supported by social criticism and pressure for conformity'.
That is true, but it should not lead us, as perhaps it has
led Hart, to ignore the important affective elements in
the 'internal aspect' or the 'internal point of view'. There
is an important, indeed essential, volitional as distinct from
cognitive element in the internal aspect of rules, understanding of which is essential to an understanding of rules.
When Hart himself speaks of the 'acceptance' of rules in
a social group, he seems to have in view precisely such
a volitional element as that which has been discussed here,
though one of the weaknesses of his account taken as a
whole is that he fails to give anywhere a single specific
explanation of the relationship between the various inter-
twined conceptions which throughout the book are central
to his theory— namely the 'internal aspect', the 'internal
point of view', 'internal statements', and 'acceptance

of rules'.[10]

What seems beyond doubt is that the volitional element of the 'internal point of view' must be recognized as central thereto. It is the fact of people's will for conformity to a conceived pattern of action, of their preference for some rather than other possible configurations of such action in given circumstances, that is for them the primary ground of criticism and reflective appraisal of actual conduct in society. Any conceived pattern of action such as:

'People taking reasonable care to avoid harming other people'

'People marking out the perimeter of clock faces into sixty equal divisions'

could be the content of a norm; could be envisaged as a pattern for the critical appraisal of actions. But only such as are actually willed by some people as common patterns for a social group can be thought of as actual social norms.

But for the existence of a norm in a social group, not all its members need have this volitional commitment to it. Some indeed must, but others may simply 'play along' not out of conviction but from a kind of salutary hypocrisy. Different again is the 'delinquent' position, that is, the position of those who accept and prefer the common patterns, subject to exceptions for themselves, so far as they can get away with it. Thieves who are capitalists (as most are said to be) are a case in point. Again, there is the position of the 'rebels' who know and understand but actively reject the social norms willed by the more dominant groups in their society.

The 'playing along', 'delinquent', and 'rebel' positions (and any variants or intermediate types) are all comprehensible only in apposition or opposition to the volitionally committed position; it is necessarily presupposed by them while they are not presupposed by it. Of course, in the life of any complex social grouping it may be difficult or impossible to identify with confidence the members of the 'committed' group or

---

[10] Fur uses of these expressions see the passages in *Concept of Law* referred to above, p. 277 n. 1. Raz in *Concept of a Legal System* (Oxford, 1970), p. 148 n. 3, draws attention to apparent confusion as between these various phrases. But in my opinion he throws the baby out with the bath-water.

fully to understand all the cross-currents of attitude which may be in play. But understanding the social norms and rules of a group involves an assumption of some people's will as underpinning and sustaining the patterns which thus under-pinned and sustained are the norms of and for the group. Such understanding does not necessarily entail sharing in the relevant attitude.

The assumption or presupposition of that sustaining and underpinning will which is involved in understanding or *a fortiori* using and applying social rules norms and standards is of course not stated in any given judgment passed by reference to the norm; nor does the judgment *necessarily* express any such will. Understanding, using, passing judgment in terms of given social norms, are not to be thought of as acts which must themselves be accounted for in terms of an expression of the subjective will of the person who understands, passes judgment, etc. At one end of the spec-trum, critical reflective attitudes are much more markedly reflective than actively critical; though at the back of them all must rest some sense of a genuinely felt preference on somebody's part against which, ultimately, the critical reflection makes sense.

There are all kinds of statements which may be made which presuppose an understanding of given norms and all that that understanding in turn presupposes. Even to say 'It is 11 o'clock', meaning it as a statement of the time, is to make a statement which presupposes an understanding of the given conventions, whose existence as a set of operative social norms in turn depends on a widely disseminated will to maintain them as such. Yet the statement itself does not express such a will. And so too for statements of, or in, the law: 'As a seller of goods by description, you must deliver goods conform with the description', 'As occupier of these premises, you must take reasonable care for your lawful visitors', and so on. Such statements presuppose an under-standing of a set of legal norms, whose existence is explicable only in terms of some volitional commitments by some members of a society, though they do not in themselves express a commitment on the speaker's part.

Such statements belong to the category of what Hart has

called 'internal statements',[11] on the ground that they can
only be made 'internally' to the norm systems which they
presuppose by way of truth conditions. And at least at some
points in his narrative, he assumes that to make such statements is to evince the 'internal point of view'. But it will be
noted that what determines the 'internality' of a statement is
the *understanding*, not the *will* of the speaker. So far as that
goes, indeed, an entire outsider to a given society could form
an understanding of its norms, to the extent of being able to
make 'internal' statements, 'internal' to the social norms of
that society. I take it that that is precisely what social anthropologists try to do.

To observe that is to observe a crucial ambiguity in the
internal/external distinction as drawn by Hart: is it a
distinction between levels of understanding, or a distinction
between degrees of volitional commitment? There are, it is
submitted, two very important distinctions there; yet it
seems to be the case that Hart has to some extent at least
conflated them. We started this appendix by considering the
'externality' of the Lilliputian commissioner's report, which
was external in the sense that it revealed a failure to understand Gulliver's conduct except in its overt behavioural
manifestations. In a similar way, the study of human beings
from certain scientific perspectives might involve ignoring the
norms which people as agents would regard as guiding their
conduct; to do so would be to study human behaviour only
in its external aspect.

Whoever seeks to go beyond that level of understanding,
and to appreciate conduct in terms of the categories which
for the agent are crucial, is taking a radically different view of
it and one which deserves to be described for some purposes
at least as 'internal'. But this is 'internality' only at the
level of understanding, for the observer in this case may
remain entirely detached and uncommitted as regards the
norms understanding of which is vital to his enterprise.

[11] Op.cit., pp. 99–100. See also p. vii, 'neither law nor any other form of
social structure can be understood without an appreciation of certain crucial
distinctions between two different kinds of statement, which I have called
"internal" and "external" and which can both be made whenever social rules
are observed.'

But of course that sort of detached understanding, like the not dissimilar uncommitted attitude of the person who plays along, or the delinquent, is parasitic upon and presupposes the position of volitional commitment which we have seen as essential to the existence of norms, and central to the internal point of view. For that reason it is important to draw a further line of distinction here in terms of differing dispositions of will.

To summarize the point: There is a genuine distinction as drawn by Hart between 'external' and 'internal' points of view with reference to human activity. But the 'internal' point of view as characterized by Hart contains essentially distinguishable components, which ought to be distinguished. There is 'cognitively internal' point of view, from which conduct is appreciated and understood in terms of the standards which are being used by the agent as guiding standards: that is sufficient for an understanding of norms and the normative. But it is parasitic on—because it presupposes—the 'volitionally internal' point of view: the point of view of an agent, who in some degree and for reasons which seem good to him has a volitional commitment to observance of a given pattern of conduct as a standard for himself or for other people or for both: his attitude includes, but is not included by, the 'cognitively internal' attitude.

I do not think that in *Concept of Law* Hart has observed the need to distinguish between differences in levels of understanding and differences in degrees of commitment, and to that extent I find his account ambiguous. But if there are defects in his account, that is merely a challenge to others to improve it. That is what I have here tried to do.

INDEX OF STATUTES CITED

Acts of Union, 1707: 130–1
Divorce (Scotland) Act 1964: 98
Drugs (Prevention of Misuse) Act 1964: 50–1
Foreign Compensation Act 1950: 143–4, 195–6, 199, 232
Hire Purchase Act 1964: 206
Increase of Rent and Mortgage Interest (Restirction) Act 1920: 200–4, 213, 232
Malicious Damage Act 1861: 180–2
Matrimonial Homes Act 1967: 206
Murder (Abolition of Death Penalty) Act 1965: 208–9
Occupiers' Liability (Scotland) Act 1960: 216–7
Offences against the Person Act 1861: 181
Race Relations Act 1965: 154, 211, 235
Race Relations Act 1968: 66–8, 77–9, 148, 154, 210–3, 235
Race Relations Act 1976: 66
Rent Act 1968: 205–6
Royal Style and Titles Act 1953: 131
Sale of Goods Act 1893: 20–2, 28, 30–1, 73–4, 198
Sex Disqualification Removal Act 1919: 237
Supply of Goods (Implied Terms) Act 1973: 26
Supreme Court of Judicature Act 1925: 183
Vehicle and Driving Licences Act 1969: 182–3

GENERAL INDEX

Acceptance of rules (see also 'internal aspect') 55, 64
Acceptability, consequences, 104-5, 110, 173
Acquittal, logic of, 41-52
Adultery, 93-4, 146-7
Analogy, argument by, 120-1, 146, 155-6, 160
  closeness of, 159, 190-2, 231-2
  cognitive aspect, 185-6
  elements, 185
  evaluative aspect, 185-6
  examples of, 180-5
  explanation, 161-3
  inconclusiveness, 186-8, 189, 231-2
  incremental quality, 160, 225, 237-8
  statute and case-law, 187, 192-4
Animals, liability for, 142-3, 169
Appraisal, normative, 277-8, 285-91
Aquinas, 61
Arbitrariness, 76-7, 100-1, 268-9
Aristotle, 2, 24
Attwooll, E., 4
Austin, John, 55, 60, 127, 277
Austin, J.L., 25, 35
Authority, 25, 29, 55, 134
Autonomy, 123-4, 273-4
Averments, specificity of, 49-52
Bankowski, Z., 47, 234
Barrow, G.W.S., 55
Behaviourism, 6, 284
Bentham, Jeremy, 55, 60, 105, 115, 252
Bindman, G., 237
Blackstone, Sir W., 59, 60, 61
Cardozo, B.N., 40
Categories of illusory reference, 145-6
Choice, 33-4, 79
Classification, problem of, 95-7, 147-8, 197, 198, 203
Code, codification (see also 'interpretation'), 68
Coherence, argument from, 39, 106-8,

119-218, 152-194, 266-7, 270-1
  as criterion of truth, 90-92
Command theory of law, 59-60, 287
Common law, 6-13, 194, 211, 228
Common sense, 105, 111-2, 149-150, 166, 187, 195, 206, 252
Consequentialist Argument, 105-6, 108-119, 129-151, 171-3, 178, 186-7, 196, 198, 206, 208, 212, 214, 219, 252-3, 270-1
Consistency, requirement of, 39, 106, 179, 195-228, 266, 270-1
Constitutions, 129-132, 242-4
Construction, canons of, 207-8, 210, 212
Convenience, argument from (see also 'expediency'), 1, 3, 58, 105, 114-5, 178
Correspondence (truth), 91
Cooper, Lord, 40
Cour de Cassation, 9, 95
Courts as legal institutions, 8, 54, 55-8, 242-4
Criteria
  of argumentation, 12-13, 77, 122
  of evaluation, 105, 110-112, 114-6, 138-140, 148-151, 253
  of recognition (see also 'rule'), 54, 56, 138-140, 155, 229, 238, 240, 244
  of truth, 23-27, 32, 90-92
Cross, R., 82, 203, 207, 215, 225
Deduction: see 'Logic', 'Justification',
Delict, law of, 166-7, 191-2
Democracy, 64, 264
Derham, D.P., 87, 197
Devlin, Patrick (Lord), 35
Dias, R.W.M., 82
Disagreement, speculative/practical, 246-9
Discovery, process of, 14-16
Discretion, 230, 246-255
Duty (see also 'Obligation')
  of care, 121-2

Duty (see also 'Obligation') cont'd
 of counsel, 119, 122-3
 judicial, 32-3, 54-6, 65, 122,
   181-2, 186-7, 242-4, 250
 public, 46
 statutory, breach of, 192
Dworkin, R.M., 112, 153, 155, 160,
   229-274 *passim*
Economic circumstances, 4-5, 60, 172
Economic loss, 140-2
Efficacy of law, 55
Equilibrium, reflective, 245
Equity, 56, 60-1, 97-9, 112, 128
Erskine, J., 59, 60
Esser, J., 104
Evidence, 16, 82, 88-9, 92, 101-2
Expediency, argument from, 105,
   114-5, 135, 144, 206
Expectations, normative, 11, 17-18, 274
External point of view, 139-40, 241-2,
   275-277
Fact skepticism, 36
Facts, 2-4, 29, 32-7, 250
 decisions on, 86-97, 200
 evidentiary, 27
 material, 84, 117-9
 operative, 27, 45, 47, 50, 51, 53,
   67, 94, 121
 primary, 93
 secondary, 93-7
Ferguson, Adam, 4
Fiction, 48
Frank, Jerome, 16, 36
Fuller, L.L., 61
Functionatism, 14, 16-18
Garner, J.F., 96
Generality, relative levels of, 78, 117-9
Gottlieb, G., 34, 45
Goodhart, A.L., 84, 117, 225-6
Grotius, 59
Guest, A.G., 201, 225
Habits, 277-8, 280
Hacker, P.M.S., 232, 247
Halsbury, Lord, 39-40
Hard Cases, 195-203, 227-8
Hare, R.M., 78, 123
Harris, D.R., 201
Hart, H.L.A., 54, 61, 63, 64, 66, 133,
   197, 229-31, 240-2, 276-292
   passim
Haward, L.R.C., 87
Hercules, 252, 254, 255, 269

Hodgson, D.H., 15, 116
Holmes, O.W., 40
Hume, David, 2-8, 17, 77, 247, 267-9
Hypotheses, testing of, 16, 101-3
Impartiality, 17-8, 234
Institution, legal, 56-8, 242-5
Internal aspect of norms, 63-4, 133-4,
   139-140, 229, 239, 240 273,
   275-92
 volitional and cognitive elements,
   286-92
Interpretation
 problem of, 68, 77-9, 94, 97,
   195-228
 statutory, 106, 143-4, 147-8, 196,
   203-13, 221-2
 – in codified systems, 68, 218-9
 – 'liberal' approach, 210-11
 – rules of, 204, 207-8, 210-11
 – obvious meaning, 203-4, 207-11
Intuitionism, 110, 257
Irrationalism, 265-9
Judge, law making power, 188, 194
 – position of, 54-7
 – power of, 59, 61, 129-35, 173,
   183, 187-8, 249-5
 – recruitment of, 10-11
 – duty of: see 'Duty, judicial'
Jury, 34-7
Justice, 63-4, 105, 206, 239
 – according to law, 32, 59, 74,
   107, 250
 – arguments from, 135, 144,
   149-50, 166, 178, 195, 253
 – formal, 73-82, 99
 – forward-looking, 75-6, 78-82
 – judicial conceptions of, 105, 114,
   228
 – natural, 49, 178-9, 194, 223,
   259-60
 – substantive, 17, 73-5
 – theories of, 253-5
Justification
 – deductive, 19-37, 41-52, 58-9,
   65-72, 100, 187, 183-4, 197
 – of factual inferences, 88-92
 – process of, 14-16, 19, 52, 62,
   73, 77-82, 270
 – of rules, by principles, 152-3,
   156-7, 166
 – scientific, 101-3
 – second order, 101-108, 156

Justification (cont'd)
— two level procedure, 116
Kahn-Freund, O., 95, 119
Kamenka, E., 4
Kames, Henry Home, Lord, 112
Kant, I., 6, 123, 267
Kelsen, H., 53, 55, 62, 63, 64, 245
Kenny, A., 24
Lamont, W.D., 273
Law reports, 8-9, 13, 273
Lawson, F.H., 68
Legal system
— civilian, 8-9, 10, 11, 41
— English, 8-11, 40-1, 46
— French, 8-9, 68, 95, 119, 227,
229, 233-4, 258
— Roman, 165
— Scottish, 8-11, 40-1, 46, 142-3
233-4
— South African, 239
— Soviet, 233-4
— U.S.A., 8, 40-1, 118-9, 129-130
— theories of, (see also: 'Natural
Law' 'Positivism'), 53-65,
139-40, 229-264
Legalism, 272
Legitimacy, 55-7
Legislation, 57-8, 188, 209, 235-8
Legislatures, 57-8, 59, 173, 188, 204
Lessnoff, M., 16, 101, 102, 279
Lester, A., 237
Levi, E.H., 238
Lévy, C., 95, 119
Llewellyn, K.N., 75, 198-9, 207
Logic
— deductive, 19-38, 41-52, 53,
92-3, 197, 271-2
(see also 'justification, deductive')
— formal, 21-29
— of formal justice, 81
— modus ponens, 24
— ordinary usage, in, 27-41, 179
— propositional, 24-28
Lyons, D., 105, 115
McCallum, G.C., 209
MacCormick, (D.) N., 55, 57, 126,
154, 233, 245, 256, 272,
Marx, Karl, 4, 5
Medawar, Sir P.B., 16, 101
Megarry, R.E., 190
Miers, D., 45, 58, 112
Millar, John, 4

Mitchell, D., 24, 28
Morality, 2-4, 123-4, 236-9, 267-8,
271-4
Mungham, G., 47, 234
Nature of things, 1-2, 269
Nature, human, 5, 268
Natural law, 1-2, 54, 58-62
Neumann, Franz, 268
Norms: see 'Internal Aspect'
Obiter dicta, 157, 215, 222
Obligation, 33, 55, 122, 191, 240,
282-3
Open texture of law, 66, 209-10,
230
Ought/is, 3, 17
Passions, 3-7, 270
Paterson, A.A., 11, 123, 199
Paton, G.W., 87, 197
Performative Utterances, 25, 35
Perelman, Ch., 14, 75, 104, 233, 234
Persuasion, 14-15
Plato, 2
Policy, 39, 159, 161, 178-9, 185,
189, 195
— explanation of, 262-4
— public policy, 105, 135, 149-50,
172, 253
Political question, 132-3
Politics, 60, 64, 230, 235-6, 240
Popper, K.R., 16, 101
Positivism, legal, 54, 60-1, 62-5, 231,
233, 239-40, 258
Possession, 200-2, 204-6
Pound, R., 231
Practical Reason, 1-8, 266-74
Precedent
— doctrine of, 60, 82-6, 134-8,
213-28
— 'distinguishing', 106, 121, 185,
196, 219-24
— 'explaining', 85, 106, 121, 196,
220-24
— following/applying, 216-9
— not following, 134, 137-8, 227
— statute, similarities, 213-4,
217-9, 221-2, 223, 226-7
and see 'Ratio decidendi', 'Obiter dicta'
Presumptions, 46, 148, 159, 165, 212,
222
Principles, 4-6, 39, 58-9, 78, 110-111,
120-1, 123, 149-150, 259

Principles of Law
— in analogical argument (see also
  'Analogy'), 163-4, 186-7
— change over time, 155, 160,
  223-4, 235-8, 266
— of common law, 211
— conflict of, 127-8, 167-73
— establishment of, 154, 157, 230
— explanation of, 152-7, 186-7, 238
— inconclusiveness, 161, 178-9
— instances, 167-9 (strict liability);
  170-2 (contract); 173-6, 218,
  254 (damages); 178 (natural
  justice); 223 (family law);
  154-5, 235, 237 (race discrimination); 196 (public law)
— modalities of, 260-2
— moral principles, and, 235-6,
  238-9, 256, 260-1, 274
— 'neighbour', 125, 157-60, 178,
  253
— and policies, 166-7, 230, 259-64
— political principles, and, 230,
  235-6, 238-9, 256
— as rationalizations, 152-3, 155,
  156-7, 166-7, 187, 232-3, 235,
  238
— and rights, 256-8, 259, 264
— and rules (distinction), 231-2,
  245
— and rule of recognition, 133, 230,
  233-6, 240-6
— statutes, and, 205, 206-7, 211,
  218
— 'weight', 155-6. 160
Procedure, 44-5, 48, 49, 71
Proof, burden of, 44-5, 47-8
— problem of, 87-93, 250
— process of, 26-7, 47, 87-93
Prosecutors, 46-7
Rationality, 1-8, 48-9, 58-9,
  76-7, 100-1, 125, 179, 265-74
Ratio decidendi, 60, 82-6, 117-8,
  157, 212, 215-6
Rawls, J., 73, 245, 272
Raz, J., 54, 61, 232, 247, 289
Reason, 1-8, 254, 265-74
Reasons, underpinning, 64-5, 138-40,
  240-1
Reasonableness, 61, 96-7
Recognition: see 'criteria', 'Rule'
Relevancy, problem of, 70-72, 80-82

Reid, Lord, 105, 137, 148-50
Reid, Thomas, 3, 6, 77, 247, 267
Rescher, N., 91
Rhetoric, 14
Rights, 46, 177-8, 230, 255-8, 264
Ross, Alf., 265, 266
Ross, Sir W. David, 257
Rule
— 'all or nothing' quality, 155-6,
  231-2
— consequential, 57
— institutive, 57, 244
— form, canonical, 43, 45
— of law, 54
— legal, 29, 233, 240
— mandatory, 156, 157, 164, 179,
  180, 183
— primary, 229
— principles, and, 232-3
— of recognition, 54, 56, 133-4,
  138-40, 155, 229, 230, 233,
  240, 241, 242-5
— secondary, 229
— social 240-2, 277-280
— terminative, 57
Rule scepticism, 197
Ruling, 67-8, 71-2, 78, 83-4, 94, 96-7,
  101, 104, 118, 196, 197, 214-6,
  218, 243-4
Sartorius, R., 133, 240
Scientific method, 6, 87, 88, 101-3,
  269
Shklar, J.N., 272
Simpson, A.W.B., 55, 225.
Skinner, A., 4
Skill, conventional, 281-2
Smith, Adam, 3-5
Smith, S.A. de, 134
Society
— industrial, 46
— forms of, 4-5
— order in, 5, 107
— values of, 187
Sociology of law, 11, 123, 199, 270
Socrates, 269, 274
Stair, James, 1st Viscount, 1-2, 58-61,
  142, 143, 153-4
Statutory interpretation: see 'interpre-
  tation'.
Stein, P., 165
Stone, J., 117-8, 145-6
Style, 12, 198-9, 207

Summers, R.S., 119, 133, 209
Tapper, C.H., 179
Tort, law of, 166-7, 191-2
Touffait, A., 10, 68
Toulmin, S., 70
Truth, 23, 25-7, 32, 90-92, 113-4,
    271-2
Tunc, A., 10, 68
Twining, W., 45, 58, 112
Universality, universalizability, 6, 78,
    81, 84-6, 97-9, 100, 123-4,
    215
Utilitarianism, 105, 115-6, 132, 259,
    271-2
Validity
  — legal, 54, 57-8, 61-2, 65, 71,
    155, 196, 241, 242-4
  — logical, 21-29, 32, 71

— thesis, 62, 65, 71, 107, 139,
    155, 194, 242, 244-5
Value, 5, 19, 62, 105-6, 107, 152-3,
    180, 187, 234-5, 243, 270
Value-freedom, 233-4
Verdict, 34-6
Walker, D.M., 40, 71, 118
Warrant, legal, 70, 72, 107, 127,
    164-5, 187, 196
Wasserstrom, R.A., 15, 116
Weber, Max, 279
White, J.J., 119
Whitehead, A.N., 24
Will, 3, 267, 286-92
Wilson, B., 279
Winch, P., 279
Wittgenstein, L., 24, 279